W9-AYW-359

THE ADVENTURES OF EDDIE FUNG

CHINATOWN KID · TEXAS COWBOY · PRISONER OF WAR

EDITED BY JUDY YUNG

UNIVERSITY OF WASHINGTON PRESS · SEATTLE & LONDON

The Adventures of Eddie Fung *is published with the assistance of a grant from the*
NAOMI B. PASCAL EDITOR'S ENDOWMENT, supported through the generosity of
Janet and John Creighton, Patti Knowles, Mary McLellan Williams, and other donors.

University of Washington Press
P.O. Box 50096, Seattle, WA 98145, U.S.A.
www.washington.edu/uwpress

Library of Congress Cataloging-in-Publication Data
Fung, Eddie, 1922–
The adventures of Eddie Fung : Chinatown kid, Texas cowboy, prisoner of war
/ edited by Judy Yung.
p.   cm.
Includes bibliographical references and index.
ISBN 978-0-295-98754-5 (pbk. : alk. paper)
1. Fung, Eddie, 1922– 2. Chinese Americans—Biography. 3. Chinatown (San Francisco,
Calif.)—Biography. 4. San Francisco (Calif.)—Biography. 5. Cowboys—Texas—Biography.
6. World War, 1939–1945—Participation, Chinese American. 7. World War, 1939–1945—
Prisoners and prisons, Japanese. 8. Soldiers—United States—Biography. 9. Prisoners of war
—United States—Biography. 10. Prisoners of war—Burma—Biography.
I. Yung, Judy. II. Title.
E184.C5F86 2007   940.54'7252092—dc22   [B]   2007019488

The paper used in this publication is acid-free and 90 percent recycled from at least 50 percent
post-consumer waste. It meets the minimum requirements of American National Standard
for Information Sciences—Permanence of Paper for Printed Library Materials, ANSI Z39.48–
1984.♾ ♻

Cover photo: Eddie lighting a firecracker in Chinatown during the New Year celebration,
1935. Courtesy San Francisco History Center, San Francisco Public Library.

FOR LOIS AND ALL MY BUDDIES IN THE LOST BATTALION

CONTENTS

PREFACE

first met Eddie Fung in the summer of 2002. I was working on my fifth book, *Chinese American Voices: From the Gold Rush to the Present*, and I needed a World War II story, preferably one told from the perspective of a Chinese American veteran. I asked Colonel Bill Strobridge, a military historian who had conducted a study of Chinese Americans in World War II, if he could find me someone to interview. He came up with two possibilities. The first person had fought heroically in the front lines at Normandy, but he turned out to be a poor storyteller, one who gave short answers and stuck to the facts. Even though I conducted the interview in Chinese and did my best to make him feel comfortable, I could not get him to elaborate on the story or share his feelings on the matter. So I made arrangements to meet the second possibility, Eddie Fung, hoping that he would prove to be a more engaging storyteller.

We agreed to do the interview at Colonel Strobridge's home in San Francisco. Prior to the interview, I did some background checking on Eddie Fung. I found out that he was an American-born Chinese who had grown up in San Francisco Chinatown like me, only he had preceded me by two decades. I was fifty-six years old, and he had just turned eighty. Colonel Strobridge also told me that Eddie had the dubious distinction of being the only Chinese American soldier to be captured by the Japanese during World War II and that he had worked on the Burma-Siam railroad made famous by the film *Bridge on the River Kwai.* Not knowing much about that history, I made a point of seeing the film before the interview. I was horrified by the brutal treatment of the prisoners under the Japanese and impressed by the courage and heroic actions of the POWs in the film. I hoped that Eddie would be forthcoming with details about how he as a Chinese American had fared and survived under such circumstances. The other interesting thing that I found out about Eddie was that he had run away from home to become a cowboy when he was sixteen. I was intrigued—a Chinese American cowboy? Although it was the World War II story I needed, I decided I would start at the beginning with his family history in order to get a fuller picture of his life and to put his World War II experience into a larger context.

Having conducted over 400 interviews with Chinese Americans for various book projects by then, I thought I had allowed plenty of time for his story—three whole hours. This interview, however, turned out differently. A solidly built man of short stature—5 feet 3 inches, and 120 pounds, to be exact—Eddie proved to be a natural storyteller with a fantastic memory for details, a precise way of expressing himself, a wonderful sense of humor, and a strong determination to tell the story right. In essence, he is every oral historian's dream come true. He also proved to be an unusual interviewee in that he was both introspective and analytical in his responses. I soon found out that he had an indirect way of answering my questions, often recreating conversations and connecting specific incidents from the past to make his point. Regardless of how long-winded he got, Eddie was never boring. In fact, he held me spellbound at our first meeting, and before I knew it, three hours had passed and we had not even gotten to World War II! Somehow, I got the rest of the story out of him in the next two hours before I had to leave for my next appointment. He gave me a pile of books to read about POWs and the Burma-Siam railroad, and I promised to send him the transcript and edited story for his approval.

It was not until I transcribed his interview that I realized what a gold mine I had found. I thought, this had to be how historian Theodore Rosengarten must have felt when he happened upon Nate Shaw, an illiterate black sharecropper in Alabama with a story to tell, or how Alex Haley felt when he was asked to write Malcolm X's autobiography. They both spent hundreds of hours interviewing their subjects and countless more writing their classic oral histories, *All God's Dangers: The Life of Nate Shaw* and *The Autobiography of Malcolm X*. I knew instinctively that there was a larger book to be written, although I did not think at the time that I was the right person to write it. Six months later, after I had completed a draft of his World War II story for *Chinese American Voices,* I contacted Eddie and hand-delivered the transcript and story to him for his approval. At the same time, I urged him to consider writing his memoirs, but he said with modesty that his story was not that unique or interesting. "Besides," he said, "I'm not a writer." I continued, however, to press him, and suggested that we do a longer interview. "If nothing else," I said, "we could deposit the tapes and transcript in an archive for the historical record and for the use of other researchers." He reluctantly agreed. Retired and a recent widower, he had the time. For me, the time was right as well, because for the next nine months I was on sabbatical from my job as professor of American Studies at the University of California, Santa Cruz. Until then, my research and writing had primarily focused on Chinese American women. I never thought that I would be working on a book about a man's life, but the opportunity was too good to pass up.

We began meeting on Saturdays in the kitchen of his North Beach flat. I would set up the tape recorder and come prepared with questions about a certain period or aspect of his life. The agreement was that we would see how far we could take his story and that he would be completely open and honest with me. Although I kept reminding him that he had the right to refuse to answer any questions that made him feel uncomfortable, he never did—not even when I asked him about how he lost his virginity. At one point in our interviews, Eddie said, "You're the only one who knows the intimate details of my life. I've never even told my wife Lois." I felt honored by his complete trust in me and pleased by his willingness to cooperate with me fully. Each session ran for about four hours. I became enthralled by his story and by his voice. In between our sessions, I would transcribe the entire interview and come up with follow-up questions for our next session. One thing for sure, I felt very comfortable with him and looked forward to each of our weekend sessions.

Into our fifth session together, the unthinkable happened. We were sitting on opposite sides of the kitchen table, as usual, and were on the topic of post-traumatic stress disorder and how Eddie had found a way to deal with the anger he felt after the war. "The first thing to do is to admit you have a problem and then what are you going to do about it?" Then he slipped in, "Just like I would like to come on to you, except that I know that our age difference—I mean, there's just no percentage for it. So the only thing I can do is enjoy your company while you're here, and that's it. You understand?" Then, almost in the same breath, he moved on to an incident in his childhood when his father taught him how to quell his flash temper. Later, when I listened to the tape and heard what he had tried to tell me, I felt flattered and troubled at the same time. I did not want to jeopardize or compromise our professional relationship and the book that was materializing so well. And there was the age difference—he was old enough to be my father. After some lengthy telephone conversations in the next few days, we decided to give in to Cupid's arrow but continue on with the book project. Fifty more hours of interviews later, we were married on April Fool's Day 2003. We deliberately chose that date because we did not think any of our family or friends would believe us.

In retrospect, our marriage helped rather than hindered the interview process and my understanding of how Eddie's character has been shaped by his family background and upbringing, his life as a cowboy in Texas, and his POW experience during World War II. His life story confirms the wise sayings "We are the sum total of our experiences" and "What does not break us makes us stronger." As his wife and (as he calls me) "his Boswell," I had immediate access to him and his extensive library collection on World War II, and I was able to ask him many personal questions as well as conduct follow-up interviews whenever I wanted. Indeed, I learned to keep the tape recorder ready and close by in case he came up with anything important and relevant in our daily conversations. In this way, we completed another twenty-five hours of recorded testimony. I also had access to his family and relatives, and his POW buddies, all of whom I met after we were married. However, as I soon discovered, no one really knows Eddie Fung very well, since he is a very private person. He has been especially reluctant about speaking of his POW experiences except to other POWs who share a similar past. As he said, "There is a common bond between survivors that you cannot get membership into unless you have paid the initiation fee. This is true of all survivors—they can talk between and among themselves, but with great reluctance and difficulty to anyone else."

As my husband and the subject of the book, Eddie entrusted me with the writing of his story, but he had the final say over every word in the telling of that story. I gave him every chapter to review and correct as I wrote it, and we went over the final revisions together with a fine-tooth comb. Admittedly, I have influenced the outcome of the interview in my choice of questions and emphasis of focus because of my interest in Chinese American and women's history, but I have tried to provide Eddie with ample opportunities to add subjects or delete anything he did not want included. After transcribing all the interviews, which amounted to over 1,000 pages of text, I edited and rearranged selections from his interviews for a smoother read, while trying to remain faithful to his actual words and way of speaking. At times I relied on other published accounts and oral history interviews (see the bibliography) in order to add details or corroborate Eddie's version of the story. Ultimately, *The Adventures of Eddie Fung* is very much a collaborative life history project and autobiography of a Chinatown kid, Texas cowboy, and POW survivor, as told from his memories and in his own words. Using Rosengarten and Haley as my models and marshalling all my knowledge, sensitivities, and skills as a Chinese American historian and writer for this monumental task, my goal has been to do justice to Eddie's story as a survivor and to share with readers the many lessons in life that his story has to offer.

ACKNOWLEDGMENTS

O ur deepest gratitude goes to the late Colonel Bill Strobridge, for introducing us to each other, and to Ruthanne Lum McCunn, the Fung family, and the Yung family, for their unflagging support and encouragement from the beginning of our relationship through the end of this book project.

We wish to also acknowledge the following people for assisting us with our research. Members of the Lost Battalion and the Fung family who shared their memories of Eddie's past with us include the late B. D. Fillmore, Willie Hoover, George Lawley, the late Paul Leatherwood, Luther Prunty, the late Otto Schwarz, Jessie Jing, and Raymond and Fair Fung. Ronald Marcello, director of the Oral History Program at the University of North Texas, provided us with transcripts of interviews he had conducted with Eddie's war buddies and guided us to other important sources of information. Harry Ogg, librarian at the Midland County Public Library, kindly ran down answers to our questions regarding the history and culture of Texas. Him Mark Lai and Hiroshi Fukurai helped us with the Chinese place names and Japanese phrases. And the interlibrary loan staff at McHenry Library, University of California, Santa Cruz, tracked down every book we asked for.

Our difficult search for photographs to go with Eddie's story was greatly facilitated by the resourceful staff at the Bancroft Library, California Historical Society, San Francisco Public Library, Southwest Collection Library of Texas Tech University, and Australian War Memorial. Assistance and photographs were also provided by Robert Dana Charles, Philip Choy, Bill Fung, Grace Fung, Raymond and Fair Fung, Rosalie Griggs, Fred Haring, Herbert and Esther Ho, Ken and Yoshiko Ho, Montgomery Hom, Otto Kreeft, Amanda Lee, Joy Rasbury McLaughlin, Luther Prunty, and Vivian Thompson. The maps were drawn by cartographer Ellen McElhinny.

Our heartfelt thanks go to Gavan Daws, for his advice and inspiration; to the following reviewers, who gave us critical feedback on the manuscript: Valerie Matsumoto, Ruthanne Lum McCunn, Franklin Ng, Irene Reti, Juliana Rousseau, and Helen Zia for their critical feedback on the manuscript; and to Naomi Pascal, Kerrie Maynes, and the staff at the University of Washington Press, for their expertise and assistance in bringing *The Adventures of Eddie Fung* to light.

INTRODUCTION

T he way Eddie Fung tells his life story, it has been one adventure after another, beginning with the time he ran away from home to be a cowboy to the time he joined the army and became a prisoner of war. At one level, *The Adventures of Eddie Fung* is a coming-of-age story, of a young man's quest to explore life to its fullest and in the process grow into manhood. At another level, Eddie's story offers us valuable insights into Chinatown life in the 1920s, the myth and reality of the American cowboy, and the survival tactics of a POW.

Very little has been written about the experiences of American-born Chinese in the early twentieth century. Only two autobiographies exist: Pardee Lowe's *Father and Glorious Descendant* and Jade Snow Wong's *Fifth Chinese Daughter*. Both books were published by major publishing houses at a time when U.S.-China relations were at their best and little was known about Chinese Americans.[1] The authors go to great lengths to explain Chinese family life and customs to an American audience and at the same time recount their problems dealing with intergenerational conflict at home and assimilation into mainstream society. Ultimately, Pardee Lowe and Jade Snow Wong demonstrate to readers how it is possible to "blend the conflicting streams of Chinese and American thought" and transcend racial prejudice without feeling embittered or immobilized. As Wong wrote in the 1989 edition of her book, "Despite prejudice, I was never discouraged from carrying out my creed; because of prejudice, the effort is ongoing."[2]

Eddie Fung tells a distinctly different story of Chinese American life in the 1920s and 1930s. He does not speak in the voice of a cultural ambassador, to satisfy the curiosity or assuage the guilt of white America, but from the retrospective perspective of a wayward son who has come to terms with his ethnic identity. Eddie has fond memories of his childhood, bathed in the love and protection of his family and the old bachelor society of Chinatown. He recalls how the family and neighbors pulled together during the Depression and how his immigrant parents taught him to be frugal, self-reliant, resourceful, and a responsible member of society.

There is, however, also a dark side to living in Chinatown that Eddie shares with us. Growing up in the shadows of Chinese Exclusion, when anti-Chinese laws prohibited Chinese immigration and severely restricted Chinese American life, he resented the ghetto conditions and mentality of Chinatown. Many of the Chinese were illegal immigrants who had come to this country posed as "paper sons" of a merchant or U.S. citizen in order to circumvent the Chinese Exclusion Act of 1882, which barred the further immigration of Chinese laborers to this country.[3] Eddie's own father crossed the Canadian border surreptitiously as the "manservant of a Caucasian gentleman." He later found a way to bring his wife and two adopted sons from China as a "paper wife" and as "paper sons." Always fearful of being discovered and deported, his father never explained to him why Eddie's older brothers had different surnames from the rest of the family or why he could not return to Canada or China for a visit. At the time, Eddie thought this duplicity and secrecy was just the way it was for people in Chinatown. Just about everyone lived in overcrowded tenement apartments and seemed afraid of venturing outside the boundaries of Chinatown. It was not until Eddie left home for summer camp and work as a live-in houseboy that he realized other people did not live the same way. They had spacious houses with front yards and backyards. "Okay, people don't have to live in Chinatown in cold-water flats," he reasoned. Certainly, he did not want to continue living that way, so he began to plan his escape.

Eddie had another reason for wanting to leave home—he resented his strict upbringing. Like many other second-generation Chinese Americans, he was expected to do well in American school and Chinese school, to help out at home, to be obedient and respectful to his elders, to follow Chinese customs, and to never bring shame to the family by misbehaving. Yet at American school, through books and movies, and in his contacts with the outside world, he was encouraged to be a rugged individualist, to speak his mind, and to pursue any line of work or lifestyle he pleased. Many Chinese Americans at this time were torn between following the Chinese ways of their parents and following the American ways of mainstream society.[4] Eddie learned to accommodate cultural conflicts as they arose. "You might say that our generation had split personalities," he explained. "When we were inside the house, we were completely Chinese. When we were outside the house, we could be either all Chinese or all American or half and half." Being the curious and rambunctious kid he was, Eddie could not always meet his parents' expectations, nor be satisfied with the restrictions of Chinatown life. Yearning to explore the wider world and to pursue the romantic life of a cowboy on horseback, he decided to strike out on his own and try his luck in Texas. This decision would set Eddie apart from his Chinese American peers, most of whom remained stuck in Chinatown until World War II, when racial discrimination lessened and opportunities opened up for them.

By the time Eddie arrived in Texas in 1938, the Depression was drawing to a close and the cowboy days of cattle drives and open ranges that he had dreamed of were long gone. After the railroads came to Texas, getting the cattle to market became easier. Fewer men were needed to drive the smaller herds of cattle to the shipping points. Fenced ranching allowed ranchers to keep track of their cattle and to improve on their breed, but it meant that cowboys could no longer roam the open range with the cattle. Most work became seasonal, when cowhands were needed for the spring and fall roundups and branding. The rest of the year they were put to work maintaining windmills, repairing fences, and doing farm chores. Instead of the idyllic life Eddie had imagined, where "all you have to do is ride a horse and maybe herd a few cows," it turned out to be nothing but hard work. Any experienced cowpuncher could have told him, "He [would be] poorly fed, underpaid, overworked, deprived of sleep, and prone to boredom and loneliness."[5]

Considering how small in stature and how inexperienced Eddie was, it is amazing that anyone hired him. Eddie credits his success in landing a job to his eagerness to learn and his willingness to accept the low wage of ten dollars a month. His success also attests to the openness and friendliness of ranchers who were willing to give a young man an opportunity to prove himself. As Eddie found out, there was less racial discrimination on the ranch than in town. In 1940, African Americans and Mexicans made up 15 percent and 12 percent of the population in Texas, respectively. They each formed about 14 percent of the cowboy population. Although Jim Crow codes were still strictly enforced, cowboys of color were tolerated on the ranch as long as they had the skills to do the job.[6] In contrast, there were only 1,785 Asians (Chinese and Japanese Americans) in Texas in 1940, accounting for less than 1 percent of the population. Most of the Japanese were rice farmers in the Houston area, while the Chinese operated laundries, cafés, and grocery stores, and lived in segregated communities in El Paso and San Antonio. Small in number and not considered an economic threat to the Anglo population, the Chinese occupied a "gray area" in the black-white racial hierarchy in Texas. They were tolerated and better treated than African Americans and Mexicans, although in 1937 Anglo competitors did try to get an anti-alien land law passed that would have driven Chinese grocers out of business. The measure failed, however, due to opposition from the Chinese community.[7]

Eddie Fung may well have been the only Chinese cowboy in West Texas at the time, and as such he was treated more as a novelty than a threat. As he said, "I was only five feet tall and nonthreatening, so most people took me to be nothing more than a young adventurer." The one Chinese stereotype that stuck to him, however, was that of the proverbial cook or houseboy. Eddie was offered that job more than once, but each time he refused, even though it meant higher wages and easier work. He had come to Texas to be a cowboy, and by the end of his second year he had proven to himself and to others that regardless of ethnicity or size he could do any job assigned to him.

From the vantage point of a Chinatown kid, Eddie shares with us what it was like to be a Texas cowboy in the 1930s. His first job at the Scarborough ranch taught him that cowboys worked hard from sunup to sunset. He had to be a jack-of-all-trades—part mechanic, part vet, and part carpenter—in order to do all the tasks required of him. At his first roundup, Eddie learned how to flank a calf that was three times his weight. He also came to appreciate the code of conduct that most Texas cowboys still abide by—a mixture of rugged individualism, neighborly cooperation, and a strong sense of honor. "If a man gave you his word, there would be no need for a contract," Eddie said. "And if you wanted to be formal about it, you shook hands—that was ironclad." Contrary to the image of the uncouth and uneducated cowboy he had seen on the movie screen, most of the cowboys he came to know were gentle, courteous, and knowledgeable, and they were more than willing to show this greenhorn the tricks of the trade.[8] By the time Eddie was ready to move on to his next adventure, he realized how much he had grown under their tutelage. What he did not know then was how this education would help him become a good soldier and survivor in prison camp.

Most young Texans who joined the National Guard in the 1930s did it for the pay. Some did it for adventure or to make military service their career. But as far as Eddie was concerned, "Here's another place where I can be around horses—I can join the cavalry!" By the time he got to Lubbock, Texas, to inquire about joining the army in May of 1940, Italy had seized Ethiopia, Japan had invaded China, and Germany had swept through most of Europe. Unbeknownst to Eddie, the United States was heading for war, and plans were being made to call for the draft and to mobilize the National Guard. Too young to be admitted into the army without parental consent, Eddie signed up with the Texas National Guard instead. Although he was the only Chinese American in his military unit, he never felt out of place and recalls that he got along fine with all the other men. His size posed more of a problem than his race or ethnicity. But once he proved that he could pull his share of the weight and pass basic training, he earned the respect of his officers and fellow soldiers.

Approximately one million African Americans, 33,000 Japanese Americans, and 15,000 Chinese Americans served in the U.S. armed forces during World War II. Until desegregation in the military was banned by executive order in 1948, African Americans were segregated into separate barracks and units and generally assigned menial duties. Because Japanese

Americans were considered "enemy aliens" after Japan attacked Pearl Harbor, they were only allowed to serve in the Military Intelligence Service in the Pacific theater or in the all-Japanese 100th Battalion and 442nd Regimental Combat Team in the European theater. In contrast, Chinese Americans were integrated into all branches of the military, with the exception of 1,200 men who were assigned to two all-Chinese units in the China-Burma-India theater.[9] With China and the United States at war against Japan, many Chinese Americans joined out of a strong sense of Chinese nationalism and American patriotism. Like Eddie, they experienced no blatant discrimination, and many would agree with Private Charles Leong, who wrote in 1944, "To G.I. Joe Wong in the army, a 'Chinaman's Chance' means a fair chance, not based on race or creed, but on the stuff of the man who wears the uniform of the U.S. Army."[10] In truth, Chinese Americans were caught between the white-over-black paradigm of race relations in the army. They did not suffer the same bigotry directed at African Americans, but neither were they fully accepted as equals by their white counterparts.[11]

While Eddie was training to be a machine gunner at Camp Bowie, Texas, war escalated on the two continents. Germany attacked the Balkans and Russia, and Japan, now a part of the Axis powers, took the French colonies of Indochina. As negotiations with Japan deteriorated, President Franklin D. Roosevelt froze all Japanese assets in America, stopped oil supplies to Japan, and made General Douglas MacArthur commander of the U.S. Army in the Far East. Paralyzed financially and starved for the raw materials needed to keep its war machine going, Japan activated its plans to take over Asia. In November of 1941, Eddie's battalion was sent to the Philippines as reinforcements. En route to the Philippines, he recalls, Pearl Harbor was attacked, and his convoy was diverted to Australia. From there, the 2nd battalion was sent to Java to help the Netherlands defend its colonial outpost. They were no match for the Japanese army. Within a few days, the battle for Java was over, and Eddie became one of 140,000 Allied soldiers to be captured by the Japanese in the Pacific theater.[12] Along with 61,000 American, British, Australian, and Dutch prisoners, Eddie was sent to work on the Burma-Siam railroad—the largest use of POWs in any single project in the Pacific war. For the next forty-two months of captivity, the men would suffer unimaginable brutality, diseases, and starvation in the POW camps. Those who survived the harrowing ordeal would bear the physical and mental scars of incarceration for the rest of their lives. Thus the refrain that is familiar to all of them, "We can forgive, but we can never forget."

Many books have been published and films made about the Pacific war, the experiences of POWs, and the building of the Burma-Siam railroad— the most well known being *Bridge on the River Kwai*. The 1957 Oscar-winning movie, however, gives a misleading account of how the bridge was built and destroyed as well as an erroneous impression of the relationships between the Japanese military, British commander, and prison labor force.[13] More accurate accounts can be found in Gavan Daws's *Prisoners of the Japanese: POWs of World War II in the Pacific* and Clifford Kinvig's *River Kwai Railway: The Story of the Burma-Siam Railroad*.[14] By now, there are also numerous oral histories and memoirs by POW survivors, many of whom worked on the "Death Railroad."[15] They each tell a different story about the life of a POW because no one was alike in their reaction to and interaction with their captors, nor in the way that they perceived and remembered the same events. Gavan Daws points out in his book, "Nationality determined the way POWs lived and died, and often *whether* they lived or died."[16] As Eddie's story bears out, personality and ethnicity were determining factors in the matter. What makes *The Adventures of Eddie Fung* different from other first-person accounts is Eddie's unique perspective and experiences as the only Chinese American to be captured by the Japanese.

According to Eddie, the first thing that crossed his mind after Allied forces capitulated to the Japanese on March 8, 1942, was, "My God, what are they going to do to Foo and me?" Eddie Fung and Frank "Foo" Fujita were the only two Asian American soldiers to be captured by the Japanese in what has been termed a war between the "yellow" race and the "white" race.[17] The assumption was that both would be immediately spotted by the Japanese, then tortured and killed for betraying the "yellow" race. Foo, whose father was Japanese and whose mother was a white American, was able to hide his racial background until his Japanese surname betrayed him in Nagasaki, where he was sent to work in the shipyards while Eddie was sent to Burma to work on the railroad. Foo steadfastly refused to denounce the

United States and participate in propaganda work in Japan, and as a result he was brutally beaten and assigned to latrine duty.[18] As for Eddie, although he was sometimes beaten because he was Chinese, he was never tortured. Instead, he found that his Chinese upbringing made it easier for him to adjust to the meager rice-and-vegetable diet, and to find ways to supplement it with throwaways such as animal organs and fish heads. Even his limited command of the Chinese language came in handy. It allowed him to trade with the local Chinese and to help his commanding officer communicate in writing with the Japanese engineers. Moreover, the domestic and scrounging skills he had acquired as a Chinatown kid proved useful in the camps. For example, Eddie was able to show the cooks how to use a wok, and the food and medicine he scrounged helped him and others to survive. In fact, it was while a prisoner of the Japanese that Eddie learned to appreciate his Chinese background, "I had finally come to terms with my past, and I was looking forward to going home and telling my mother, 'Okay, Mom, I understand what you and Pop have been trying to get through to me—about what it means to be Chinese—and I'm going to try and live up to it.'"

Ultimately, what kept Eddie alive and what makes his story so unique and interesting were his curiosity and desire to learn from his adventures and encounters in life. Even the details of railroad work come alive when seen through Eddie's curious eyes—how the Japanese organized the work crews, how jungles were cleared for the right-of-way, how bridges were built, how the tracks were laid, and how the men were practically worked to death during the "speedo" period. To Eddie, "any job is interesting as long as I'm learning something new." At the lowest point of his captivity, when he was hit with dysentery and malaria and down to sixty pounds, Eddie convinced himself to stay alive for no other reason than to satisfy his curiosity: "I wanted to see what the next day would bring; whether it was good, bad, or indifferent, I just wanted to know."

After the war was over, how did Eddie deal with the scars from his excruciating POW experience? In the final chapter of the book, he talks about going on eating binges, hoarding twenty pounds of coffee at a time, having nightmares, going without sleep for a whole year, and losing his temper over trifling matters. Some of his buddies became alcoholics. A few committed suicide. The V.A. Hospital was of no help, because at the time no one understood what we now know to be posttraumatic stress disorder and survivor's guilt. Even so, Eddie found a way to deal with the problem, and he managed to turn the negative experience into a positive learning experience. By the time we get to the end of Eddie's story, we can discern that he is finally at peace with himself. Upon reflection he said, "I've never regretted the war or the hardships I've suffered, because it made me a better man."

The Adventures of Eddie Fung is an important contribution to our understanding of Chinese American life, cowboy culture, and the experiences of American POWs in World War II. It is also a remarkable chronicle of a Chinatown boy's journey to manhood that will leave a lasting impression on our hearts and minds.

—JUDY YUNG

THE ADVENTURES OF EDDIE FUNG

ONE · GROWING UP IN CHINATOWN

Pop named me Man Quong, which means "intellectually bright," so my father had high expectations of me. Years later, when I visited our ancestral village in China for the first time, they knew right away who I was, because Pop had sent money back to celebrate my birth and I was written in the village genealogy book. From all of this, I suspect that he must have been very disappointed in me as I was growing up. But unfortunately, I cannot change my nature. I don't know why I had itchy feet, why I was born curious, so curious that I had to see what was on the other side of the hill.

MY FATHER, FUNG CHONG POO

My father, Fung Chong Poo, was a wetback—he sneaked in from Canada. According to people I talked to later, at one time he lived in Chinatown and worked as a kitchen helper in a downtown hotel in Nanaimo. He crossed the border posing as the manservant of a Caucasian gentleman—that was how he got into the U.S. My guess is that it was in the late 1890s, when he was in his early twenties. Dad was from Lei Yuen (Pearl Garden) village in Enping District, Guangdong Province (near Hong Kong). My mother, Ng Shee, was from Si Ji Yim (Lion's Loin) village, also in Enping District. The funny thing about the Enping people, if you meet a married woman with the surname Fung, the chances are she used to be a Ng from somewhere around Si Ji Yim. And if you meet a married woman with the surname Ng, the chances are she was a Fung. You see, most villages in China at this time were inhabited by people with the same surname, and young people in one village were often arranged in marriage to prospective spouses in nearby villages. We're so intermarried within that area, it's almost incestuous!

I had two older adopted brothers who were born in China, and four older sisters and a younger brother who were born at home like me. My father, being a progressive man, chose to use a lady doctor instead of a midwife. The reason we had two adopted brothers was because after my parents got married in China and before Pop came over to America, it was thought that Mom was barren. So since he was going to find his fortune in the West, he decided to adopt two sons to keep her company in China. But when he finally got her over here in 1914, one year later, my older sister Mary was born! How did Pop get his wife and two sons over here when he was illegal? He had a brother in San Francisco who had a wife and three sons in China. As a merchant, he could have brought them to America, but he never intended to do so. Instead, he sold the papers to my father. Mom came over legally as my uncle's wife, and my oldest adopted brother, Al, came as my uncle's ten-year-old son, Ho Li Quong.[1] Somehow, Pop knew the Chinese consul general, and in 1939 the consul fixed it so that Mom and Uncle were divorced, and Mom and Pop got married. As to my second adopted brother, Francis, or Pee Wee as we called him, Pop was able to buy immigration papers for him to come in 1920 as Hom Sin Kay, the nine-year-old son of a native-born citizen. Both Al and Pee Wee retained their paper names because it would get too complicated. The consul general could only do so much.

This would create all kinds of problems for us later, like when I went overseas in November of 1941 and my mother said, "You stop in Honolulu and find out how Pee Wee is doing." At the time he was a seaman on the Matson lines. We had one day in Honolulu, so I went to the Seamans Union. I was in uniform, and I said, "I want to find out if my brother is in port." "What's your brother's name?" I said, "Hom Sin Kay." He said, "What ship is he on?" I said, "*Lurline*." And he said, "*Lurline* is not in." So he said, "Who are you?" I said, "I'm his brother." So I pulled out my dog tag. He said, "You're Fung, Edward. How can he be your brother when his surname is Hom?" I said, "I don't know, but he's always been my brother." This "paper son" business— I just never thought anything of it because it was so common in Chinatown.

FIG. 1. *Studio portrait of the Fung family, 1924. Left to right, front row: Grace, Minerva, mother Ng Shee (holding William), father Fung Chong Poo (holding Eddie), Mary, and Jessie; back row: cousin Tom Fung, Albert, cousin Harry Fung, and cousin Fung Woi Quong.*

According to hearsay, Pop was a hell-raiser. When he was a young man, he wore a pigtail, which was required of all Chinese subjects during the reign of the Manchus (1644–1911). One day he was running an errand for his boss and he was impatient. He jumped off the cable car before it stopped and his queue wound around the stanchion. Basically, he fell under the cable car—that was how he lost his leg. He learned to be a jeweler and watchmaker because he had to find some job he could do sitting down. I remember when I was about eight, he gave me an alarm clock and showed me how to get started taking it apart. I took it all apart. He said, "Now put it back together." I couldn't do it, and he tried to show me. He said, "It's perfectly logical. This has to go in first, then this goes on top of this, and this goes alongside of it." It all made sense, but I couldn't do it. And, theoretically, the alarm clock is the easiest to repair!

My father was not the kind of man you asked personal questions about.

If he wanted you to know something, he would let you know. But I could tell through our little sessions—like the time he taught me how to make a bow and arrow—that he had many experiences to draw from. One time in 1937, when we had the coldest winter in many years, he said, "Do you think this is cold? In Montana I was at a ranch house, and when we threw a basin of water out the back porch, it would freeze before it hit the ground. Now *that's* cold." In retrospect, then, you can kind of backtrack and say, "How did he get into the United States from Canada?" It wasn't straight down through Washington and Oregon; he must have taken a roundabout way, going down through Montana. Another time when I saw the movie *San Francisco*, with Clark Gable, Spencer Tracy, and Jeanette MacDonald, I came home and he asked, "What movie did you see?" And I told him. He started reminiscing about the 1906 earthquake in San Francisco, and how he had to stay at an encampment in the army presidio designated for Chinese people. He recalled how as soon as the bugler sounded retreat, which is the time to lower the flag, the horses would know exactly what they were supposed to do—pull caissons in formation. He said, "Just like the fire horses when they hear the fire alarm, they know that they have to go. All they need is the direction from the driver as to where." So he was telling me about the army life that he saw as a refugee from the earthquake. Of course, I later found out that it was an advantage for the Chinese that the earthquake happened, because with all the birth records destroyed, they could then claim U.S. citizenship and help bring in a number of fictitious sons from China.

My father spoke fairly good English and he was a Christian, so I gather the reason I was named Edward was because of Reverend Edwards, a Methodist minister who had taught him English. When we were kids, every Thanksgiving my father would roast a turkey with all the trimmings, and he would also bake pumpkin pies. Then the whole family would take the streetcar and troop out to Sixth Avenue, where the Edwards sisters lived after the minister died. We always had Thanksgiving dinner with the spinster sisters until they went to live in a retirement home. We knew from *that* that Pop felt an obligation to Reverend Edwards. And when Chinese incur an obligation, it's lifelong—it's never paid off.

I also learned later from old-timers about how my father made his first

$10,000. They said that during World War I, he was buying and salvaging gunnysacks used for bagging potatoes. If they were in good shape, he would pay a penny for it. If not, people would give it to him and he would spend his nights patching them. Everyone thought he was crazy because he rented a warehouse to store all these bags. He foresaw the scarcity of gunnysacks (used for bagging potatoes) after the war—that's how he made his first bundle of money, selling gunnysacks. Pop was one of these guys who in the 1920s could see "strip cities," all the way from San Francisco to San Jose. He was always traveling to Vallejo, Walnut Creek, and all sorts of places outside San Francisco, scouting out business opportunities. But if he made any money, he would use it to help people, not hoard it.

I think Pop helped at least four kinsmen come to the United States. I used to ask him why, because we could have used the money ourselves. He said, "No matter how rough you think you have it here, it's much worse than you can imagine in China. So anytime I have a chance to help bring someone over, I will." And he said, "I will not deprive you of any food, shelter, or clothing—you have the basics. All I want to do is give someone else the opportunity to have the same things." He used to buy land in China from my uncle, who wanted the money more than the land, since he had no intention of ever going back to China. Pop was always helping out his village. I think they had some bandit problems one time. I remember so distinctly—Pop and Al were wrapping cartridges of .38–caliber bullets in toilet paper. Then they hid them in a grindstone before shipping it to China. I asked Al years later what that was all about, and he said, "We had to smuggle these cartridges to the villagers who had guns but could not buy any ammunition. Bandits were extorting money from the villagers for so-called protection." So that was why they needed the bullets—to try and fend off the bandits.

My father kept a book of the monies that he had lent or expended to help bring people over from China. Theoretically, there was an agreement that the person's family would pay him back if and when they could afford it. In other words, the debt was on the book. When my father passed away in 1940, Mom asked Al to try and collect some of the money. It turned out that people were not as ethical as Pop had thought. Many of them said, "We've already paid the debt back and your father must have forgotten to mark it down." Other people would deny that they were even indebted to my father. So after a couple of weeks of that, Mom told Al, "Put a notice in the Chinese papers that the Fungs do not owe anyone, nor are the Fungs owed by anyone else." In other words, the slate's wiped clean. She figured if anyone was going to honor his debt after the notice, he would still pay it. And it was at that point that the Fungs got a reputation for being *choi gee lo* (wealthy people), because they could afford to write off the debts. But that wasn't true—Mom just didn't want the aggravation.

You might say that my father was progressive in the way that he treated the girls in the family. Whenever his friends kidded him about having so many girls, he would say, "My girls are better than any of the sons you have." Back in those times, that was high praise because girls didn't really count for much. But he was that kind of a person. He didn't care whether you were male or female. If you brought pride to him, you were bringing joy to him. When my sisters graduated from the prestigious Lowell High School and they wanted to go on to college, my father encouraged them to do so. All his peers laughed at him, "Why are you letting your girls go to college? They're just going to get married and raise families." He told them that education was something no one could take away from you. It didn't matter if his daughters got married and had families, they could still be educated. All the girls went to the University of California, Berkeley. Mary went for optometry in 1938, and upon graduating she opened her own office at the corner of Sacramento and Grant. Jessie majored in anthropology and worked as a bookkeeper for Sherwin–Williams Paint Company before marrying Bill, an electrical engineer, and moving to Bakersfield. Number three, Minerva—we called her Mints—studied literature at Cal. She met and married Jim, a Caucasian guy who later became a psychologist. My parents did not approve; neither did his mother. Back then, they could not get married in California, so they got married in the state of Washington, where it was allowed.[2] My fourth sister, Grace, never attended college because she had asthma. Early on, when she was twelve or thirteen, she was sent to live with a family in Fresno, which would hopefully help her asthmatic condition.

Although my father was gentle and supportive of his daughters, he was hard on his sons. Have you ever heard the term *sa heng*? It's a rattan whip.

That was what Pop used on my younger brother Bill and me whenever we did something bad—the usual kid stuff, like fighting or sneaking into theaters without paying or shoplifting at the dime store. We didn't have any toys, so naturally when we were in a variety store and saw all these things, we would shoplift. Whenever Pop found out about it, he would whip us in no uncertain terms, saying that he didn't want this sort of thing happening again. Anytime he whipped us, we had given him a reason—there was no question about that. It wasn't child abuse. He was just trying to get a point across: there was proper behavior and there was improper behavior.

I would not go so far as to say that my father was a dictator. He often tried reasoning with me. One time after I had been reported fighting again, he took me aside and said, "Men reason, animals fight." Another time he admonished me by saying that my behavior reflected poorly upon him as the father, and, by extension, the family name and the clan. He never went any further than that. He probably decided, if nothing else—even if I were puzzled by what he had said—maybe I would start thinking about it. I remember I used to have a flash temper and I would go around slamming doors in the house. One day my father was home and he saw that I was mad about something. After about four doors, he said, "Do you feel better now?" And I said, "What?" He said, "All that door slamming, what are you mad about?" And he said, "After you're done slamming all those doors, do you feel any better? Has your problem gone away? Whatever you were angry about, it's still there, right?" And I knew he was right.

MY MOTHER, NG SHEE

If Pop was the head of the household, Mom was the heart of the house. If we had a scrapped knee or a skinned elbow, we would go to Mom, and she would kiss it and make it well. If we had a problem that needed solving, we would go to Pop, although he just basically handed out edicts. Mom came from a fairly poor background, judging by the fact that she did not have bound feet.[3] As far as I know, Mom's father was an itinerant herb dealer, and her brother was physically handicapped, so she had to take care of him all the time.[4] She never talked about herself except in a very peripheral way. For instance, when Bill and I would come in hot from play and we would stick our heads under the faucet to drink cold water, Mom would be horrified, because she had seen cholera in her village. Of course, we told her, "Mom, this is America. Things like that don't happen." Every morning, she boiled a pot of water, put it in the tea caddy, and that was the water she drank. It was only when I saw the effects of cholera in the POW camps that I realized why it had made such a deep impression on her. When the girls started working and had a little money set aside, they asked my mom, "Would you like to go back to China for a visit?" She said, "Me go back *there,* where there's no running water and flush toilets? Absolutely not!" So Mom didn't have any romantic notions about what she had left. She was perfectly content, even though we didn't have much. One of the things I remember she always said when people were having problems adjusting to a new environment, she would always say *jun sui,* meaning "change of water." In other words, they had gone to an area where the water was different. I will never forget that, especially later in the camps, where every drop of water that passed our lips had to be boiled.

My mother was a housewife and she worked as a seamstress at home. She did very fine hand sewing of tailored suits, where she put in the linings in the suit coat, the vest, and the pants. And she hand made the buttonholes and sewed on the buttons. All she got was twenty-five cents a suit. It was considered a favor by the tailor to even give her that kind of work, because there were lots of people who would have been glad to have the work. She also made all our clothes—pants and shirts—on a Singer foot-treadle machine. When she found out from the sewing ladies that there were such things as hemmers and buttonhole attachments, she expressed one time that she wished she could have these attachments. So Pop went down to the Singer sewing machine display room and looked to see how these things were made. Then he came back to his shop and with scrap pieces of tin and copper, he tried to make what Mom wanted. Now these things were for electrical machines, so he would make it, try it out on Mom's machine, and if it didn't work exactly the way it was supposed to, he would take it back and modify it until he got it just right. So Mom got all these attachments meant for electrical machines for her foot-treadle machine, and that made her job a lot easier.

My dad never went to school, but he was self-educated. My mom, on the other hand, was illiterate in both Chinese and English. I guess with all those kids, she never had time to learn English, even if Pop were willing to teach her. So when we started learning to speak English, Pop said, "Inside the house you will speak Cantonese, because it would be disrespectful to your mother. She would not understand a word you're saying." He also told us that in the company of strangers we should not speak Chinese because, regardless of what we were saying, they might take it the wrong way. When Mom wanted to go shopping, like at the Emporium, she would come to Commodore Stockton School and ask for me. The principal would know why she was coming. I would take her wherever she wanted to go and help her carry the packages. Then, of course, she always bargained. My sisters would tell her, "If the Emporium says it's nineteen cents a yard, you can't bargain." She might buy ten yards and she would say, "Ask the salesgirl if it would be cheaper." So I said, "Mom, they won't." She said, "Ask them anyway." I loved my mom dearly, so I would always ask. And the salesgirl would inevitably say, "No, it's not our policy." I would tell Mom. Then she was happy that I had asked. She couldn't make change, so she would hold out the money in her hand. She was never cheated, as far as I could see. We were never embarrassed by what my mom did because we realized that there was something in her background that made bargaining a part of her character. I remember her saying that in China she saw meat for sure once a year, and that was at New Year's, and maybe on her birthday. None of us, even living as we did in Chinatown, could quite picture that, because we always had food on the table.

My fondest memory of my mom has nothing to do with her working and slaving her fingers to the bone. My oldest brother's wife and Mom both had long hair, and we're talking about as far down as to the waist if it's hanging free. I remember Ah So (Auntie) and Mom would sit sort of side by side and they would groom each other's hair. Then, of course, they would braid it and wear it in a *gai* (bun). Mom had enough hair that she had to have two buns. Back in those days, we didn't even have shampoo. Mom used Chinese soap to wash her hair and *pow fah* (paste made from wood shavings) to dress it. Then I think it was around 1933 or '34 when the girls talked Mom into cutting off her hair. I know that for a lady it is a lot of weight on her scalp, and the care of the bobbed hair is a lot easier, but I sure missed that long hair.

My other fond memory of my mother would be her cooking. Mom was a good cook. I don't know where she got the training or how she learned it, but whenever relatives from Stockton came to town, they would hand Mom fifty dollars and all they wanted was for Mom to cook her specialties. And we all got to be participants in this feast—we were all going to eat. Now, her specialties were always bird's-nest or shark-fin soup—depending on which one the relative wanted: fried squab; West Lake duck; fried prawns; a dish of sea cucumber, abalone, and mushrooms; steamed chicken; steamed fish; and a vegetable dish.

The chicken and squab had to be fresh. There used to be poultry stores on Grant Avenue, right across the street from the old opera house. Mom would feel the breast and pick the one she wanted. She never had the market do the killing or cleaning—same thing with the squabs, even though she might be buying as many as four or six, depending on the size. She didn't want me to see her kill the squab, so she would strangle it inside a bag. Then we would defeather them, which was made easier by dipping them in hot water first. The reason she retained the blood in the carcass was so that when she deep-fried it, it would have that nice moist, dark color. With the chicken, she would cut the throat and drain the blood. That was when I learned about blood pudding. She would put the blood into a bowl and steam it. Blood pudding wasn't served at the banquet; it was just a question of not wasting it. Then Mom would have me help her pluck the chicken, and she would clean the insides and save the gizzards, the liver, and so on. If she had time, she would even save the chicken intestines and clean them thoroughly on the outside. Then she would take a chopstick and turn the intestines inside out and clean the inside, and then do the outside again, do the inside again, and make sure it was thoroughly clean. The intestines she would serve as a side dish to the family on another day. I learned early on from my mother that nothing should be wasted. So it was fairly natural for me, when I was in the prison camps, not to waste anything either.

My mom hardly left home except to go shopping. Naturally, every chance we had, we would try to get Mom out of the house and basically not be so concerned about whether all the clothes had been washed and ironed. I mean, the chores were endless when you consider there were six kids and no modern conveniences. Aside from the Chinese opera, she loved the movies, especially the comedies, so every once in a while, my sisters would take her downtown to see movies like *Alice in Wonderland* or *Tom Sawyer*. The girls said Mom couldn't understand a word of English, but she knew exactly when to laugh and when to cry. Once they found out that she could enjoy a movie without understanding a word of English, they would take her more often. But usually her movies were confined to Chinatown. There were at least three theaters that showed Chinese movies during the daytime because at night they were converted to opera houses. She went maybe once or twice a month. I know it was only a nickel for me, and maybe ten cents for an adult. I didn't especially like the Chinese movies, but since Mom enjoyed them, I didn't mind going with her. But she definitely liked slapstick, and we never figured out how she picked that up.

GROWING UP POOR AT 842 WASHINGTON

Our family was not dirt-poor. There were no luxuries, but we had the basics—a roof over our heads, clean clothes—even if they were mended—and nutritious food. For the first nine years of my life, we lived at 842 Washington Street, on the third floor. There were five families on that floor. We had two rooms, for a total of nine people. All four girls slept in one room, and the three boys had the front room, which served as the living room in the daytime, the dining room at night, and our bedroom after dinner. There was a hall closet in between, where Mom and Pop slept. And they cut off an area no more than two feet by three feet for Mom's three-burner gas stove—that was her cooking space. There were two toilets and one community kitchen on our floor, and all the water came from that kitchen. Every Saturday night, we would bring water in by the buckets and use every container we had to boil water, and everyone would take turns taking a bath in the number-two washtub. It was a continuous water-bucket parade! Everyone in Chinatown lived like this. There were people in the building who lived in more restricted circumstances than us—four or five people in one room. Yet they managed as we all did.

I remember hand-me-downs in the sense that we didn't always have new clothes and new shoes. There was one pair of shoes that I just hated. I don't even remember where they came from. They had no shoelaces and required

FIG. 2. *Storefronts below 842 Washington Street, where Eddie lived in the 1920s. The waiter is delivering a tray of restaurant food that he balances on his head. Courtesy Bancroft Library, University of California, Berkeley.*

a buttonhook to connect the mating hooks together. I could have sworn the shoes were made out of iron, because they never showed any signs of wear. Thank goodness I finally outgrew them! Even when we bought new shoes, we always bought them much larger so that we could grow into them. The one thing that I resented about hand-me-downs was sometimes I had to wear my sister's undies. Hand-me-downs, *that's* exactly what it means—handed down. When the girls had outgrown them, they were passed down. And if it just happened you were a boy—that was tough!

With my father's earnings as a watchmaker, we always managed. I don't remember ever eating breakfast until we started junior high school, but for lunch we had a piece of pastry or bread with milk. Our main meal together was supper, and that was when Mom would cook rice, soup, some vegetables, and a little meat. She would send me down to the Chinese grocery store to buy two and a half cents' worth of beef, two and a half cents' worth of pork, and that would be the meat ration for the day. Then, of course, the vegetables—two bunches of *gai choy* (mustard greens) for a nickel, three bunches of bok choy for a nickel. In our time, you could *chaan* (ask for free) some *chong* (green onions), *mien seen jeong* (bean paste), or some liver. Any of the animal organs were free. Butcher town was down on Evans Street, and every Friday a big truck would come to Waverly and Washington with all these organs—tripe, hearts, stomachs, livers, kidneys, and so on, from all kinds of animals—and we could take anything we wanted. Any other time we wanted liver, we would go to any Chinese grocery store, preferably one that relatives ran or had shares in, and we would ask for a piece of liver for our cat. Everyone knew that the Fungs didn't have a cat, but they knew that we had six kids, so they would give us a commensurate-size piece of liver. That was so that we didn't lose face. We were going to help each other out, period. Otherwise, nobody was going to survive.

The only time we ever splurged was at Chinese New Year's. Mom would make the traditional vegetarian dish, *jai*, and we would have chicken for a change. She would also take out the beautiful, ornate wooden case with the compartments for the various sweetmeats. We could look, but "no touch," and definitely "no take." We knew it was for display and to impress the guests. Even the guests never really took things from the trays. If someone were visiting with kids, the parents would make sure that they didn't try to empty out the compartments. Later on, we would get a treat, and my favorite was the sugared coconut peelings. Of course, we always looked forward to getting *li see* (lucky money in a red envelope) from the adults. This was how we worked it: We had six kids in our family, and the Wong family on our floor had two girls. Now, suppose Mrs. Wong gave six of us a quarter each—that would be a dollar and a half. So Mom would keep track, and what happened was that Mom would make sure that the Wong family got back a buck and a half. The Wongs couldn't afford to give us a buck and a half, and we couldn't afford to give them six bits for each girl. But on the other hand, if we kind of kept track, we could each follow the tradition of giving kids *li see,* and there would be no net loss. We never kept the money from the *li see,* but every once in a while, Mom would say we could keep a nickel. The money was usually kept in circulation.

Everyone was expected to help out as much as they could. Mom sewed at home, and I remember the girls started out picking shrimp at a factory on Clay Street. But after they got lice in their hair, Mom said, "No, no, we're going to do this at home." They basically worked in the living room of our small apartment. But after a year of that, my father put a stop to it, saying that it was more important for the girls to keep up with their schoolwork. I remember one other job we all took a hand in was wrapping Chinese characters that were printed on sheets of paper for the Chinatown lottery. We would all sit around the dinner table and bundle up sets of Chinese characters and put them in boxes. It was a lot of work for a penny a box. Later, the girls took on babysitting jobs outside Chinatown to bring in extra income.

If you didn't help out earning spare change, you could always help out at home— cleaning house, getting water from the common kitchen, cooking, and so on. But everyone was expected to help in some way, and as we got older, we had more responsibilities. So I never had what was called a "childhood." I started helping around the house when I was five or six years old, and I started working as a shoeshine boy when I was eight. It was a nickel for a shine. I would go over to Portsmouth Square with my shoe box filled with shoe polishes and brushes and ask people if they wanted a shine. Another place I would go to was the bail bond office on Merchant and Kearny, where the policemen sometimes hung out. By and by, I developed a steady clientele, and certain people would wait for me to come by to give them a shoeshine.

Then, when I was about nine years old, I started delivering newspapers. Tommy Yip, who lived across the hall from us, had a paper route with about 100 papers or subscribers. He offered me ten dollars a month to deliver half of the papers. Tommy was responsible for delivering the other half, and also for collecting from each subscriber. Later, I found out that each subscriber paid seventy-five cents a month for their subscription. So, for 100 papers, that would be seventy-five dollars. From that seventy-five dollars, Tommy paid *San Francisco News* fifty dollars, so he got twenty-five dollars. Well, he paid me ten dollars, so he was still ahead by fifteen dollars. But then, he could lose money if a subscriber defaulted, and ten dollars seemed like pretty good money to me. The first month I got my ten dollars, I walked up to Mom and I handed her the ten dollars, and I told her how I had earned it. She said, "No, Man (my Chinese name), I keep half and you keep half."

FIG. 3. *Two boys—possibly Eddie and his brother Bill—shine shoes in Portsmouth Square, 1930s.*

That's the way it was—she would never take all my money. When I got my own paper route and was making a little more money, she still only took half.

THINGS GET BETTER AT 130 TRENTON

Somehow Pop saved enough money to buy a two-story house at 130 Trenton Street in Chinatown, and we were able to move there in 1931. Compared to 842 Washington, it was luxurious. We had four bedrooms—one for Mom and Pop, one for the girls, one for Al and his family, and one for Bill and me. There was a living room, a kitchen with hot running water, and a bathroom with a bathtub and toilet. The house also came with a back yard that Pop made into a garden. He loved to garden, and I remember he had a camellia bush that was the envy of Chinatown. We had a light well and windows in the front rooms, so the place was well lighted and ventilated.

I remember my sister Grace telling me years later that as soon as she got her first full-time job, she decided, "I'm going to get Mom a treat." She went to Montgomery Ward and she picked out a range and a refrigerator. She told the store to deliver it to 130 Trenton and set it up. She came home that night from work, looked around—no range, no refrigerator. She asked, "Mom, didn't someone deliver anything today?" She said, "Oh, some crazy *lo faan* (foreigner) tried to bring a stove and an icebox in here. I told him I didn't order anything and shooed him away." She said, "But Mom, that was for you, I got them for you." She looked at Grace and said, "I don't need a range; I don't need an icebox—don't spend your money that way." Finally, Pop went down to the used furniture store on Pacific and Stockton and picked up a range for ten dollars, and, of course, like any sensible Chinese woman of her time, Mom used the oven for storing pots and pans. As for the range, Mom said, "I don't need a range; gas burner is fine." Pop said, "No, now you have four burners." So, okay, she won't fight it, and she went ahead and started using it.

After my sisters started working and making more money, they asked her, "Don't you want a washing machine?" She said, "I don't need that." We're talking about hand scrubbing the sheets and cleaning all our comforters every once in a while. She would have to unbaste the linen and the cover, and she would wash all those and air out the batting, and all this by hand. Mom was one of these people who can always manage, even if a catastrophe were to hit. I mean, as far as she was concerned, she had hot water that came out of a tap, she didn't have to boil it on the stove—that was good enough for her. Mom taught us to work under any condition. Most people would call it primitive, but I think to her, it was just basic survival. I never heard her complain, although she had plenty of reasons to. She just took the attitude, "What good is it going to do to complain? The conditions aren't going to get better because you complain."

It was strange that I got to be so close to my mom, because it's usually the girls who get close to their moms. What was it Oscar Wilde said? "All women become like their mothers. That is their tragedy. No man does. That's his." You know, he's right! The first time I realized I could help Mom out was after we had moved to Trenton Street. She was washing sheets and clothes for at least eight people in a number–two washtub. She now had a hot water tank, but she still had to heat up the water, because the hot water heater couldn't keep up with her. After she rinsed out the wash, I would help her turn the crank on the mangle while she fed the sheets or clothes through. Then I would help her hang the wash on the line to dry out over the backyard. She would be in front, and I would hand her the sheet so that she could clip a clothespin on it before feeding the line out. When it was dried, I would help her fold it up. Then I also found out that when she was preparing the evening meal, I could help her wash the vegetables, cut them up, and so on. That was my way of being close to my mom without being in her way. Of course, the girls were busy with schoolwork and trying to maintain good grades, so it felt almost natural that helping Mom would fall on me. She never complained, she never asked me, but, on the other hand, whenever we worked together, we coordinated pretty well.

There was only one time Mom got peeved at me. She was making rice wine, and, of course, any Chinese knows that rice wine is not wine—it's distilled whisky used for cooking. So Mom got everything started, and we were in the distillation process. She had all these empty bottles waiting, and it was drip, drip, drip. She told me, "I want you to watch these, and when a bottle gets full, I want you to slip in an empty bottle." It was going so slowly that I went out to play. I didn't realize I was out that long. When I came back, there was wine on the floor. I had never seen my mother so mad—she was ready to kill me! But she finally simmered down, and she said, "I want you to sit right here and watch. No going outside." She never struck me, but I knew she was peeved at me, and I knew she had cause to be peeved. So from then on, whenever she made rice wine, Mom would make absolutely sure I had a chair so that I could sit right there and watch every drip, drip, drip.

Things got better after we moved to Trenton Street, but our parents continued to stress the importance of being frugal and self-reliant to us. There were never leftovers as such. The only thing that we needed the cupboard for was Pop's marmalade, the unused butter, and a can of evaporated milk, usually with a piece of wax paper stuck into the opening. That was all we needed; everything else was in daily use. Once in a while, we got canned goods like corned beef from a family that was on welfare—this was during the Depression. I remember asking my father, "Why don't we just go ahead and apply for welfare and get it ourselves?" He said, "No, these people are giving these things away because they don't want to waste it. We'll take it, but we're not going to ask for anything as long as we can get by." To this day, I call it *haan* (being frugal), and other people may call it something else. There are people who have thrown away canned meat or boxes of cereal. And when I see anything thrown away, I'll pick it up because I can't stand wasting food. I would literally throw away a five-dollar bill before I would throw away food, because food is food in hand; the five-dollar bill only represents the purchasing power to buy food.

I wasn't designated to be the scrounger for the family; it just came about naturally. The produce section used to be on Davis Street—a five-block spread between Jackson and California streets—before they moved to South San Francisco. When we needed vegetables, I would go down to the produce section, because I knew it from my paper route. I would scrounge carrots, potatoes, tomatoes, and whatever was available and bring them home to supplement our vegetable diet. On Clay Street, right below Kearny Street, was the poultry and fish wholesale area. The poultry market would put chicken feet, duck feet, and turkey feet in separate fifty-gallon drums, and anyone could come by and grab a sackful. Turkey feet were the primary pick because they had eatable tendons; then duck feet next. The fish markets would filet the fish, and fish being one of the cheapest meats you could buy at the time, they didn't worry about taking every bit of meat off. I would bring home fish heads and fish tails, and Mom would make a stew or use them to make a fish stock to go with the vegetables. The first time I brought vegetables home, Mom said, "Where did you get these?" I said, "From the produce section." And she said, "How much did it cost you?" I said, "Nothing, it's free. Anytime you want vegetables, I can get it for you." I added, "Different kinds, too." She said, "I understand." She didn't say, "You have to do it." She just appreciated the fact that I did it; the same thing with the fish heads, the turkey feet, and so on.

We never bought fresh bread or fresh pastries. On a weekly basis, my mother would hand me a quarter and I was supposed to run down to Eighth and Howard, where the day-old Langendorf Bakery was, and buy the weekly supply of bread and breakfast rolls. I had acquired a pair of roller skates, so without my mother's knowledge, I would use the roller skates to skate down to Eighth and Howard. It was a pretty fast trip if I didn't fool around, except that I usually did. Crystal Palace used to be at Eighth and Market. It was at least half a square block, and it was all enclosed. They had different vendors selling cheese, smoked meats, bacon, hams, and staples—anything that you wanted to buy in the way of food. There were, of course, people like the snake oil salesman, who would put on a show to attract customers to their stands. And there were always free samples of squares of cheeses and salami, boloney, or whatever they were trying to push. So once I got to Eighth and Market, I would take off my skates and casually walk through Crystal Palace, taking in the food displays and spectacular demonstrations. Then I would put on my skates again and go to Eighth and Howard to do my shopping and come back. The bread was used to make sandwiches and the rolls for breakfast. Every afternoon at 4:00 Mom and Pop had toast and coffee. That was their daily ritual, when they both sat down for half an hour and relaxed.

We didn't start celebrating birthdays until we got more settled on Trenton Street, and, of course, with six kids, there was always someone's birthday or another. Mom had one rule—we could pick pork chops or hamburger, and there was always a cake from Victoria Pastry. If we wanted hamburger, she would go down to Duck Hing, which was on the corner of Washington and Wentworth. The butcher would say, "How many pounds do you want, Mrs. Fung?" And she would say, "X number of pounds." He would cut up a big chunk of chuck and show it to her. Then he would go and grind it. She didn't want hamburger that was already ground; she wanted to know exactly what went into that hamburger. Strangely enough, we would usually all pick hamburger. She would cook it and serve the patty on a sourdough bun—a regular American hamburger, but no French fries. I'm not sure where Mom picked it up, but she decided, "Okay, now that we can afford it, we're going to do it."

FAMILY RELATIONS

The birth order in our family was Mary, Jessie, Mints, Grace, me, and Bill. Regardless of the birth order, there's always someone who takes more responsibility than the other siblings, and in my family that was Jessie. She was always the one who looked after us outside the house. She was bossy, but not to the point where it would bother me. There was no question that if she wanted you to do something, she would make sure you knew. When she and Mary were going to UC Berkeley, and on their way home one afternoon they encountered a masher, Jess took off her shoe and just beat him over the head. That's the kind of person Jess is. I mean, if you don't bother her, she's a perfectly cordial person, but if you bug her, you better stand aside because she's going to do something about it. I never could figure out why my father felt that I had to be the chaperone when Jess was perfectly capable of handling any situation. But then again, my father was old-fashioned. He believed that it was the responsibility of the

FIG. 4. *The interior of the Crystal Palace Market at Market and Eighth streets, 1935. Courtesy San Francisco History Center, San Francisco Public Library.*

men in the family to protect the women. "I don't care if you blush, I don't care if you're standing one foot to the other," he said to me. "You're a man in the family, and you're to fulfill your obligations." And that was that!

When I was at the playground and people asked me who Grace was, I would say, "That's my *dei* (older sister). I always liked that about the Chinese family system. There was no question about whether your sister was older or younger, or whether an uncle was on the maternal side or the paternal side, and so on. I loved it because it was so orderly and you knew exactly where you stood in the family. When we were growing up, I didn't just say, "Hey, you, kid," to my brother Bill. I always addressed him as "*sai lo* (younger brother)," and he would call me "*gor* (older brother)." It was perfectly natural, and each member of the family would look out for the others in the family. All my sisters would have the responsibility of looking after me, and I would have to pay attention and answer to their authority. And I was supposed to take care of my younger brother. If I said anything to him, he was supposed to respond to my authority. But Bill, being much taller than I, always resented the fact that I was big brother and he was little brother. That was enough for us to get into a fight every day. Then, of course, Pop would hear about it. We always thought he was omnipotent. Here he was stuck in his watch repair shop, but he knew exactly what we had been up to because Chinatown was such a close-knit community.

In a way, I hated the fact that the boundaries of Chinatown were limited by Sacramento Street on the south, Pacific Avenue on the north, Kearny Street on the east, and Powell Street on the west. It was basically twelve square blocks. I didn't know the word "ghetto" then, but I knew that we were confined to living within these boundaries. On the other hand, the thing I loved about Chinatown was the fact that we were a very close-knit community. Everyone looked out for all the kids to make sure that they didn't get into trouble and that no one tried to molest them. And if any of us got into a fight, it would be reported to our parents. Just like this business about "It takes a village to raise a child," it was literally true in Chinatown. In our time, Chinatown was comprised largely of bachelors, because men couldn't bring their wives over for one reason or another, so all children were loved and appreciated. We knew that everyone cared.

FIG. 5. *From left to right: Eddie with his nephew Raymond, sister Grace, and brother Bill, 1930.*

GOING TO SCHOOL

It was a big deal for me when I started preschool at five years old. It was held in the backyard of the Gum Moon school for girls on Washington Street—only a block away from home. I was only there from 9:00 to 12:00 in the morning. But I remember it was a big adventure, because when my mother took me to school in the morning, we had to cross Stockton Street. Then when I started first grade at Commodore Stockton Elementary School, I remember some of the kids who were homesick started crying almost immediately. But I loved school because of the novelty of being in a new situation. We were exposed to so much that we didn't know about— the multiplication tables, English grammar, classical music, geography, and so on. We used to read the Kiplinger newsletter, which showed us statistics on what a lawyer, doctor, engineer, or teacher earned—I guess to start us thinking about career choices. The teachers also exposed us to current events and economics—it was all new to me.

The only time I was ever absent from school was when my mother needed me to go downtown to interpret for her. Well, there was one other time I missed school. I remember it was a nice day, and I decided I was just going to take a walk and enjoy the day. The next day, the principal, Miss Crow, called me into her office. She said, "Eddie, do you have a written excuse from your parents?" I said, "For what?" She said, "You were a truant yesterday." I said, "What's a truant?" And she said, "You know, playing hooky." I said, "I didn't think I was playing hooky. It was such a nice day, I just wanted to enjoy it." She said, "Okay, I'm going to let it go this time, but until you graduate from Commodore Stockton, you're supposed to attend school every day no matter how nice the day is." So I never did that again, because all she had to do was threaten to notify my parents, and that was enough to put the fear of God in me.

One other time, when I was in the third grade, Miss Crow asked the school nurse to measure our height and weight. The nurse was completely befuddled because we all refused. She didn't know what to make of it, so she consulted the only Chinese teacher at that time—Miss (Alice) Fong. She told her, "I'm coming across a disciplinary problem that I've never had before. All I asked them to do was to come up to the nurse's office to have their height and weight recorded. The kids all refused and they said, 'Tomorrow, we'll do it tomorrow.'" So Miss Fong told the nurse, "If you had come to me with the assignment, I would have told you not to do it today but notify the class that you're going to do it tomorrow." The nurse asked, "What's the problem?" And she replied, "The problem is that they want to be sure that they come to class with socks that don't have holes in them, or at least mended. That's why they're not willing to do it today, because some of the kids may have holey socks." The nurse thought that was real funny because she didn't care and she couldn't understand why we cared. We were only nine, ten years old, but we were already conscious of the fact that we had a standard to uphold. Sure enough, the next morning, the class marched right up to the nurse's office, took their shoes off, and had their height and weight recorded. I guess the teachers were learning about us at the same time we were learning from them.

I loved going to American school, but Chinese school was another matter. It went from 5:00 to 8:00 Monday to Friday, and from 9:00 to 12.00 on Saturday morning. I was probably seven when I started at Nam Kue, which was supposed to be the best Chinese school. Unfortunately, I was not a good student because I just had no interest in what they were trying to teach me—

things like Chinese calligraphy, literature, and history. By then, I had discovered a wider world outside of Chinatown, and that was what I was interested in. I flunked out of three Chinese schools before I finally persuaded my father to let me drop Chinese school altogether. When I realized it was costing him a buck and a quarter for each child he sent to Chinese school, I told him, "You're just wasting your money. I'm not getting anything out of it." So he decided, "Okay, we'll let you drop out before they throw you out again."

You might say that our generation had split personalities. When we were inside the house, we were completely Chinese. When we were outside the house, we could be either all Chinese or all American or half and half. When we were in American school, one standard applied, whereas another standard applied when we were in Chinese school. If I were out at a formal dinner, I would naturally spoon my soup outwardly and I would not slurp. If I were home, it would not matter how I dipped my spoon, but I would know to pick food from the part of the communal dish nearest me. In that sense, we always behaved according to where we were. But gradually I became more comfortable speaking English than Chinese. That is why my Chinese is frozen more or less as if I were an eleven-, twelve-year-old Chinese kid, and why I am not proficient in Chinese even though I grew up in Chinatown.

RECREATIONAL ACTIVITIES

Growing up as we did, recreation was something that required ingenuity. In other words, everything we did, we did with anything. If we needed something like a shuttlecock, we made it—we didn't buy it, or we used a beanbag instead of a shuttlecock. Basically, aside from playing jacks, hopscotch, and double jump rope with my sisters, we boys played "kick the shuttlecock" and flew kites. When I was nine, I joined the Boy Scouts at the Chinatown YMCA. I remember distinctly one of the group leaders was Chester Lee, and he helped us through tenderfoot class, where we were taught how to tie knots, how to camp and start a fire without matches, and basic things like that. I remember that they tried to get us to buy uniforms, but we didn't have the money. They said it was possible to buy just one piece of the uniform to

FIG. 6. *The Nam Kue Chinese School at 765 Sacramento Street.*
Courtesy California Historical Society, FN-23698.

FIG. 7. *Eddie (center right) trying to light a firecracker in Chinatown*
during the New Year celebration, 1935. Courtesy San Francisco History
Center, San Francisco Public Library.

indicate that you were a member. So we decided on the kerchief, since it was fairly reasonable in price. But I only stayed about a year because I didn't particularly care for the group activities. The other thing was that you had to pass a swimming test. I tried, but I was so lean and had so little body fat that I literally did not float. Now, they say that's impossible—you fill your lungs with air and you're supposed to float. But for some reason, I swam like a rock.

I remember spending a lot of time at the public library in Chinatown, and that was how I accidentally found J. W. Schultz. He wrote about the Plains Indians, particularly the Blackfeet, who were enemies of the Crows. No one told me about his books, but I read everything he wrote and just got more and more interested in the Plains Indians and how they lived off the land: "You're not a farmer, you're a hunter, and maybe a gatherer." It seemed like such a natural way of life: "You're not trying to conquer nature, you're part of nature." Indians didn't feel that they owned the land; rather, they were stewards of the land. They respected what Mother Nature had provided for them, so they only killed animals for their own survival and subsistence, not for profit. However, I didn't care for the part when they went on raiding parties against the Crows. I never thought of Indian life in those terms. I just thought it seemed like such a neat way to live.

I especially enjoyed *Seizer of Eagles*, a story about how this Indian boy hid himself in a hideout near the eagle's nest and waited for the chance to get his hands on some eagle feathers that he needed for a war bonnet. When the eagle landed, he reached up and grabbed both the legs, and held the bird until the eagle got tired of beating its wings or pecking at his hands to get free. Then he was able to take the feathers. Stories like this attracted me to the Indian way of life. A bow and arrow was just a natural implement to help them survive. And the way they utilized every bit of the buffalo for making teepees or clothing or moccasins, and boiling the hooves for glue—to me, it was just a natural way to live. Of course, I probably would not have lasted a week with the hardships that they had to endure every day. But on paper it sounded very romantic.

I remember one time we had a school project to design an Indian head. I don't know where I developed this tendency to go right to the source, but I decided the way to go about it was to ask an artist directly. So my

FIG. 8. *The Chinatown public library at 1135 Powell Street. Courtesy San Francisco History Center, San Francisco Public Library.*

classmate Ronald Ong and I marched over to Maynard Dixon's studio on Montgomery Street, and I said to him, "Mr. Dixon, we have a school project to try and design an Indian head for a trademark. Can you help us out?" Maynard Dixon was a well-known painter of Western art, and he had just returned from a painting trip to Boulder Dam. He started pulling out artifacts from his loft to show us—like Indian headdresses, blankets, peace pipes, and moccasins. He said he had done a lot of paintings of Indians, and he proceeded to show us some of the things that he had done. Then he made us a sketch. Here I had been exposed to the writings of J. W. Schultz, who wrote about the Blackfeet Indians, and now I was lucky enough to find an artist who not only specialized in painting Indians, but he had been up in Montana living and painting among the Blackfeet Indians! That evening I ran home and told my mom, "There's someone who's willing to teach me how to paint." Mom said, "No, no, no, you can't make a living doing that." Of course, she was right. In our time, we had to be very practical.

One of the customers on my paper route was a friend of C. S. Howard, who owned the famous racehorse Seabiscuit. Noticing my size—I was about four feet eight and eighty pounds soaking wet at the time—he asked me, "Do you like horses, Eddie?" I said, "Yes, but I've never been around them." And he said, "My friend C. S. Howard is looking for an exercise boy." I said, "What's an exercise boy?" He said, "Well, he's the person who takes the horses out in the morning and exercises them." So I went home and told my mother, "I can be a jockey!" And she said, "I don't want you hanging around with those gangsters." To this day, I still wonder how in the world did she know horse racing was an unsavory trade when she lived and died in Chinatown, she didn't read English, and she didn't socialize with a lot of people? But my tendency has always been to do what I'm told not to do. So when Mom said I couldn't be a jockey, I decided to find out what it was all about. I went out to the polo fields and began walking the horses between chukkers. For that, I got two bits per horse.

A TASTE OF LIFE OUTSIDE CHINATOWN

The school nurse was always concerned about the fact that some of us were underweight, so every summer they would send a group of us—about forty Chinese kids—to Hills Farm in Marin County to try and fatten us up. The farm was run by the school district, and there was no cost to our families. It was my first exposure to an American diet. We had things like prunes and cornflakes for breakfast, sandwiches and fruit for lunch, and spaghetti or macaroni and cheese for dinner. On Sundays we would have something special, like pot roast. I remember distinctly the first time we had beets. I thought it looked pretty bloody, but when I tasted it, it was sweet. I thought, "Holy smoke, this is entirely different from Chinese vegetables!" We ate three American meals a day, so that I gained four or five pounds by the end of summer. But within a month after I started school again, I would go back to my normal weight, which was underweight by the school nurse's standards. So every summer for the next three years, they would schedule me to go to Hills Farm, and that was basically where I spent my summer vacations.

At Hills Farm, we had to take showers and recite the Lord's Prayer before we went to bed each night. There were planned group activities, but I was allowed to roam around on my own as long as I made it back in time for the meals. That was when I discovered things like lizards and dragonflies, and when I got interested in archery. I would cut a piece of rattan and string it, use reeds for the arrow, and put acorns on the tip of the arrow for the arrowhead. They had a dairy farm, and I would go out early in the morning to watch them milk the cows. That was my first encounter with rural life and the outdoors, and I was fascinated by it, mostly because I was a city kid who had always lived in very crowded quarters.

Later, Bill and I began spending our summers in Stockton, where Pop had a financial interest in a potato farm. We would stay there for a month or two, and that exposed me to farming life. Of course, Stockton was god-awful hot, and during the Depression years, you couldn't make money in potatoes, but it was all a matter of timing. The farm employed thirty Chinese and Filipino men, who mainly worked out in the fields, plowing with horses. We got to feed the horses, drive the horse-drawn wagon, play around with a Caterpillar tractor, and learn to trap fish with a basket. We had chores to do, like gathering firewood, getting the eggs from the chicken coops, tending the vegetable patches, and helping the cook prepare meals, but it wasn't hard work. Most of the time we went fishing and just ran around the farm. The cook grew long beans, tomatoes, and bok choy to feed the farmhands, and that was when I found out how sweet fresh vegetables could taste. It was also my first time using an outdoor privy, and I learned how human waste could be used for fertilizer.

At least once or twice during the summer, we would go into town with the workers after they were paid. Most of them would give us a nickel or dime to buy candy or go see a movie. While they went to the brothel or gambling house, Bill and I would cool off at the movie house. Most of the Filipino workers would dress up and spend their money freely in town, but there was one Filipino who never went to town and never gambled. I noticed that in his spare time in the evenings, he would make fishnets. He told me that he was hoping to go back to the Philippines and start a small fishing business. I always wondered what happened to him. Did he make it back to the Philippines and realize his dream? I couldn't help but admire the man. Here he was working at slave wages during the Depression, but instead of blowing his earnings in town like the others, he was saving to build a future.

There were other occasions when I got a taste of life outside Chinatown. One time we drove to San Jose to visit the Duk family. It was a weekend adventure because it took us half a day to get there on the two-lane road. Mrs. Duk had fig trees, and we were there at the right time of the year when the figs were ripe. Of course, we overdid it and had to run to the john frequently. A bunch of the ladies, including my mother, had a *balut* party. I was horrified when I saw these half-hatched eggs, and I thought, "Holy smoke, they're going to eat the things, feathers and all!" I found out later that they were supposed to be a delicacy.[5] That was the first time I had ever seen anyone with a house, a front yard, and a backyard. I thought, "Okay, people don't have to live in Chinatown in cold-water flats and conditions like that." That was also the first time I had ever met someone who looked Chinese but was, as I heard the ladies saying very softly, *boon tong faan*. I didn't know what that meant, so I asked my mother after we got home. She basically said, "He has a white father and a Chinese mother." And she told me that sometimes they look more Chinese and sometimes they look half and half, but very seldom do they look white. That was my first experience, besides Hills Farm and Stockton, going outside San Francisco. Those were the kinds of experiences that got me thinking, "There's got to be another world outside Chinatown!"

A HOUSEBOY IN ANTIOCH

I was determined to get out of Chinatown. The first time I ran away from home, I was thirteen. I got a job as a houseboy in Antioch with Dr. and Mrs. Nevius. Mrs. Nevius had a sister who worked at the Emporium, and she had put an ad in the paper for a houseboy. When I saw the ad, it said, "Five dollars a week and found." Well, the only definition I knew for "found" was the past tense of "find." So I went to the public library and there was this big unabridged dictionary on the stand, and I was looking for the word "found." The librarian saw I was puzzled and asked if she could help me. I said, "Well, I've got this word, 'found,' and I'm trying to find out what it means." I showed her the ad. She said, "Oh, I understand. That means you get room and board." She said the reason they used that word was because "room and board" involved three words, and they were paying by the word for the ad. Anyhow, that was how I found the job.

Mrs. Nevius had to teach me how to be a houseboy. Like the first morning, when she was cooking breakfast, she fried some bacon. So, naturally, I expected her to fry the eggs in the bacon grease, because that was what we always did at home. What happened instead was that she took the bacon out and put it on a piece of paper towel to drain. Then she set out another pan, put in a pat of butter, and fried the eggs in that. And I was thinking, "Holy smoke, these Americans are strange people!" When it came to washing dishes—here I was used to bowls and chopsticks, and that was it. We wound up with a bowl of soapy water, and she told me, "First we wash the glasses, because they're the least dirty. Then you go from the least dirty to the dirtiest—pots and pans." All this was new to me. Like vacuuming— that was strange too. But she was very patient, and she eventually got me to do what she wanted me to do.

This was during the summer, when I got the job, and my brother found me within one day. I asked Al years later how he found me so quickly. He said, "It was very simple. I just went down to the bus station and asked if they had seen a Chinese kid, four and a half feet tall, going anywhere." He said he hit it on the first try because there were only two bus stations— Trailway on Fourth Street and Greyhound on Seventh Street. He went to Fourth Street first, and, sure enough, they said, "Yes, a little Chinese kid got on the bus to go to Antioch." After he found me, he called my dad. Pop said, "Okay, let him finish the job this summer, but he's to come back and finish school in the fall." When I got home, he said, "Aren't you happy at home?" I said, "Yes." Then he said, "Then why did you run away?" I said, "Well, you've always taught us to be independent and self-reliant." And he said, "There's a time and place for that. Not now! I want you to finish high school first."

LIVING IN GRASS VALLEY

In the fall I went back to Francisco Junior High School. I didn't really need the money from the houseboy job because I was making better money with the paper route, but I had wanted to strike out on my own. As it turned out, I didn't finish junior high because my father retired from the watch repair business, turned it over to my brother Al, and became a partner in a butcher shop in Grass Valley. One reason he got into the butcher business was because my brother Pee Wee was a meat cutter on a passenger liner. He wanted to see if he could entice Pee Wee to be a land lover instead of a sailor. My father asked if I wanted to go along, saying how nice it would be to see snow in Grass Valley. He wasn't foolish enough to try and get me up there to work. He knew the change was what I wanted. So I went up there and started working in the meat market while I went to school.

The butcher shop was in the Hills Flat area, in a market that was owned by a Chinese family with the surname Yee. We just owned and operated the butcher shop. There were four meat cutters, my dad, and me—six people altogether. Basically, the shop was open from 8:00 in the morning to 10:00 at night. I remember the last thing we did at night was to put everything back into the walk-in icebox, so that the first thing we did in the morning was to put everything back out in the display case. It was kind of like a jewelry store, where the jeweler would put all the jewelry in a safe at night, and in the morning, he would put them back out. During the school day, I would get up early in the morning and start the display case. That would basically be the lunchmeats, hot dogs, bacon, and the hams—things that didn't require a lot of finesse—because the butchers preferred to put out the chops and the steaks themselves. Then I would head for school at around 7:30, stay there until 3:00 and sometimes 4:00, then come back to work at the meat counter until closing time. On weekends, I would put in full days.

I basically did all the grunt work, like slicing the lunch meat, keeping the meat trays full, grinding the hamburger, making sausage, and washing the windows on the display case inside and out. When the meat cutters were through with their jobs at the end of the day, they would take off. It was my job to stay behind and scrape off the butcher blocks, clean up the meat grinders and all the hand tools, put the knives away, and make sure that things in the walk-in icebox were neatly arranged. I was fourteen when I learned to be a meat cutter—that's really the only trade I know. The first thing I learned to do was how to bone—take the meat off the bone. That was how I learned to handle a knife, because I couldn't do any harm getting pieces of meat off the bone. We used to get calves with the skin on and Pop would always take care of the skinning. I would watch him and he would show me what he was doing and why he was doing it that way. I learned that it was important not to cut the skin; otherwise, it would lose its value after it was cured. There was a knife for everything in the butcher shop— boning knife, skinning knife, steak knife, all kinds—and I learned how to use each one of them.

I was also given the responsibility of tallying the receipts at the end of the day. We had a lot of charge accounts, because most of our customers worked in the gold mines and they would get paid either by the week or the month. Every Friday night I would take all the checks and the monies and make up the deposit slips. This was even before I had had a business class in high school, and Pop would just show me what to do. He would check me out the first few times to make sure I had done everything right and that I had totaled everything up correctly. Then I would put every-thing in a tin cottage-cheese can and walk it over to the bank on Saturday morning. Here I was, no more than five feet tall and eighty-five pounds, walking from Hills Flat to downtown where the bank was—about a mile and a quarter. I was carrying money in this tin can—sometimes as much as $400—and not once was I ever accosted. We were living at a time when you could do that.

We lived behind the supermarket in two cabins that we rented from a Mr. Coffin. I'll remember that name until the day I die! The cabins were at least ten feet wide and about sixteen feet deep, so we basically had two rooms easily. One room was for the bunk beds, and the other we used for eating, reading the newspaper, and so on. We had a cooking arrangement in the middle of the room, with cupboards, sink, and stove, so that was a natural partition between the two rooms. Mom, Pop, and I stayed in one cabin; Pee Wee and the other butchers stayed in the second cabin. As I recall, my mom was there about four months out of the year. She would prepare the meals, and people would eat in shifts because we couldn't all leave the shop at the same time. Other times, Pop would cook so the guys wouldn't have to do their own cooking. We were eating high on the hog because we could eat almost anything we wanted. We could have hamburger every day, or steaks and chops—that was something new for me. And I would use all the scraps from the lunchmeats to make all kinds of sandwiches to take to school.

I started my first year of high school in Grass Valley. The thing I remember the most was English class, because they had a wide range of reading material that I probably would not have gotten in the San Francisco schools. It was all about old England, knighthood, and chivalry, like *Ivanhoe* and "The Charge of the Light Brigade." I also remember reading *Scaramouche* and *A Tale of Two Cities*—mostly historical novels. I probably had history, math, and science, but I don't have any recollection of those classes. But in woodshop, I remember guys were making their own skis. I asked Mom if I could learn to ski, and she said, "Oh, no, you'll break a leg, you'll break an arm, or break your neck." She was always so protective; her hair would probably turn gray if she knew what I had been doing without her knowledge. But as much as possible, I tried not to make her too apprehensive. So I didn't get a chance to ski—not even bobsledding or any of the snow sports. The other thing that was memorable was the fact that the creamery was about a block away from high school and they gave you a milkshake that was all you could do to finish for ten cents. Because they had their own dairy, the ice cream was homemade and fresh. I often ate my lunch there, but since I was lactose intolerant, it wouldn't do for me to have a milkshake every day.

As far as I can remember, most of the students were white, which was different from junior high school in San Francisco. But I had no problems with that. I remember one boy—a Jewish refugee from Germany—told us stories about how regimented life was in Germany and also how badly Jews were treated. That was why his family left, and that was the first I had ever heard of things like that happening in Europe. Except for another Chinese kid, George, I had very few friends. But then, even when I was attending school in San Francisco, I had no close friends. George and I weren't what you would call buddies. He was a year older and he had his own interests. But he had a car, so if I needed a ride, I would ask him. One time, we drove to San Francisco together for the opening of the Golden Gate Bridge—the only time I got away from Grass Valley.

It was in Grass Valley that I first started learning how to run. In P.E. they required everyone to get into some kind of physical activity. But when

FIG. 9. *Eddie's parents with one of the butchers (left) behind the store in Grass Valley in 1937.*

I asked the gym teacher if I could take archery, he said, "No, you can't, you're not a girl." I said, "How about fencing?" And again he said, "Girls only." So I had to let that go too. I didn't want to play baseball, football, or any team sports like that, so I decided, "Okay, running is one activity I can do by myself." In the beginning, I would be lucky if I could make a quarter of a mile around the track. So the coach said, "What are you trying to do, Ed?" I said, "I'm going to try and run a mile." I was thinking of Glen Cunningham, who had overcome injuries from a fire at fifteen to become a world-renowned miler. He said, "Well, you're going to have to learn to jog first. If you have to, just walk." I said, "I already walk a lot." He said, "Jog then." So he showed me what to do. Pretty soon I could jog a mile. And he said, "Now, go for two. What you have to do is build up your legs so that you can go for five, six miles." This was long before the jogging craze took over. He said, "What you want to do is be able to get your second wind." That was the first time I had ever heard the term "second wind." He explained to me, "What happens is that you get to the point where you think you can run forever—that's when you have your second wind. Once you do that, you can start thinking about running. You'll be doing good if you can do a mile in six minutes. If you can do it in five, you'll be in top class." And he said, "Don't worry about the time. Try to build up your stamina first."

Well, I never did get my second wind. He would tell me, "You're pushing too hard. Just work on it gradually. Don't worry about the time. Just build up your stamina." So that's what I did—I would just run to build up stamina. I would jog at about nine minutes to a mile, which is very slow, but it was more important to me that I jog long distances rather than run distances fast. I wasn't running for the team, relays, or anything else. I was just running for the enjoyment of it, even though I didn't enjoy it at the beginning, because it seemed like I wasn't making any progress. I was hoping to run five-minute miles, but I knew that I wasn't even close to that. So I just kept jogging.

The other thing I learned to do in Grass Valley was to shoot. I think it was one of the customers who first told me about the NRA club downtown. We were talking, and he found out I was interested in shooting and that I owned a single-shot, Irving .22 rifle—something I had purchased with earnings from my paper route. Back in those days, they weren't that strict about gun control, and the weapon only cost me a dollar and a half. Mom and Pop allowed me to keep it, after telling me to be sure not to hurt anyone with it. So this customer told me about the indoor course they had at the NRA, and he said, "They have people there who can teach you how to take care of guns and all the safety rules." I never became a member, but I would go there and try to learn to shoot accurately in their indoor range. That was when I got the most use out of my Irving .22. I wasn't interested in shooting game. I just wanted to learn to use a weapon, and that was all.

The first time I experienced snow was not in Grass Valley but in San Francisco in 1931. I remember Bill and I went out to an empty lot behind Chinese Hospital and we tried to gather up enough snow to make a snowball. But it was so soft and fluffy that by the time we put our hands on it, it would melt. So when Pop told me that Grass Valley had a lot of snow, I was fascinated by the idea of just seeing snow. I was only there for one winter, but it turned out to be one of the harshest winters they had ever had in the Grass Valley and Nevada City area. In fact, the whole city was closed off for several weeks, and supplies were running low, so they were kind of worried about that. On the other hand, they knew that sooner or later, the weather would break and they would be able to get trucks up and back from Sacramento, where they got their supplies. But the first time it snowed, it was great because I didn't know what was involved. Eventually, I found out that there was snow to be shoveled off the sidewalk, and when I walked to school, I had to be careful about slipping or falling on the icy spots. Then I found out that even out in the hills, I couldn't just walk around, because I would be waist deep in snow. But still, it was a new experience for me, stomping around in the snow.

Living in Grass Valley was quite an experience, because coming from San Francisco Chinatown to wide-open country turned out to be a revelation for me. In San Francisco we had had to live in segregated quarters, whereas in Grass Valley we could live like other folks. Even though I didn't have all the time in the world to enjoy the outdoors, I didn't have to go far, because the Hills Flat market was in the outskirts of town. All I had to do was walk a couple of blocks and I would be out in the forest, so I did a lot of hiking. Since then, I've always enjoyed being outdoors and more or less by myself.

LOSING MY VIRGINITY

I was fifteen when I lost my virginity at a house of prostitution in Grass Valley. I used to deliver their order from the meat market and the grocery store, usually in the late morning or early afternoon. The ladies were not working during those hours. They were more or less just getting up and having their coffee, cigarettes, and so on. The first time I delivered their order, they kind of teased me. At that time, I blushed easily, and, of course, the more I blushed, the more they teased me. The madam came in and said, "Girls, girls, girls, don't tease the help." So that was basically my first encounter with the ladies.

Now, I had never had what is now commonly known as sex education. I had never asked my older brothers, who were raising their families, and I didn't talk to other guys about it in school. I knew nothing about sex. So gradually, each time that I delivered an order, the ladies would tease me. Then they invited me in for coffee. That was how we got started as casual acquaintances. I wasn't one of their clients at that time, and I had no thoughts about becoming one. This was the first time I had ever talked to ladies who were not my sisters or my mother, because I had never talked to any of the girls at school. Little by little, I got to know them as ladies. When they found out I was from San Francisco, they started telling me how sometimes when they had spare time, they would go to San Francisco to do weekend shopping for clothes and so on.

I guess it was a couple of months later when I got up the nerve to walk up there one evening. A colored maid came to the door, and I guess she must have heard about me from the girls, because she yelled to the madam, "Eddie's here!" I almost turned around and ran down the stairs, I was so embarrassed. The madam said, "Are you here for what I think you're here for?" I said, "Well, I've never been *there* before." And she said, "Well, I think I have just the person to introduce you to the joys of sex." Of course, I found out later that there is no such thing as the joys of sex for a prostitute. They want to get the man to climax as quickly as possible and get him through in the shortest time possible. Of course, I wasn't aware of that then. But the first time, this young lady Marie treated me almost as if we were on a date. She gradually took me through the steps, and that night was when I lost my virginity.

I think I went back two or three times over a period of a year. And I always asked for Marie. I was bashful at the time, and I thought that if I stayed with one lady, it would make it a lot easier for me. The first time she had her period, and I went up there, the maid told me, "She's in flower." I didn't know what that meant, and she said, "Well, ladies have these periodically—usually once a month. But the other ladies are available." And I said, "No, I'll just wait." When I saw Marie the next time, I asked her, "What was all that about?" And she explained it all to me. They always treated me as a plaything in the sense that here was a kid who knew absolutely nothing about sex. In a way, they gave me a sex education. In return, I always treated them not as prostitutes but ladies I knew. The fact that I could purchase their favor or their time didn't make them any less ladies. And they treated me not as a client but as a special person.

As far as I can remember, they were all white ladies. I think the youngest one was probably twenty-one or twenty-two, and the oldest, as much as thirty-three to thirty-five. For the year that I was in Grass Valley, the same five ladies worked there, so there wasn't a big turnover. At that time, it was a dollar and a half, and a man could pick any of the five. With Marie, we were always cordial to each other. I never asked her why; I mean, I had no idea how people got into this business. The madam was responsible for the welfare of the girls, and, as far as I could tell, there was no coercion. To them, it was just a way of making a living. I had heard stories in China-town about how slave girls were brought over and forced into prostitution, but these ladies didn't appear to be in that situation at all.[6]

A HOLIDAY IN VANCOUVER

In 1937 my father decided that he was going to send my brother Bill and me to China for a Chinese education. Of course, we had no say, but I remember Henry Fung, a close friend of the family, saying, "You guys are going to have a lot of fun. You'll get to sit on a water buffalo with a little flute and just tend the cows." That was probably what first put the idea of becoming a cowboy in my mind. We had our ID cards ready, and we were to ship out from Seattle. That was when Pop decided, "Okay, the whole family is going up there." That included my mother, my father, my four sisters, Bill, and me. Then he decided, "While we're here and the ship's not going to be sailing for a while, why don't you kids head up to Vancouver and have a holiday." He didn't want to go with us because he wasn't legal and he was still leery about being discovered. And Mom didn't want to go because she was afraid of getting hassled by the immigration authorities. So the six of us went to Vancouver by ourselves and spent about four days there. That was my first encounter with "blue Sundays," when everything was closed—all the theaters and all the shops—and we thought that was strange. Then when we came back to Seattle on the cruise ship, Pop decided the war situation in China looked too unsettled, and he said, "Nope, I'm not going to send you boys back."[7]

To show you how inexpensive that trip was, when we first got there that evening on the train, we went to a Chinese restaurant. Pop ordered food for the eight of us, and the whole meal was ten dollars. And for the first

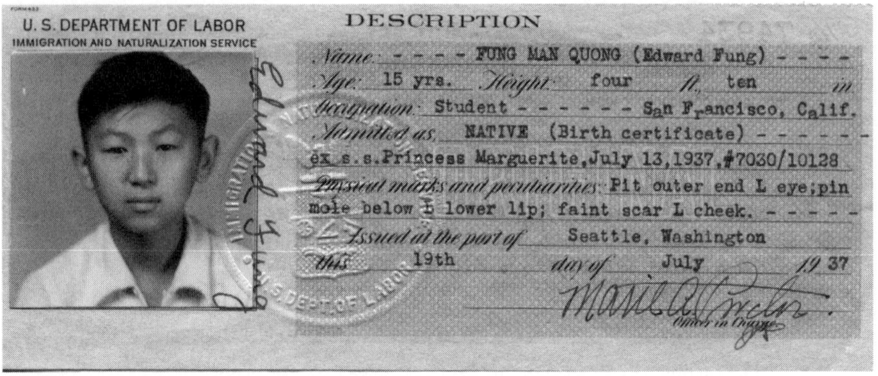

U. S. DEPARTMENT OF LABOR
IMMIGRATION AND NATURALIZATION SERVICE

DESCRIPTION

Name — — — — FUNG MAN QUONG (Edward Fung) — — — —
Age 15 yrs. Height four ft. ten in.
Occupation Student — — — — — — San Francisco, Calif.
Admitted as NATIVE (Birth certificate) — — — — —
ex s. s. Princess Marguerite, July 13, 1937, #7030/10128
Physical marks and peculiarities Pit outer end L eye; pin
mole below ½ lower lip; faint scar L cheek. — — — — —
Issued at the port of Seattle, Washington
this 19th day of July 19 37

FIG. 10. *Eddie's certificate of identity—required of all Chinese persons to prove their right to remain in and return to the United States.*

time in my life, I saw my dad leave a silver dollar for a tip. My dad was worldly in the sense that even when he went to a coffee shop and had a twenty-five-cent lunch special, he would leave a tip. He had, in his vest pockets, nickels in a certain pocket, dimes in another, and so on. He told us, "Always leave a tip. You don't have to be extravagant, but leave something appropriate, even if it's only a nickel." We were always stringent in our spending, and we thought this was outright extravagant. But he told us, "When you're traveling, your behavior has to be different from what you do at home." As a Chinese businessman, he was always careful about protecting his character—how he was seen and how he behaved towards others.

The Vancouver trip reminded me of the time our family went on a picnic to Fleishacker Zoo. We made up a suit box full of sandwiches, dessert, fruits, and drinks. There may well have been as many as two of these suit boxes. The same thing was true when we went on the train to Seattle. We didn't eat on the train, except what we brought. I'll never forget how we walked from Fleishacker Zoo to the Playland. Give or take, it had to be at least two miles, and Pop could still outwalk us. He had an artificial limb and no knee joint, but that never stopped him.

LEAVING HOME

When we got back from Seattle, I told my father that I had had enough of Grass Valley and that I would prefer to finish high school in San Francisco.

Back then, the high schools in the city were specialized. Commerce High School was exactly that—people went there to learn business things. Mission High was like a trade school, Galileo High was general ed, and Polytechnic High was basically polytechnical. Lowell, of course, was academic— college prep. I thought I wanted to become a mechanical engineer, without knowing what it was all about. It almost sounds foolish, but I saw one of these signs they have when they're putting up a building. The architect's name was followed by the mechanical engineer's name. For some reason, "Mechanical Engineer" caught my eye. I remember when I got to our drafting class at Polytechnic High School, Mr. Walker saw that my report card had been signed by Al as my guardian. He asked me, "How is Mr. Albert Quong your guardian?" And I said, "Well, he's my oldest brother, and my father wasn't around to sign the report card." So he said, "Albert Quong is your brother? Well then, I will expect you to make drawings as neatly as he did." And I thought, "Holy smoke, after twenty some odd years, he recognizes his name and remembers his work!" That sort of put me on my toes.

I finished my first year of high school, then I was thrown out in my sophomore year for being a wise guy. We got two grades in high school—one for academics and one for deportment. I could always get by with academics, but I always got low grades in deportment because I would talk back to the teacher. I didn't like authority, and I was getting antsy about leaving school. What happened at Poly was that the teacher in my English class gave me a failing grade for both. I protested because I didn't think I deserved the failing grade for my academic work. But she said, "Because your deportment was so bad, I'm failing you in both." When I protested to the principal, he said, "I have to go along with the teacher." I was already in the frame of mind to quit school anyway, so it didn't matter to me. It just gave me an excuse to leave school earlier.

I had been making plans to leave home from the time when I was in Antioch. I found out that when a student turned sixteen, he could no longer be considered a truant. So I decided that on my sixteenth birthday, I was going to leave home and go far away so my folks would no longer fuss over me. By then I was really into horses, and I figured the way to be around horses was to work on a ranch. I got a map of the United States and told my brother Bill to blindfold me. I said, "I'll take any state that is from Montana down to Texas. Somewhere along there, I'll find a cattle ranch." It was like "pin the tail on the donkey"—he spun me around and moved the map around, and where I pinned the tail turned out to be Midland, Texas. Of course, I didn't know that Midland was not a cattle town but an oil town! I had saved about a hundred dollars, and I figured *that* would last me at least two months if I didn't find a job right away. Then, of course, I had to have the bus fare. I decided to get a half-fare bus ticket for kids under twelve, so I got Bill, who was four inches taller than me, to go with me to Trailway to buy the ticket. He was the only one who knew what I was going to do, and he was sworn to secrecy.

I took off to the bus station by myself, lugging my belongings in my father's carpetbag. I had an alarm clock to make sure that I got up on time for work, and some toiletries. I even scrounged a bed sheet from home, just to be sure that I had linen. I had two extra shirts and just the pair of pants that I had on, because I figured if I were going to work at a ranch, I would have to buy Levi's and work clothes like that later. And I brought along a pair of cowboy boots that I had picked up during my first year at Poly. That was basically what I had when I left home. It was the beginning of an adventure. I never had any qualms about being able to make it on my own, even at that age. If I couldn't find work on a ranch, I would work elsewhere doing anything. I wasn't worried. One thing for sure, I was not about to go home any day soon.

TWO · A CHINESE COWBOY IN TEXAS

I've always had this romantic notion that as a cowboy all you have to do is ride a horse and maybe herd a few cows. Then I found out, no, no, you have to do things like build fences, maintain water tanks and windmills, and at some of the ranches you might even have to plant a crop or two to feed the horses and hogs. It was nothing but hard work. So, right away, my illusions of the movie cowboy were shattered. It was up to me to face the reality of the situation and start learning from that point.

LOOKING FOR WORK IN MIDLAND

When I got off the bus in Midland, the first thing I did was to ask people at the bus depot where I could find a room. At the time, it never occurred to me that someone might not want to rent a room to a Chinese person. I didn't think of myself as a Chinese and I didn't project myself as a Chinese. Besides, I was only five feet tall and non-threatening, so most people took me to be nothing more than a young adventurer. In fact, many of my Texan friends later told me, "We thought it was pretty funny. Here was a big city boy coming to Texas wanting to be a cowboy when most Texans would give their eyeteeth just to get away from that kind of life." Anyhow, this person at the depot told me about the Haley Hotel. He said, "It's very moderately priced and clean and not far from downtown."

When I got there, I found out that the weekly rate was five dollars, but that the monthly rate was even cheaper. I told the desk clerk, "I'm not sure that I'll need a whole month, so why don't we start on a weekly basis." Actually, the rooming part wasn't that expensive, and the eating part wasn't that expensive either, because I ate very simple meals. I found a small café near the hotel, since the hotel charged higher prices. Back in those days, most cafés ran a "blue plate special," which provided good quality food in adequate amounts. There was one thing that I found strange, though. We had fish one day, and I asked for a glass of milk, and they said, "No, we can't serve you milk when you're eating fish." I said, "Why not?" He said, "It's against the law." I said, "What?" Apparently, there was some notion that drinking milk with fish was injurious to your system. I still don't know the medical reason behind it, but I found it absolutely strange.[1]

I soon learned that there were other strange things—like the poll tax. In San Francisco, where I was from, voting was everyone's privilege and right. But in Texas, a person had to pay before he could vote.[2] I later found out that the tax was to keep blacks and Mexicans from voting. It wasn't that I agreed with all the things I heard; I just found it enlightening that customs in various parts of the country could be so different. Then I found out that the poll tax of $1.50 could be covered by any of the candidates running for office. During one of the campaigns for senator, I was taken to a political rally where they served a free barbeque and the politician handed out dollar bills to prospective voters. Now, a dollar and fifty cents may not sound like much, but if you were being paid forty dollars a month as a top hand, that was at least a day's wages. These were the sorts of things I was learning that were completely unfamiliar to me. So each day was an adventure in itself because I never knew what I was going to find out, who I was going to encounter, and how they were going to react to me.

I found out from the people at the Haley Hotel that the Scharbaum Hotel downtown was where most of the cattlemen stayed when they came into town. The people who were looking for work usually stayed in that area as well. So I decided, "Okay, I'll go down there." I started asking people, especially the people who were looking for work, "How do you go about it?" They asked me, "Why do you want to know?" I said, "I'm looking for a job." And they looked at me—this skinny little runt—and they said, "If we hear of anyone who wants someone who's absolutely green, we'll let you know. We'll even spread the word." Within a few days, everybody in town knew about the Chinese kid from California. This was my first taste of Southern hospitality, which I took to be all part and parcel of the South, including Texas. I think, on the whole, they were more amused by the idea that this kid who couldn't fight his way out of a wet paper bag would want to work on a ranch, where there was nothing but hard work.

A SHORT STOPOVER IN KERMIT

After hanging around the Scharbaum Hotel for two weeks, I finally found a job with W. F. Scarborough. His ranch headquarters was in Kermit— about eighty miles southwest of Midland. Since I had no experience whatsoever, Tom Lineberry, the ranch foreman who interviewed me, said, "Would you be willing to accept ten dollars a month with room and board?" And I said, "Of course. I know I don't know anything about ranch work, and the fact that you're willing to pay me ten dollars is quite generous." As I said, a top cowhand at the time was earning forty dollars a month. He didn't tell me what I would be doing, but I knew intuitively that as a greenhorn, I was going to have to do any kind of work asked of me.

The stopover in Kermit was no more than a week while I waited to be transported to the ranch I was going to be working at near Seminole. During that time, I was put to work at whatever odd jobs needed to be done. Of course, as the low man on the totem pole, I was assigned the unpleasant jobs. I would be shown how to clean the chicken house, and the guy would leave as quickly as he could. Another job I was given was unloading gravel off what they called a stake body truck, which was not a pickup but a truck with a flatbed and holes alongside the bed for side boards. I had never done any pick-and-shovel work, and I didn't know the first thing about it. I was told to work with Frank Lewis, a Negro gentleman who was one of the ranch hands. So I got a shovel and I was shoveling away as if my life depended on it, and Frank got up there with a shovel and he said, "Eddie, take it easy. You're not going to last if you go at that pace. We got this whole truck to unload." So he taught me, in other words, how to pace myself. He told me, "Relax, a ranch day is a long day. You're not gong to even last through this job if you don't slow down and pace yourself." Frank was very friendly, and he was kind enough to take me under his wing and show me the ropes. In hindsight, I wonder how long I would have lasted if there hadn't been people like Frank Lewis around to teach me. This lesson would serve me well in the prison camps, where the workload was much harsher and pacing could mean the difference between life and death.

A GREENHORN AT THE SCARBOROUGH RANCH

There was a total of five ranch hands at the Scarborough ranch—Tom Lineberry, his brother Robert, two other hired hands, and me—and that was considered a medium-size ranch. The owners had the main house, and we had the bunkhouse. Bunkhouses were very simple arrangements—a wood structure about twenty feet in each direction. That was plenty of room for a couple of bunk beds and for the guys to play cards if they wanted. We ate at the main house, and the bunkhouse was merely for sleeping. Of course, there was an outhouse; most ranches didn't have septic tanks. Even growing up in Chinatown, we had flush toilets, so I had to get used to the fact that conditions in Texas were fairly primitive. But once I got used to the idea, it was not all that bad.

It was a learning process right from the start. We got up at four in the morning and did what most would consider a full day's work before we even had breakfast. For instance, we would milk all the cows, feed the chickens, pick up the eggs, feed the horses, and then go have breakfast. So I learned right off the bat that the livestock was more important than anything else on the ranch because that was what the ranch was for—raising cattle. Then after breakfast we started the ranch work. This involved keeping the fences mended so the cattle wouldn't wander all over and repairing the corrals in case any cattle needed to be brought in for "dipping." Basically, the cattle were driven through the chute and dipped into a trough filled with antiseptic fluids in order to get rid of any ticks. Whenever a fence needed to be built, we didn't buy the cedar posts; we had to cut them, trim them, and then dig the holes, put in the fence posts, align them, and string maybe four strands of barbed wire. Then we might go out to various parts of the ranch to check on the water tanks, which were just pack-dirt reservoirs to hold extra water, and see if the windmills needed repairing. This was long before the days of irrigation, pumps, and using motors to draw up the water. In the wintertime, when the tanks would freeze over, we had to chop holes in the ice so that the cattle could drink. And we had to make sure that the salt licks were not depleted, because the cows need to lick salt for their system, just like people need salt in their system. These were all routine things that needed to be done around the ranch but that were never in the movies. Even riding a horse—it was not for pleasure, but for doing a job.

I learned that a cowboy was like a vet. Most cowboys carried a small supply of medicine with him so that he would not have to go back to the ranch house, which might be five, ten miles away. If he saw that any of the cattle needed doctoring, he would just routinely doctor them on the spot. If it were serious, he would call in a vet. Usually, they were minor problems, like doctoring a sore. During the season when heifers had their first calves, they sometimes had trouble with their uterus. If it came out, you had to put it back in. Here was where I found cowboys could be very ingenious. When they pushed the uterus back in, they would shove the big part of a wine bottle in to hold the uterus in position and then tie the neck of the bottle around the tail to hold the bottle in place until the uterus got settled again. If a cow needed a vaccination, they would just rope the cow, push it down to the ground, and vaccinate it. In essence, the cowboy was a jack-of-all-trades—he had to be part mechanic, part vet, and part carpenter.

The spring and fall roundups were the main events at any ranch because they were raising cattle and calves to sell. The rounding and branding was to help the rancher keep track of how many calves he had as well as take care of their health. It basically involved dehorning, vaccination, castrating if it were a bull calf, and branding. To do all of this, four men formed a branding crew. First, the calf had to be dragged to the branding area with a rope. Then one man would force it to the ground and hold its hind legs, while a second man would use his knee to keep its neck down and hold its front legs. Once the calf was immobilized, a third man would dehorn and vaccinate while a fourth man would castrate and brand it. I swear that it didn't take more than a minute, because once the calf was dropped, each

FIG. 11. *Dipping cattle to get rid of ticks. Courtesy Southwest Collection/Special Collections Library, Texas Tech University.*

person knew exactly what he had to do and he just did it. Then when it came time to trade off, someone would say, "Let's trade off," and everyone would know who was trading with whom and how to do all the jobs. This was just to give everyone a little variety and a break in the muscles, because the smoke was very acrid and the men might be branding for eight, ten hours.

My first time, they had me flanking and holding the hind legs. I was only ninety pounds at the most, and the calf was at least 250 pounds, so naturally I had trouble manhandling the calf down. Finally, one of the old-timers said, "Eddie, you're not going to last half an hour. Let me show you." And he said, "What you have to do is grab him under the front leg and under the flank." And the flank was that loose flap of skin from the belly to the hind leg. As soon as the calf made a little jump, he put his knee under to help him jump. He then flopped him on the ground and practically knocked his breath out. And before the calf knew it, someone was dehorning him,

FIG. 12. *Branding cattle. Courtesy Southwest Collection/Special Collections Library, Texas Tech University.*

someone was vaccinating him, someone was castrating him, and he was even branded. By the time they shook the rope off his neck, he was running back to his mama, and the calf was probably screaming at the top of his lungs, "Look what those men did to me, Mama!" At that point, he was not even feeling the pain; I mean, the shock hadn't set in yet. That was when I realized, "Okay, Ed, you don't have body mass, you're not even strong, so you're always going to have to find an easier way to do things." Little did I know then how useful this lesson would be in prison camp, where the bulk of our work involved carrying heavy loads.

Because all the ranchers had a limited time frame to complete the roundup—about thirty days—there was usually a mutual agreement among them to help each other out. All the small ranchers would get together at the big ranch and take care of its roundup first. Then all the men from the big ranch would help all the small ranchers do their work. It was all done in the spirit of cooperation and friendship. Same thing would happen if anyone ever got sick and couldn't put in the crop—people would automatically help plow his fields and seed it. And if he were still sick at harvest time, they would not only harvest it, but also take it to the gin and give him the money as if he had done the job himself. When all the roundup work was done, the big rancher would throw a barbeque or party. It wasn't payback in the real sense of the word, because you could never pay back obligation, but it was to acknowledge their friendship. And it was a time to relax and enjoy each other's company.

I thought it was a great way to live because, sure, it was hard work, but the friendship among the ranchers was real. They didn't keep score, like "You handled X number of heads of cattle and I'll help you do X number." It didn't work that way—everyone just helped each other out, period. It felt so natural and so right that I thought *this* was the way it should be. I learned that cowboys had a code of ethics that was so stringent that most people would probably not be able to live up to it. Their word was the most important thing in the world, because that impinged on their honor. If a man gave you his word, there would be no need for a contract. Unless he dropped dead, the deed would be done. And if you wanted to be formal about it, you shook hands—that was ironclad. Most people think of a cowboy as being uncouth, uneducated, and so on, but I found them to be gentle and courteous, especially when they were around women— then courtesy was extended tenfold. And when they danced, they were light on their feet—and I'm talking about some big men. Some of them were very well educated, both in the scholastic sense and in a self-educated way. And some had traveled a bit with rodeo shows the equivalent of Buffalo Bill's. So a cowboy wasn't anything like the movie cowboy I had envisioned him to be.

I got along fine with the other ranch hands. I don't remember any problems, other than the fact that they had to teach me everything, like how to milk a cow. About a week after I started milking the cows, the milk production went down, and one of the guys said, "Eddie, that milk cow is holding back on you. What you have to do is learn how to out-trick her and take the milk that she's holding back for her calf." Of course, the implication was that I was pretty dumb to be outfoxed by a cow. He showed me how to strip or squeeze the udders some more until all the milk just flowed out naturally. In the two years that I worked on the ranches, I never met anyone with a mean bone in his body.

Although the ranch was owned by Mr. Scarborough, I answered to Tom Lineberry, the foreman and son-in-law. But one of the things I remember about Mr. Scarborough—he had a glass eye and false teeth. Being the low man, aside from helping Miss Evelyn (Scarborough's daughter and Tom's wife) around the house, I was assigned to bring him a glass of warm milk before he went to bed at night. The first time I saw his glass eye and false teeth in the glass tumblers, I didn't know what to make of them, because in all my time in Chinatown, I had never heard of false teeth, nor seen a glass eye. Being out on my own and being exposed to different facets of life like this, there was something new every day. I never thought about the hardships; it was just one adventure after another.

After about four months at the Scarborough ranch, Tom said that Miss Evelyn wanted me to work as a houseboy at her home in Midland. I suspect that Tom realized that he really didn't have the time to teach me how to become a good cowhand, since he was often away from the ranch taking care of the family's oil leases and other enterprises. Not wanting to hurt anyone's feelings by saying that I didn't want to be a houseboy but a cowboy, I decided to look for another job at another ranch. By then, I had become acquainted with Red, who ran a ranch nearby. He used to come over to our ranch in the evenings to play penny-ante poker. So the next time I saw him, I asked, "Red, do you know of anyone around here who might need someone as inexperienced as me?" And he said, "Eddie, you can come work for me." The understanding was that he would pay me ten dollars, same as what Tom Lineberry was paying me. Then he said, "What are you going to tell Tom?" I replied, "Well, I think I'll go ask him right now." So I went up to Tom and I said, "Mr. Lineberry, would it be okay if I leave here and go work with Red?" I added, "He needs someone to help him around the ranch." He knew that Red ran a small spread all by himself. "Oh," he said, "if you can help him, sure, go ahead." I said, "No problem with leaving here?" He said, "No, no, we'll get along." So that was how I moved out to work with Red. His Christian name was Harvey—but it was at the peril of your life to use that—and his last name was Craddock.

LEARNING TO BE A COWBOY AT THE CRADDOCK RANCH

I started learning more with Red because we had a one-to-one tutor-and-student relationship, and from his perspective, the quicker I learned and the more I learned, the better I could help him out. Red was about forty years old, so we're talking about a twenty-five-year age difference. I realized that it was an education for me to be around older people like Red, who had lived some of their lives already and knew something of the world. One evening, he opened his equivalent of a footlocker and I saw his gun belt and holster, and I said, "Gee, Red, you've grown up in a very interesting time. You've seen the airplane come in, automobiles, trains, telegraph, telephones, and all sorts of things." He looked at me and said, "Eddie, when you get to be my age, you're going to look back and say, 'Poor Red, he hasn't seen anything yet.' " His father had been a sheriff, and he said back when he started out as a cowboy, everyone packed a gun. And he said, "It's not what you think, Eddie. We don't shoot each other. It's for rattlesnakes and things like that."

His mother had been a schoolteacher, and I found Red to be well informed and well educated. He was always correcting my grammar and spelling. Like many other cowboys, he was well aware of the politics involved in running a ranch. For instance, the Craddock ranch didn't have a road from Seminole, so Red suggested, "Eddie, if you go to school, the county will have to build a road to the ranch house so that the school bus can come get you." I said, "Gee, Red, I left school to come here." And he said, "Well, it sure would be nice if you did, because we'll get a road built right out to the ranch." Of course, I didn't enroll in school, and he didn't push me. I just didn't realize that the county, in order for the school bus to get to a particular place, would do a thing like that.

Even though the Craddock ranch was a lot smaller than the Scarborough ranch, the basic work was the same. Red just had fewer heads of cattle to run and a smaller spread to run it on. I was absolutely flabbergasted when he talked in term of sections. I was so used to thinking in terms of acres that when I first heard the term, I didn't know what it meant. So Red explained to me, "A section is one square mile—640 acres. We don't think in terms of acres out here, Eddie, because an acre won't even support a cow." And he said, "We think in terms of a section, which will support maybe ten, fifteen cows." That means you need sixty-four acres for one cow, and sixty-four acres is a lot of land! It never occurred to me until we started riding around the ranch that it was mostly sand hills. There was basically sage and a brush called "shinnery," and lots of mesquite. It was practically all weeds out there, and that was what we used for firewood. As Red said, "West Texas is fairly dry country, and grass is very scarce—that's why we need so much land to raise cattle." Again I had to expand my field of vision, because I had grown up in Chinatown, where buildings were stacked next to each other and we had ten people living in two rooms. San Francisco is roughly seven by seven miles and approximately forty-nine sections—that's not even a good-size horse pasture as far as Texans are concerned! I had to think entirely on a different scale. Red got a big kick out of it because he had worked in the rodeo and been to California. "I know how you people think," he said. "You think in terms of acres."

One of the first things Red taught me was to be observant around the ranch. For instance, he could tell from a long distance whether something was a cow or a horse. I used to be puzzled by this. He said, "Eddie, think about it. A cow is more rectangular and a horse is more an elongated, oblong thing." Then he said, "It's basically the difference between how a cow and horse gets up." And I said, "There's a difference?" He said, "Yeah, these are the things you have to observe." I got lost easily out in the open range, and Red used to like playing a trick on me. We would get about four or five miles away from the ranch house, and he would say, "Okay, which way do you get home, Eddie?" I would look around and say, "I don't know, Red." He'd say, "Well, you haven't been observing where you've been going and what direction you've been going." I said, "Gee, you must have a compass in your head." He said, "No, no, I don't. What you have to do is observe everything going on around you at all times." So he said, "Since you have such a poor sense of direction, if I'm not with you, here's what you do if you get lost. Drop the reins so the horse knows that he's not being con-trolled. Let him loose—he knows where home is." It was simple, common sense things like this that I learned all through the time that I was with Red. I'm sure that there were people who probably thought I was dumb as a fence post, and I was—there was no question about it. But they took it all in good humor.

One time I was digging a water tank with a Fresno (a big horse-drawn shovel) and I practically fell in. We had a team of two mules hooked up to the Fresno, and we were scooping dirt out of the ground to make a water tank. Well, when the Fresno gets full, you're supposed to lift the handle—

FIG. 13. *A ranch near Lubbock in West Texas. Courtesy Southwest Collection/Special Collections Library, Texas Tech University.*

what they call the Johnson bar—and the natural forward movement on the lift will help tip the load over. I was working the team when Red said, "Let go of the Johnson bar." I didn't know what the Johnson bar was, so when the lift of the Fresno hit a rock, it just tipped over. I went right with the handle, head over heels, on top of the mules. The mules got scared and started jumping around, and Red was on the side laughing his guts out. He said, "Why didn't you let go of the Johnson bar?" And I said, "I don't know what the Johnson bar is!" And he said, "You're hanging on to it." It was one of those situations where you do these stupid things and you get away with it, because you're young and you're green. As he said, "A lot of things we do is common sense, Eddie. You just have to start using it." He never got mad at me—this green kid who probably didn't even know how to get out of the rain if he didn't tell me. No, he was very good-natured, and willing to teach me as long as I was willing to learn.

I helped Red build a three-room cabin from scratch. We each had our own bedroom, and there was a kitchen and an outhouse. Red told me that as the junior member of the firm, I would be responsible for the cooking. I said, "I don't know how to cook." And he said, "I'll show you." It was fairly simple—basically meat, beans, and biscuits. We would butcher a steer in the fall and have four hundred pounds of meat to eat for the whole winter. Red's mother sent him things like *Good Housekeeping*, *Ladies Home Journal*, and *True Stories*, and *that* was our reading material. Since I didn't know much about cooking American food, the recipes in *Good Housekeeping* were a great help, except that some of the dishes were not exactly what you would call ranch fare. But I managed to try a pineapple upside-down cake, and since we had lots of eggs, milk, and cream, I even tried making custards.

One day, we went to town to do some shopping. Red left a grocery list with the clerk and he said, "We'll be by later to pick these up." I stayed behind and I said to the clerk, "Ten-pound sack of flour, and I'll pay for it now." He said, "Is this part of the ranch supplies? It's all taken care of." I said, "No, this is my ten-pound sack of flour." So he told me what it cost, and I paid him. Red found out when we were unloading and storing the supplies. He said, "Where did this extra ten pounds of flour come from?" I said, "I bought it." He said, "Why?" I said, "Well, I goofed up some recipes and I wasted some flour. I figure if I goofed up, I should replace it." Red looked at me and he said, "Eddie, don't ever tell an owner that. If I had to pay for everything that I goofed up, I'd be in the poorhouse!" He said, "That's part of the learning experience; you don't pay for it. It's allowed that you screw up once in a while." And he said, "Don't do that again, Eddie." And I said, "No, that's the way I am." Even though I was only sixteen years old at the time, I just knew from my upbringing that I should always pay for my mistakes.

We also raised hogs at the Craddock ranch. Perry (Red's brother) had traded a one-eyed horse for thirty hogs, so we built an enclosure for them. We made a wet mixture of corn to feed the hogs because we didn't have any slop to speak of. A ready supply of meat was always kept down at the well house by the windmill, which served as a cooler. We had to do our own slaughtering, so Red said, "Okay, you've been a meat cutter, Eddie. You can do the butchering." I said, "Red, I'm a meat cutter—I've never done any butchering." "Well," he said, "I'll show you how to do one hog, and then you can do the other two." It wasn't difficult, except that hogs give almost a human squeal; they almost know what's going to happen. First, we cut the throat and bled him. Then, to remove the hair, we dipped the hog in a fifty-gallon drum of hot water. Then we cleaned the insides. Red told me about keeping the head for headcheese—basically making a jelly out of the meat from the hog's head. When I started cutting the hindquarters for the hams, Red said, "Save us a mess of spare ribs, and we'll have some barbequed spare ribs." I had the knife right at the bone and I was just about to start cutting when he said, "Eddie, what are you doing?" I said, "You said you wanted some spare ribs." He said, "Yes, I want spare ribs, but I don't want it that spare." He moved the knife up about an inch, so that there was more meat on the spare ribs. And he said, "That's what we call spare ribs." We saved some of the fat to render the lard, and the rest of the fat and meat we ground up to make sausage. Then I asked, "How are we going to keep the sausage?" Red said, "I'll show you." He used a hand grinder to grind the sausage, then seasoned it and put it in these muslin socks that his mother had made. I said, "They're going to spoil, Red." He said, "No, they won't." After we had rendered out the lard and put it into a container, Red showed me how to put the sausage socks in the fat so that it was preserved in lard. As I said, everything I encountered was a learning process.

Red also had to show me how to cure the ham. At that time, the most famous brand for curing was Morton's. All we had to do was mix up the formula and soak the ham in it. Then, after a curing period, we hung it up to dry and then pack it with salt—that was how we preserved it. At that time, no one ever worried about things like salt intake. We had lots of cream, lard, butter, and all those things that are considered "no-no's" now. One of the favorite things we used to do was to mix some molasses with butter and spread it over hot biscuits—it was delicious! I never craved Chinese food, even though ranch food was meat and pinto beans and we had very little vegetables unless it came out of a can. To me, having a steak all to myself was a luxury. And no one ever told me how much I could have—we cooked and ate until we were satisfied.

Aside from curing ham, we also cured bacon. Then, during the roundup, there was always that special feature—Rocky Mountain oysters. As the calves were castrated, they would throw these testicles into a pan, and those were your fresh mountain oysters. They would coat them with flour before throwing them into the frying pan. I was a little squeamish about trying it in the beginning, but then I remember the time when Mom cooked a special lunch for Pop because he was going away on a trip, and it was fried oysters. I had helped my mother wash them and drain them and pat them dry. I thought they were kind of slimy, so when lunch was served, Pop noticed I wasn't reaching for the oysters. He said, "Why don't you try an oyster, Ed?" I said, "I don't think so. They don't look very appetizing." He said, "If you try one, I'll take you with me to Santa Barbara." So I took an oyster and I swallowed it almost without tasting it. All of a sudden, I realized, "Gee, this is pretty tasty!" From then on, I decided not to prejudge anything because I learned to love oysters. So although I was a little apprehensive at first about the Rocky Mountain oysters, I decided to give it a try. As soon as I took the first bite, I knew why they called them Rocky Mountain oysters. Aside from the shape, the texture was pretty much the same, and they were also quite tasty.

Out on the ranch we were basically cut off from the outside world. There was no electricity, no phone, no radio or newspaper. Our closest neighbor was twenty miles away. In retrospect, it was almost as if I were preparing to become a POW. I never thought of it as an inconvenience, because once we got our work done, had our supper, and it got dark, it was time to go to bed. The isolation didn't bother me a bit. Having grown up in Chinatown, I was used to living under very crowded conditions. So even though we had a small cabin that we had to share, it was a luxury for me just to have my own bedroom. On the contrary, I rather enjoyed the isolation.

Occasionally, I got mail from home. In the first letter I got from Jess, she told me, "In a way, Pop is proud of you because you showed so much gumption; and in another way, he's disappointed because you're not getting your education. But he knows where you are." Jess indicated that my parents would appreciate hearing from me and that Pop wasn't mad enough to cut me off. In fact, when I turned seventeen, Pop sent me a birthday check for twenty dollars, so I took that as a sign that he had forgiven me. I would send postal cards home almost regularly—at least three times a month—because they cost only a penny. I distinctly remember one postcard I sent to Jess. I wrote, "It snows in Texas!" That was the whole message in *big* print. Red, of course, was the one who took care of the mail. He said, "Eddie, what did you think happens in winter time here?" I said, "I don't know, Red, I always thought Texas was hot." He said, "Yeah, it is hot, but not in the wintertime." Jess would write me with news from home— about Bill graduating from high school, passing his Subject A for entrance to UC Berkeley, and so on. In that way, I wasn't totally cut off.

One time Jess sent me a red sports shirt. When I opened the package, Red said, "What in the world are you going to do with *that*, Eddie?" We wore Levi's and blue work shirts—that was our standard uniform for work. And he said, "You're never going to be able to wear *that* in Texas." People had never seen a sports shirt without shirttails. I don't think I ever wore that shirt. Imagine my having the nerve to tell Jess not to send me any more! I just told her that I was adequately supplied with work clothes and I didn't really need any more sent from home. At that time, Levi's were a dollar a pair and work shirts were fifty-five cents. I had four shirts and four pairs of pants that I kept washing and rotating. My first cowboy hat cost eighteen dollars—that was two months' pay. The salesman had tried to steer me toward the cheaper straw hats, but I decided, "No, I have wanted to be a cowboy all this time; I'll buy a real Stetson."

The first time I encountered any racial discrimination was when we went to Lubbock with a load of cattle to sell. When we got into town, Red told me he had to run down to the stockyards to attend to the cattle and make arrangements for the sale. He parked me at the hotel, and he said, "I'm going to give you five dollars, and you don't even have to spend it down at the hotel café, because you can sign a check for that." Then he asked me, "Okay, what are you going to do while I'm down at the stockyards?" I said, "First thing I'm going to do, Red, I'm going to take a hot water bath." We didn't have bathtubs or showers at the ranch. Then I said, "I'm going to see a movie even before I get a haircut." I had not had a haircut in six months, so it was fairly long. He said, "Okay, I'll meet you back here in the lobby at five o'clock so that we can go have supper."

The theater was about three blocks away from the hotel. At one o'clock in the afternoon. I walked up to the box office, I put down some money, and I said, "I would like to buy a ticket." The girl at the booth looked at me and she said, "Can't sell you a ticket." I said, "I'll take standing room— I haven't seen a movie in months." She said, "No, that's not the reason.

I can't sell a ticket to a Mexican." I said, "I'm not Mexican." And she said, "Well, I can't sell a ticket to an Indian either." I said, "I'm not an Indian." She looked at me and she said, "What are you?" I said, "I'm Chinese." At that point, she pressed the button for the manager. The manager came out, looked at her, looked at me, and said, "What's the problem?" The attendant said, "This man wants to buy a ticket." "Well, sell him a ticket." "But," she said, "he's Chinese." And the manager said, "Yeah, I can see that." This poor lady had never been confronted with a situation where she meets a Chinese person who wants to buy a ticket. But the manager apparently knew a Chinese face when he saw one. That was the closest encounter with racial discrimination I ever had, but in a way it was so humorous, I didn't even think of it in those terms. Most times, as the lone Chinese, I was considered more of a novelty than a threat.

After I had been at the Craddock ranch for four months, Red's brother decided that the ranch was not a paying proposition, and he sold off the land and the livestock. I was lucky to find a job working for Fred Mitchell. He was out servicing the septic tank at a neighbor's and said that he needed some help. I told him I didn't know anything about dairy work, but he said, "Nothing to it—all you have to do is milk the cows." As it turned out, I had to milk thirty cows twice a day, and fortunately he did the other half. Besides milking the cows, we raised feed for them. It was interesting work, but I didn't want to do it for life. So I was glad when Red found a job with the Jowell's up in Quay, near Tucumcari in New Mexico, and sent me a letter, saying, "Eddie, if you want to come up here to work, they will hire you." He told me to meet him at the Elkhorn Hotel in Clovis at a certain time. He said, "We're coming for supplies, and we'll pick you up." And that was how I got to work at the Jowell ranch.

RAISING HORSES AT THE JOWELL RANCH

The Jowell ranch raised horses as well as cattle. They were raising half mustang and half thoroughbred, and they were raising horses primarily for the U.S. Army—their biggest customer. So it was different in the sense that it was not just a cattle ranch—it was a horse-and-cattle ranch. The Quay area

FIG. 14. *The movie theater on Broadway Street in Lubbock, where Eddie had trouble purchasing an admission ticket. Courtesy Southwest Collection/Special Collections Library, Texas Tech University.*

was what we called high mountain mesa country. It had enough altitude that we had nice, clear mountain air, but it wasn't high enough that we would get snowed under. It was just a very pretty place to be after West Texas. For example, there was a place at the back end of the ranch called the Saddleback, where the cattle loved to go. It was fairly forested so that it was nice and cool, and there was a lot of nice feed. During roundup time, we knew that there was where we would find most of the cattle. It was about four miles from the main ranch house and a nice easy ride, loping the horses part of the way.

By now, I had some knowledge of ranch life, so that I was of more use to the owner, but I was still considered a beginning cowhand. The Jowells paid me twenty dollars a month. Basic work at a ranch tended to be the same no matter where you went. It was mainly animal husbandry, maintaining all the equipment, and in some cases you might cut hay and stack it up in the barn for winter feed. The main difference at the Jowell ranch was that I had to learn a lot more about horses. Of course, Red knew a lot about horses already. When we showed the horses for sale to the army people, Red would braid the horse's tail so that just the meaty part of the rear end would show. He would also be the one to ride the horses because he was a good horseman and knew how to show them at their best. He weighed easily two hundred pounds and was about six feet tall, but he was of solid build. When he rode on a horse, it was like one unit—you couldn't separate the rider from the horse. The army people wanted to look at the gait and how the horse moved, so you needed a good rider to show the horse off.

Myrl, the son who was running the ranch while his father, Spencer Jowell, lived in Midland, was an avid polo player. They even had a small practice field for hitting the balls with the mallets. Being left-handed, I was never allowed on the polo ponies because they were trained for right-handed hitters, even though the hitter could swing the mallet from both sides of the pony—what they called a backswing, like in tennis. For the same reason, I never got to do much roping, because, as Red told me, "Most horses are trained for right-handed riders, and if we train you with a horse for left-hand roping, that horse will be no good for anyone else except a left-handed rider." So it was just common sense. Being left-handed wasn't a big handicap because I was never going to train on polo ponies, and I was probably not going to do much roping of cattle either. But I had to learn how to trim the horse's hooves, brush their coats, clean the stalls, and do whatever else was required in taking care of horses versus cows.

When I got to Quay, Red decided, "Eddie, it's time you had a horse of your own." And he introduced me to Abe, a nice little unbroken dun. I said, "Red, I've never broken a horse." "That's alright," he said. "Abe has never been broken either, so you guys can start even." In the beginning I had this notion that all you had to do was put the saddle on the horse, get on him, and then let him buck until he got tired. But I found out that Red didn't break a horse that way. He said, "I want you to start going up to the corral where he is and let him get used to you. If he wants to smell you, let him smell you. If you extend your hand and he's willing to nuzzle it, just leave it there. You guys have to get acquainted." So little by little, we got acquainted, and after Abe was willing to let me approach him, I would slowly get him to let me put a blanket on his back, then a halter over his head, and finally the saddle and me in it. Breaking Abe in took all of four months. As

Red said, "You don't want to be in a hurry to break a horse. You want to train the horse, but you don't want to break his spirit." I thought it was a great learning process, and it did away with all those foolish notions I had about breaking in a horse. I used to also have this notion from watching cowboy movies that you ran the horse flat out. Well, the first thing I learned on the ranch is that you shouldn't run a horse flat out unless you absolutely have to. That's because you're on a horse all day, so he's not going to last two hours if you run him to death. In essence, I learned that ranching and cowboy movies had basically nothing in common.

We did a lot of animal husbandry work at the Jowell ranch. I remember one time we were taking care of this horse's right hind horseshoe, and Red was tending the forge. I was holding up the horse's foot so that the hoof was exposed for Red to clean and trim. He was ready to size the horseshoe, and the horse was leaning on me. Here I was, one hundred pounds if that, and I said, "Red, he's leaning on me." "Well," he said, "push him back. He's just lazy and wants to rest, so just push back at him." So I used my butt and pushed him back. Sure enough, the horse took some of the weight off of me. It was little things like this that helped me learn about horses. Of course, Red had been around horses all his life. It was as if the horses knew that he was boss and that they would not be able to get away with anything, so they didn't even try.

I learned another valuable lesson when I was riding Peanuts one day. He was a bay horse, a pretty tall horse, about fifteen hands. (A hand is four inches, so he was sixty inches from the ground to the wither, or where the neck begins.) We were working some cattle, and the basic rule is that you always keep the horse's head toward the cattle, so that the horse can see what's going on. Like a damn fool, I pointed Peanuts's head in the wrong direction. He knew better, so instead of turning the way I wanted him to, he went the way he was supposed to go. The horse was going one way and I was going the other way. That was the first and only time I ever fell off a horse. Red was laughing so hard, he could barely say, "Eddie, the horse knows better than you do." I said, "Okay, I'll learn from him then." I wasn't hurt, but I was sure embarrassed when I realized what had happened. So Red said, "That's probably as good a lesson as you're ever going to have, Eddie."

The ranch in Quay was a government stud station for people who couldn't afford to have their mares bred to a good bloodline. I remember there was a young stud about three years old, and he had never been bred to a mare. One day, Myrl invited all the neighbors to a show. He had a grandstand in the corral area for showing off horses, and this would be the first time that this horse was going to be used as a stud. First this brooding mare was brought in, and she was of course in heat. Then this young stud was brought in, and the lead was taken off so all he had on was the halter. I guess in a way it was comical, because you have to understand that ranch people take sex—animal or otherwise—as natural. So here this brooding mare meets up with a virgin stud, and she's looking back and saying, "What are you waiting for?" And the stud is not quite sure what he's supposed to do. He finally follows his instincts and climbs up on the mare from behind. Meanwhile, this mare is almost bored. The stud finally gets up there and he basically fumbles around until he finds the right place for his penis. He does his work and when he has serviced the mare, he literally falls backwards, and all four legs go up in the air, and he is kind of struggling. Everyone was laughing and having the greatest time. I think most of them knew what was going to happen because they had probably seen this before, but that was my first time. I will never forget that brooding mare's look. She just kept looking back, "What are you doing back there? What's taking so long?" So for me, everything was a new adventure.

Unlike the other ranches I had worked at, the Jowell ranch had electricity because they had hooked up a wind generator to storage batteries. The electric lights were used sparingly. They also had a refrigerator—a kerosene Servel-type. Another thing that they had was a hot water heater. Every Saturday night was reserved for Red and me to take our showers. And I didn't have to cook—Mrs. Jowell did all the cooking, and we took our meals at the main house. There was something else that was different at the Jowell ranch—we had two extra men living in the bunkhouse. The government had started a new project of contouring the land so that it would slow down the run-off water, and in some areas the rancher would build a small tank to store the water for use in the drier seasons. While the team was staking and marking the land for contouring, they lived in the bunkhouse and paid Mrs. Jowell a dollar a day for their meals. These two men had worked at the Boulder Dam, so in the evening, they would tell Red and me stories about how massive the project was. They were telling us about wiremen—these guys who went up and down the face of the dam, wiring the reinforcement bars together before the concrete was poured in. They were saying that wiremen made ten dollars a day, and I was thinking, "Holy smoke, that would be great," without realizing then that construction companies did not hire Chinese. But they also told us that it was very dangerous work because men had been killed falling off the project. They talked about how they had to divert the water even before they could begin the foundation work and how cement was poured literally day and night. It was hard for me to envision that large of a project because I had never seen anything like that before. When I saw Boulder Dam in 1951, I finally understood what they were talking about.

I found it fascinating because they were talking about the different phases of the construction and the many skilled craftsmen who were needed to complete such a massive project. Here again I was being exposed to people who had been around. It made me realize how big the world was, how little I had seen, and how many more things there were for me to experience. At that time, I knew nothing about heavy construction work or even how to run a tractor. When the two men were out working and we happened to be in the same area, we would watch the engineers lay out how they wanted the land contoured. This guy with the grader literally shaped the land exactly the way the engineer had surveyed and laid it out. To me, it was just fascinating that there were so many kinds of jobs, not that I necessarily had to learn and do every job in the world, but on the other hand, it was just interesting to see and hear of the many things that were being done.

I could see six months into the Jowell ranch that I was learning as much about ranching as I was going to, except that I could always get more experience. In other words, things were getting to be routine. So when these two army majors came to buy horses in early 1940, and they started talking about the good life in the army, I perked up. What I didn't realize was that they were talking about army life from the point of view of officers. They said that all they did was play polo. Of course, after I got into the army, I realized officers and enlisted men were two entirely different classes of people. But at the time, not knowing anything about the military, it sounded like maybe here was the next adventure. They asked if I wanted to be a houseboy, and I said, "No, I don't think so." Then I thought, "Holy smoke, here's another place where I can be around horses—I can join the cavalry!" I decided to give it a try, not knowing that I had to sign up for a three-year hitch, or whether I would even be accepted into the military.

THREE · A GOOD SOLDIER

The U.S. Army provided me with all the basics—food, shelter, clothing, and money on top of that. All they asked in return was that I be a good soldier. I never thought of it in terms of what we were training for. To me, it was just another adventure.

JOINING THE NATIONAL GUARD

T he next time I was in Lubbock, I went up to the army recruiting station and asked them if I could join the cavalry. The recruiting sergeant said, "No, you have to take the physical and IQ tests first." It turned out that I was underweight, and the sergeant said, "If you're really serious about trying to get into the army, eat as many bananas as you can in the morning. You'll be the first person I will weigh. If you're even half a pound off, I can fudge that, but I can't fudge a whole pound." After I passed all the required tests, he said, "Now we need your parents' permission." Back in those days, the required age was twenty-one, and I was only seventeen. I had given my mother as a reference, so he sent a telegram to her. A couple of days later, he called me and he said, "I've got your mother's reply and she *absolutely* does not want her son to be in the army." When I found out I couldn't be a soldier, naturally, I was determined more than ever to be one. The sergeant, seeing how disappointed I looked, said, "I'll tell you what—there's a National Guard armory in town, and they'll take anyone who can walk in there, regardless of age. By November you'll be in the army because the National Guard will be federalized."

I almost never forgave my mother that I didn't have a serial number starting with the number six, because that was regular army. Back then, we were called "Boy Scouts"—that's how the army looked upon the National Guard. In case of an emergency, they would call the National Guard, then the active reserves, then the inactive reserves. In fact, it was Lieutenant Ilo B. Hard, who was the sergeant, that signed me up. He always felt guilty about that when we were in prison camp, so he would always look after me. Yet he shouldn't have felt guilty, because I was willing, able, and ready to sign up—it didn't matter who the recruiting sergeant was.

I signed up in May, but I didn't move to Lubbock until June. I went back to the ranch to make sure it was okay for me to leave. I remember Red saying, "I think you're making a big mistake, but since you've already signed up, it's too late." He could see the war was coming, but he also knew that I was ready to move on to something else. We shook hands and I thanked him for everything he had done for me. I regret that I never stayed in touch with Red, because what he taught me held me in good stead. Later, when I got hooked up with the Jacksboro boys in my unit, I got along with them fine because I knew exactly where they were coming from—they were just younger versions of Red.

While I was waiting for the National Guard to be mobilized, I thought I had better find something to do, because it was just not in my nature to sit idle. So one day when I was having lunch at the Silver Grill Café, I told Tom Ng that I had joined the National Guard and that we weren't going to be mobilized until November. Tom was the only Chinese in Lubbock, and his restaurant was downtown. I said, "I know you already have a dishwasher, but is there any other job I can do around here?" He said he happened to need another cook. I warned him that I was going to be gone for two weeks of maneuvers in August, because I didn't want to leave him in a lurch. But he said, "Don't worry about that; we can always manage." That was how I got started learning how to be a short-order cook.

The restaurant was open twenty-four hours a day. It closed only one day a year—the Fourth of July. My hours were from 6 PM to 6 AM. By 6 PM, the other cook had gotten everything ready for the daily bill of fare—usually three different choices of entrées, plus vegetables, soup, salad, and dessert. All I had to do was put it together for the waitress to serve. Of course, during supper some guy may decide that he didn't want the bill of fare. If he wanted to order a steak, I had to be ready for that. I had to also take care of the breakfast trade. A person could ask for anything from dry cereal, which the waitress handled, to oatmeal, pancakes, ham and eggs, and so on. I was paid ten dollars a week—that was pretty good, considering that I had been making twenty dollars a month at the ranch and restaurant work was a lot easier. Again, I was learning something new, so I found the work interesting.

During the afternoon hours when I had some free time, I would go to the library to read the newspaper or check out books. You might say that I was catching up on almost two years of being out of touch with the world. Or I would go down to the National Guard armory to read the manuals and try to learn as much as I could about artillery. As a rule, the National Guard was very relaxed. For instance, the monthly meetings were mandatory and you were paid a dollar if you attended. But if you didn't attend, you were not considered AWOL or penalized. I found out later that where you joined up determined what you would be doing in the army. It just so happened that the National Guard in Lubbock was a firing battery, so we were basically an artillery unit assigned to provide protection for the infantry. Most of the sergeants at Lubbock had gone to college at Texas Tech, so they were a fairly well-educated bunch.

We were drilled on the French 75–millimeter cannon at the weekly meetings. There were six people in the gun crew. Two men sat near the gun, behind the shield. The number one position was the easiest job because all you had to do was operate the elevation of the gun and fire when ordered. My crew chief, Sergeant John Lee, who thought I wasn't robust enough for anything else, figured I should be able to handle *that*. Number two, who was on my left, operated the traverse. The other four men were responsible for swinging the gun around from the back, cutting the fuse and handing the shell to the loader, placing the shell in the canon, and bringing up fresh ammunition. A sergeant and a corporal were also on hand to supervise the crew. We each learned whatever job we were assigned to do, and also how to take the cannon apart and clean it. Everyone had a function, and we learned to work together as a support unit for the infantry. For example, once we knew where the infantry was and where the enemy was, it was up to us to set up our guns in a strategic position a couple of miles behind the infantry to give them fire support and yet not put ourselves under counter-battery fire from the enemy.

There were three firing batteries, one service battery, and one head-quarters battery in a battalion; two battalions made up a regiment; and the regiment was part of a division. Lubbock was C Battery in the 1st Battalion of the 131st Field Artillery Regiment and part of the 36th Division, which was an all-Texas National Guard unit. We're talking about 20,000 men from one state, whereas the National Guard in California was probably made up of men from two or more states. In August we went to Louisiana for two weeks of maneuvers in order to learn how to work with other units, how to operate as a battalion, as a regiment, a division, and so on. It was the only time that we ever had any intensive training in the National Guard. Whatever we had learned in the weekly training sessions was put to good use during those two weeks in the field. And that was when Sergeant John Lee finally decided that this little runt can handle any job that he is assigned to do.

John's daughter lived in San Francisco, so after the war, whenever he came from Texas to visit her, we would get together. That was when he told me, "Eddie, when you signed up and Lieutenant Kirshner told me that he had found a replacement for me, he said, 'I've got just the man for you, John.'" But evidently, after I reported to John, he went right up to Lieutenant Kirshner and said, "Lieutenant Kirshner, what am I going to do with that little runt?" He said, "Put him to work." John said, "He's so small, what can he do? Can't you give me another man?" And Lieutenant Kirshner told John, "Sergeant, you've been wanting a replacement for years. Now that you've got one, you want to turn him down. Give him a job and see if he can do it." So that was when John decided, "Okay, I'll give him the easy job of number one on the gun crew."

When we got to Louisiana, our bivouac area was laid out. It was marked where we were to drop a tent package—the poles and whatever else was necessary to erect a tent. We're talking about a five-man pyramid tent that weighed at least 100 pounds. It took two men to carry the tent to each site. So Steve "Brody" Miller and I were teamed off as this pair. Brody was six feet two and I was five feet three. We got our first load and, of course, we were a mismatch. After we dropped the tent package off and we were going back to the truck to pick up another load, Brody said, "Eddie, tell you what—why don't I just pick up the package and you just follow me. It's kind of difficult for the two of us to handle it, and it's probably just as difficult if you tried to carry it alone." So he got to the back of the truck and he told the loader, "Put one right there," and he pointed to his shoulder. He got his tent and he started moving off. I came up right behind him, pointed to my shoulder, and told the loader, "Put one right there!" John Lee said when he saw me staggering with that tent package right behind Brody, he said, "From now on, I'm not going to give that kid any more slack. I'm just going to put him to work." As I've learned from working on the ranch, I never let my size stand in the way of my doing a job. That's not to say that I can handle anything, but anything within reason, I'll find a way to do it.

I caught a dose of poison oak almost immediately, because where we were bivouacked, there was poison oak all over. I could see it as I was getting ready to get off the truck. The top sergeant, Glenn Jones, came by, and I said, "Sergeant Jones, I can't get down there." He said, "Why not? Just jump down." I said, "That's poison oak. I'll catch it for sure." "Oh," he said, "that won't hurt you." He grabbed a handful and he ate it. "See Eddie, it can't hurt you. Come on down." Glenn had worked his way through college being a bouncer in a Texas honky-tonk (nightclub), so he was rough and tough. Three days later, I was in the field hospital in hot, humid weather, sweating away, itching away. After we got back to Lubbock, I told Glenn, "Now will you believe me?" He said, "I've never seen anyone so sensitive!" Of course, in Louisiana we were also introduced to chiggers—a little mite. It drinks your blood and turns into a little red dot. What you have to do is take a safety pin, heat up the tip, and touch their rear end, because they bore in headfirst. The rationale is if you had a red-hot poker stuck up your butt, you would probably back up too! Then there were yellow jackets, water moccasins, and mosquitoes. Those two weeks were hell, even though most of the time I was in the hospital.

MY FATHER'S FUNERAL

My father died in September. I got a telegram at the Silver Grill because I had kept the family informed whenever I made any moves. Once the family notified me, I started looking for a way to get home. A friend of mine, whose father ran a stockyard in Lubbock, had a load of cattle going to the San Francisco Bay Area. He said, "We already have a handler. But you can ride in the caboose." So immediately, that solved my transportation problem. I told Tom that I would have to quit the Silver Grill because I wasn't sure what was going to happen afterwards.

I remember that the funeral was very old-fashioned and quite a departure from Pop's progressive ways, because we had a Chinese procession with official mourners. There was a Chinese marching band with the horns that play that strange wailing sound, and each family member was dressed in a white hemp cloak and a white pointed cap. We were each escorted, and my escort was my oldest sister Mary's husband, Tye. He had to lend me a suit jacket because all I had were ranch clothes. We marched along Stockton Street to the Chinese United Methodist Church at the corner of Washington and Stockton. Then we went upstairs to the second floor of the church, which was full with people—both relatives and business acquaintances of my father's—and Reverend T. T. Taam gave a long eulogy in English and Chinese about what an outstanding citizen my father had been, always trying to help other people. I thought it was quite a conglomeration of customs, because there was also the blanket ceremony, in which the children of the deceased lay blankets made of cotton cloth over their parent's body to provide warmth and comfort in the next life. As the first natural-born son, I covered my father with the first blanket. I didn't realize it then, but I took precedence over my older adopted brothers and sisters. In other words, I was now the head of the family. From there, we went to the Chinese cemetery for the internment, followed by a funeral meal at the Universal Café in Chinatown. My mother told us afterwards that instead of wearing the mourning armbands for three years, we would do it for one year, and that would be adequate. She said, "We're living in a modern time, and one year is sufficient to show that we are in mourning."

I was not emotionally distraught. I wasn't even overly sad that Pop was gone, because from what I heard, he had postoperative complications. According to my sister Jess, he had fourteen inches of his colon removed, so I suspect that it was probably cancer. After his recovery, Pop was on a scouting trip to look for new business opportunities, and he choked on a grain of rice, because he was in such a hurry to eat his lunch and catch his train. And, in the choking, the stitches broke loose and he bled internally before they could get him to a hospital to repair the injury. So in a way, Pop lived his life the way he wanted, because once he made up his mind to do something, he was always in a hurry to get it done. After the funeral, my mom suggested I go help out at the meat market in Lodi until the National Guard got mobilized. I didn't even know my father had a meat market there, but I figured it was going to be for a short time only, so I said, "Sure."

BASIC TRAINING AT CAMP BOWIE

Two months later, we were mobilized and made officially part of the U.S. Army. We spent the first two months training at the Lubbock fairgrounds, because they hadn't yet finished building Camp Bowie, which was to be the headquarters for the 36th Division. Basic training was for twenty-two weeks, eight to ten hours a day, seven days a week. There were three things we learned to do—firearms, group work, and maneuvers. Brody, when he made sergeant, decided to prove to the other sergeants that you don't need big men to fire a BAR—a Browning Automatic Rifle that weighed twenty-two pounds and fired a clip of twenty rounds. So he picked four of the smallest men in the battery, including me, and he said, "I'm going to make you into a BAR team." From practicing at the NRA range in Grass Valley, I was a pretty good shot with the rifle, but I had never trained with an automatic weapon. The maximum range for the BAR was 300 yards (about three football fields), and there were no scopes on the rifle. We had to learn how to estimate the wind direction, its effect on our firing, and so on. We all had to qualify on the rifle.

The army used slings on their rifles, and Brody told us that the secret to firing a weapon was to get used to tightening the slings on our rifles so that

FIG. 15. *Eddie
holding a Browning
Automatic Rifle and
a pipe in his mouth
at Camp Bowie, 1941.*

FIG. 16. *Eddie with
his buddies John
Connelly (left) and
Joe Foster (right) at
Camp Bowie, 1941.*

it literally became a part of us. When we thought it was so tight that we couldn't get into it, he would tighten it another notch. We were so solidly tied in with the weapon that when it fired, we could feel the jolt of the recoil but still maintain control of the weapon. During rainy weather, we did what was called "dry shooting," or sighting a target in close quarters. The target could be as small as a half-inch ping-pong-paddle shape. The first time we went out in the field with a twenty-round clip, we didn't know how to control the rate of fire, and before we knew it, the twenty rounds were gone. Once we got the hang of how to control the pressure on the trigger, we were able to direct the fire and square ourselves just as we would with a single-shot weapon. Firing any weapon is a matter of practice, lots of practice. I loved the smell of cordite (gunpowder) and the fact that I could handle a weapon like the automatic BAR. I never thought of it as representing power and destruction. To me, it was just pride of marksmanship.

After twenty-two weeks of training, the final graduation exercise was to march twenty-eight miles with a full field pack, which weighed seventy-eight pounds, while carrying a rifle, which in my case meant another twenty-two pounds. In the army we were trained to march at a certain pace—thirty-inch steps and 115 paces a minute—and we were expected to maintain this pace through sand, mud, rock, uphill, downhill, and so forth. We were also trained to swing our arms no more than six inches to the front and three inches to the back. Everything we did in the army was to some uniform code. When we got to the end of the march, we were supposed to set up camp and get into a position to fight. Even though we were in good shape, it taxed our stamina. But it was satisfying to know that we could do it. Even the officers were with us all the way. Maybe their packs were not as heavy, but they marched twenty-eight miles just like the rest of us.

Once we got through basic training, we operated like any army unit, with regular hours and weekends off, providing we passed Saturday-morning inspection. Most of the guys who had cars would drive home for the weekend. But since I didn't have anyplace to go, I just stayed in camp, and if someone had guard duty or KP (Kitchen Police) and wanted to get off, they would ask me if I could take their duty. You might say I was an easy touch. But what the hell, if the guy was close enough that he could go home, I thought that he should take the opportunity. Most of them would at least give me a couple of dollars for helping them out.

I never failed footlocker inspection, so some of the guys started asking me, "Will you do my footlocker for Saturday inspection? I'll give you two bits." I said, "I can't guarantee that it will pass inspection, but I'll tell you what—if you pass inspection, I'll take the two bits; if you don't, I won't take the two bits." It got to the point where I could do about ten lockers at a time because it was basically a formula, and for some reason, I had the knack for doing it just the way the army wanted it. The guys were also willing to pay me to sew on their stripes when they got promoted. The standard charge was fifteen cents per chevron. When I got my PFC (Private First Class) stripes, someone noticed that I was sewing on my chevrons with a fair amount of ease and the word got around. Henry Drake, who was from Lubbock and in the service battery, was the first to approach me when he made sergeant. He said, "Eddie, will you change all the stripes on my uniform?" We're talking about four khaki shirts, two wool shirts, a blouse, and an overcoat—that made sixteen chevrons times fifteen cents equals two dollars and forty cents. There was nothing to sewing on stripes—everything I had learned from my mom as a kid came into play.

What I liked about being in the army was the strong sense of camaraderie—we learned to work together as a team. The gun crews would have fun competing to see who could set up the fastest and who could fire the most accurate fire. We had time enough where some of the corporals and the sergeants would teach us how to box and fence. Although I never made any close friends, and we weren't at the point like the Three Musketeers' "One for all and all for one" kind of thing, the atmosphere was always there. You knew that you were not alone, that someone would help you if you needed help. It was just a nice feeling being a regular G. I. Joe and part of the group. I know that's a contradiction right there: I was a loner, and yet I felt comfortable being part of the group. If there was anything that I could do for one of the guys, even if he couldn't pay me, I would go ahead and do it.

I was known as a "chowhound"—I ate a lot more than the average guy, despite my small physique. Willie Hoover, a born storyteller who later became a top salesman for Levi Strauss after the war, used to tell a yarn about how he thought Eddie was too shy to get in the chow line. He was serving breakfast one morning—bacon, hotcakes, and eggs, and any amount that you wanted. He kept saying, "Come on, Eddie, come get your breakfast." But I waited until everyone was through. Then I went up and asked Willie for a dozen strips of bacon, half a dozen eggs, and half a dozen hotcakes. That's when Willie said, "Now I understand why he was waiting at the end of the line!" That was just a normal ranch-hand breakfast for me. Red and I used to have four sausage patties about half an inch thick, at least three eggs, coffee and cream, and biscuits. And if we weren't in a big hurry, we would make pancakes as well.

"Cotton" James was always trying to make a fast buck on bets. He walked up to me one evening and said, "Eddie, I've made a bet with a guy that you can eat a box of Milky Ways." We're talking about *twenty-four* bars. He said, "I bet five bucks—you've got to do it!" Well, I managed to down the whole box, but I'm telling you, from that time on, I could never look at a Milky Way. I just had that reputation—here was this little runt, where does he put it? It got to the point where I told the guys, "Will you stop making bets, or at least make them smaller bets?"

I don't remember any problems getting along with the guys or any instances of racial discrimination while I was in the army. That was probably because I was so small that I posed no physical threat in any way, form, or fashion; and I was not the sort of person who would go out of his way to make trouble. Even before the prison-camp days, I think the guys in my unit were already friendly to me. The camp days just reinforced it. The only time I remember ever having trouble with anyone was with Ray—one of the Gregg boys. It was after I had decided to transfer from C Battery to F Battery. F Battery people were mainly from Jacksboro, which used to be the starting point for the cattle drives, and it's still a fairly clannish community to this day. But they accepted me in a very short time, except for one of the Gregg twins. I was shocked when I learned that they were illiterate. Even people in Jacksboro didn't think much of the family, so, my being Chinese, he probably figured here was someone he could pick on. It was the usual thing, calling me "Ching Chong Chinaman." I just ignored him. I knew he was trying to get me into a fight, but I decided, "No, we're not going there." After the war, Ray committed suicide by swallowing lye.

The next time I saw his brother Robert, he said to me, "My brother told me he was sorry he gave you such a hard time. He just never had a chance to tell you himself."

After basic training was over, I started calling my mom once a month on payday from Brownwood. I had written ahead with a postcard saying that I would call eight o'clock their time, which would be ten o'clock in Texas. That way, I could just call station to station, which was the lowest rate. I had three minutes, which was usually quite adequate for what I wanted to do—say hello to Mom and see how she was doing. After that, I would talk to Jess most of the time. She was always concerned about how I was getting along. I told her that I was having a ball and that the fellows were all easy to get along with. She always asked me, "Do you need anything? Do you want us to send you anything?" I said, "No, no, the army takes good care of me. You don't need to send me any food, clothing, or anything—it's all taken care of." That was the gist of our conversation. With my limited Chinese, half a minute, even fifteen seconds, was enough for Mom. After a while, I started noticing that people would gather around the lobby just to hear this kid speak Chinese, even if it was only for fifteen seconds.

While I was in town, I would drop by the USO (United Service Organizations) to do some reading. I didn't play pool, and I wasn't interested in dancing. Sometimes I would go to the movies. The town had a choice of at least four theaters, and most theaters at that time charged a serviceman no more than twenty-five cents. I remember I saw *Gone With the Wind* there. When I got the news that my sister Mary had had her second baby, I looked around for a baby shop. I bought the baby a gift, and the lady wrapped it up for mailing. As I was coming out of the store, someone from the outfit saw me and said, "Eddie, we didn't even know you were going around with girls, much less having a baby!" I said, "I'm not, it's for my new nephew." He said, "Yeah, yeah, that's a likely story." My nephew Michael told me years later that he kept that thing until it was nothing but bare threads. It was a complete baby suit with socks and all.

Fortunately, the guys never caught me at the brothel in Brownwood, which I frequented a few times. Apparently, when Camp Bowie was first established, the general in charge of the division got together with the town's people and suggested that the army be allowed to set up one or two houses of prostitution. He told the town elders that there was going to be a bunch of young men in town, and they had a choice of either exposing their daughters to the advances of soldiers or they could give them a natural outlet. So after some hemming and hawing, the city fathers decided it was better to have facilities available for the soldiers. We all knew exactly where they were, and our battery medic gave us instructions as to what precautions to take before, after, and so on. At that time, a visit to the brothel cost about a buck and a half. That was still quite a bit of money, considering that we were only making thirty dollars a month. We were basically paying a day and a half of wages for no more than ten minutes of pleasure. It was one of those situations where you go for a specific purpose and you're done. Of course, payday was when they were the busiest.

For me, the biggest benefit of the army was the fact that I was paid. The minimal was twenty-one dollars for the "yard bird"—that's the lowest rank in the army. But most people were drawing thirty dollars a month. Back in those days, that was pretty good money. When I got my first stripe, I was up to thirty-six dollars. Of course, I had to pay six dollars and fifty cents for my insurance policy, so that left me with twenty-nine dollars and fifty cents. I decided to send twenty-five dollars to my mother. I said to Jessie, "Tell Mom this is not family money, and that she should spend it on herself." When I got home after the war, I found out that Mom had bought war bonds with the money instead of using it on herself. She knew I would survive, because it was in her name and mine. In a way, it made me sad, because she had never had money of her own, and she wouldn't even spend it on herself when I gave it to her.

ORDER AND DISCIPLINE IN THE ARMY

One day I saw in the newspaper that the Air Corps was having trouble finding belly gunners because they couldn't find people small enough to fit comfortably in the belly gun on the underside of the plane. So I decided I would write a letter to the commanding general of Kelly Air Force Base. I told him that I was five feet three, that I was trained as a BAR man, and that I would like to volunteer to become a machine gunner. I figured, "The

Air Force needs belly gunners, so why not just write the commanding general?" And I didn't think any more about it.

About six weeks later, I was told by Sergeant John Lee to report to First Sergeant Glenn Jones. He said, "You're in trouble, big trouble." When I got to the office tent, Sergeant Jones said, "Captain Wright wants to see you." So I knocked on the door. Captain Wright said, "Come in." Sergeant Jones said, "PFC Fung reporting as ordered." I was standing at attention when Captain Wright pulled out the letter that I had written to the commanding general, and he said, "Fung, did you write this letter?" I looked at it and said, "Yes, sir, I did." And he said, "We had the course in military courtesy, right? You know what the chain of command is, right?" "Well," I said, "I didn't think that this had to go through the chain of command because they're short of belly gunners, and I thought that if I volunteered, they would take me up on it." He said, "Fung, if you want to volunteer, you tell your sergeant, the sergeant tells the top sergeant, the top sergeant tells the executive officer, the executive officer tells me, I pass it on up to our battalion, the battalion sends it up to the division, the division sends it to the Department of the Army, the army will forward it to the Air Corps, and so on." He said emphatically, "You do not write directly to the commanding general!" I didn't get punished, but he said, "From now on, remember the chain of command."

There was only one other grim experience that I can recall from my Camp Bowie days. Like everyone else in the division, I had to put in two days of guard duty at the stockade, which was in a separate area from the barracks. The guys in the stockade were not convicted of anything serious, probably AWOL, being drunk, or something of that nature. Yet they were being treated as if they were career criminals. The first thing the sergeant told us when we reported for duty was that if any prisoner escaped under our watch, we would do his time. I noticed immediately that prisoners never went anywhere or did anything leisurely. They always double-timed, whether it was going upstairs, going downstairs, going to the mess hall, or coming back from the mess hall. Even in the mess hall, they were only allowed so many minutes to gulp down their food. They didn't get to sit around and relax over a second cup of coffee. As far as I could tell, they were basically treated like subhumans. That experience was an eye-opener for me, because I was still used to the National Guard attitude, what they called the "brother-in-law" treatment. Those two days of stockade duty was to teach us an object lesson—if this is what you get for minor infractions, you don't ever want to incur any major infractions.

Aside from discipline, the army also trained us to be orderly and well-mannered soldiers. For instance, we were taught dining-room etiquette. Back in those days, each battery had a mess hall. There were ten tables, ten people to a table, so it accommodated one hundred men. Each day an officer would come and have meals with us, to be sure that the food was prepared properly, that the officers were not getting better food than the men, and so on. At each table there would be a noncom.[1] When it was time for lunch, we would march in and stand by our assigned tables. We didn't sit down until the officer who was checking the mess hall that day sat down. And once we sat down, we didn't automatically start reaching and grabbing for food. We were taught to say, "Please pass the pot roast," and the pot roast would be handed to you. You would take a slice or two slices and then set it down. If someone else wanted the pot roast, you would pick it up and hand it down the table. One thing for sure, we never left anything on our plates. We were taught, "You only take the food you want; you only take the amount of food you want." Meanwhile, the corporal was watching to make sure that we were behaving like civilized people and that we were using the silverware properly. Not that we were slobs in the first place, but they wanted to make sure!

Everyone in the battery pulled duty as mess stewards. We were all trained to clean the pots and pans until they were absolutely spotless. The garbage cans were scrubbed with soap and water until you could literally eat out of them. As punishment, we were assigned to scrub the latrine with a toothbrush, and we would have to go through every crevice, every nut and bolt, until everything was shiny. That's the reason I've always said in a joking way that husbands should all go through basic training, because the army trains you to do housework thoroughly. I used to drive Lois crazy when we first got married. I would roll up my socks and underwear and arrange them in little rows so that they would line up as if I were getting ready for Saturday morning inspection. She said, "Ed, you don't have to do that." "Well," I said, "it's real neat." And she said, "Yes, but you don't have to do that anymore. You can just lay them in the drawer." I've been out of the army for fifty-seven years, and to this day, when I step off the sidewalk to cross the street, I still step off on my left foot—that's how solidly the training is grounded into you.

GOING OVERSEAS

The big Louisiana maneuvers occurred in August of 1941. That was when we had the "blue" and "red" armies fight it out in a mock battle. There were umpires on each side, and they scored you on how accurate you were and how many units you knocked out. We, of course, did not use real ammunition. For instance, when the planes came over and dropped bombs, they would drop five-pound sacks of flour, and the flour would mark where the bomb hit. We didn't always have enough tanks, so we would just use a truck with a "Tank" sign on it. Instead of mortars, we would use stovepipes. It was very make-believe, but the umpires were there to evaluate our performance, and their word was law. According to Gavan Daws's book *Prisoners of the Japanese*, one of the reasons the 2nd Battalion was picked over the 1st Battalion to go overseas to the Philippines was because F Battery had performed superbly during the '41 maneuvers.

I didn't have to go overseas with the 2nd Battalion because my battery—C Battery—was in the 1st Battalion. But when I found out Brody was going to be transferred to F Battery in the 2nd Battalion, I decided to go with him because I thought he was a good sergeant and I could learn from him.[2] At that point, going overseas was not such a good idea, because we were the first large group to go over as reinforcements for the Philippines. But after the war, we found out that out of 105 people from C Battery, only five survived the ETO (European Theater of Operations). Then it became a pretty good move. I could have been one of the five survivors, but the chances are slim. You make decisions at a point in time when there's never sufficient data. You make a decision because it has to be made. I was just lucky.

At first we didn't know where we were going. We were just told to pack up and stencil everything with the code word "PLUM." This was in November of 1941. All we knew was that there was a war going on in Europe and that the U.S. would eventually be involved. There was also some guessing

FIG. 17. *The Jacksboro boys setting up camp at the Louisiana maneuvers, August 1941. Courtesy Luther Prunty.*

that we might be going to Fort Sill for advanced artillery training. But when we didn't head east or north, but west, some guys figured that "PLUM" meant the Philippines: "P" was for the Philippines, "LU" for Luzon, and "M" for Manila. I found out later that when code names are assigned, they are basically pulled out of the hat and have no meaning—it's just a code word. We really didn't know where we were going, only that from Camp Bowie we were heading west on a troop train.

The train didn't make any stops, except to service the locomotives or add on locomotives. I got off the train to stretch my legs every chance I had. When we made a stop in Flagstaff, I found out from the conductor that the train would be passing through Bakersfield on its way to San Francisco, so I called my sister Jess and I told her that the train would be coming through Bakersfield in a day or so. When the train pulled in, she had this suit box filled with cookies she had baked for me. She knew I was going to share, and some of the guys never forgot that. Benjamin "B. D." Fillmore, a graduate from Texas A & M who became an agrobiologist after the war, asked me, "How did your sister know you were coming?" I said, "I called her." And B. D. said, "Don't you know you're not supposed to let anyone know about the troop's movements?" I said that I never gave it any thought. We just stopped for fifteen minutes or so. I told her, "I don't know where we're going or when we're leaving, but at the next stop I'll probably get a chance to see Mom before I leave."

We got to San Francisco about three days before Thanksgiving and immediately took the shuttle ferry at the foot of Van Ness Avenue to Angel Island. Once we got to Fort McDowell on the island, we knew *that* was going to be our point of embarkation. We stayed there for about four or five days while we waited for our USAT (U.S. Army Transport) and for our medical records to be updated. I remember B. D. walked up to the top of the hill, and right away he found out it was called Mount Livermore. He knew that across the bay was Tiburon, and here I was, a San Franciscan—I knew where Mill Valley was, but I didn't know anything about Tiburon. B. D. is one of these guys who just knows a lot of things or he finds out. When we were going through the San Joaquin Valley, he would say, "There's a cotton field." And when we passed through vineyards, and no one had ever seen a vineyard before, B. D. would say, "Those are grapes." That was when I started getting an inkling about people like B. D., who not only know how to work with their hands but also how to use their brains.

We were free to wander around the island, and one of the guys told me there was an immigration barracks on the north side of the island. But at the time I didn't know anything about Chinese American history and how the Chinese had been detained there for long periods of time because of the Chinese Exclusion Act.[3] I just knew that Ah So had come through there because Al bribed the guard so that he could peek into the women's quarters to see his bride. That's all I knew. I remember walking by the immigration barracks one evening. It was all shut down and fenced in, and I just didn't have much curiosity at the time to try and get in. Years later, I learned that there were Chinese poems left on the barrack walls by the immigrants.

To me, the most impressive thing about Fort McDowell was the mess hall. I think it could seat two thousand people at a time. I remember the pork chops were about an inch thick and they were roasted in an oven—

not fried. The dining room had several stations with big steam kettles in which the food was kept hot, and the mess stewards would serve it to us at the different tables. For Thanksgiving dinner, it was turkey with all the trimmings, and we had ham as well. After dinner, as we walked out of the mess hall, we were each handed a package of candy, fresh fruit, and a cigar. I'll never forget that, because it was the first time I had ever had a cigar. One thing for sure—when you're at a duty station, the army always feeds you well.

Everyone was allowed one day off the island as long as you weren't on KP. I was given a pass on the second day, and that's when I went home to see my mother. She asked if I would be home for Thanksgiving. I said, "I'm not sure how long we'll be in town." She said, "It'll be nice if you could have Thanksgiving dinner with us." She also reminded me about my twenty-first birthday. She said that it was important for me to mark that day no matter where I was. When I was leaving, I remember that, aside from asking me to look up my brother Pee Wee in Hawaii, she said, "Take care of yourself." That was the last time I would see her, because she died while I was overseas. In retrospect, I wished I had gone home for Thanksgiving dinner. There I was, right across the bay, with a shuttle boat that ran on a regular basis. I could have even gotten off the island without a pass—there were ways of doing it. But remembering what had happened the last time I tried to bypass the chain of command, I decided, "No, I'm going to be a good soldier and stay put."

I heard some of the officers went to the Tonga Room at the Fairmont, and they came back and told us about the rain that poured on the stage. And here I was, a native San Franciscan, and I didn't know anything about the Fairmont Hotel. There were guys who went to the Lion's Den, a Chinatown nightclub, and I didn't even know about places like that. Then the fellows who were coming back from overseas on the west end of the island told us that if we were headed for the Philippines, we were in for a treat. And they warned us about transvestites. We thought they had to be joking, but we later found out in Singapore that some of the most beautiful women who came out nightly to parade were men. I realized that even though I was born and raised in San Francisco, there was a lot that I didn't know about my city.

We boarded the *USAT Republic* at Pier 7 on the day after Thanksgiving, and I'll never forget this: The Red Cross had provided each of us with a cup of coffee while we were waiting in the assembly area, and when our group was called to board, everyone set their cup down by their right foot and marched off. As you looked back, all you could see was a formation of white coffee cups. You could see the army training right there.

CROSSING THE PACIFIC

Most of us were seasick the first few days at sea. Our living quarters got so slick with vomit that we couldn't walk on the floors. We were told to try and eat some crackers or bread in order not to have the "dry heaves"— that's when you have nothing in your stomach but you're still trying to throw up. I was assigned machine gun duty on the topside eight hours a day, and I found out that if I stayed above deck, I felt better. Basically, they were teaching us how to train the naval guns on a target while the ship was moving. But because we weren't at war yet, the machine guns were not loaded. We were supposed to be on the lookout for aircraft or any other kind of enemy movements. I just sat there wondering why we were manning an empty gun and what we were looking for, because we didn't see anything— not even birds. But at least it got me topside. Before we got to Honolulu, I had gotten my sea legs.

We arrived in Honolulu on the last day of November and shipped out on December 1. We were only there for one day. We docked at the Aloha Tower, just like the cruise ships, and were allowed to take turns going into town for four or five hours at a stretch. The only thing I wanted to do was go to the Seamans Union hall and find out if Pee Wee was in town. That was when I found out the security was fairly tight, because I got no information whatsoever, even though I knew the name of the ship he was on. But that was basically all I did. Then a day out of Honolulu, we picked up the *USS Pensacola*, and a convoy of about eight ships, carrying a total of 8,000 men, formed up. That was when we were informed that we were heading for the Philippines. We weren't told why, but the officers figured that we were going to be reinforcements for the Philippines.

We were moving in a southerly direction towards the Johnson Islands, away from the Japanese mandate islands, where the convoy might be detected. As we neared the Phoenix Islands, we heard over the P.A. system that Japan had bombed Pearl Harbor. It didn't make any impression on me at the time, because I didn't realize what that really meant. All I knew was that everyone was excited because of the fact that we had been attacked, and the general impression was, "Okay, so we're at war, but we can beat the hell out of them in a relatively short time." I remember thinking that there was Frank Fujita in E Battery, who was half-Japanese but looked completely Japanese, and me in F Battery. So here we were, one Chinese American and one Japanese American, and the thought crossed my mind, should the Japanese capture the battalion, what would they do to us? Then the news came that Cavite Naval Yard had been bombed out, so there was no point in the convoy going to the Philippines, because we would not be able to unload. General MacArthur had even blown up some of the ammunition so that the Japanese would not get it. We were told to go on to Fiji. We made a brief stop in Suva for supplies, and that was when we heard they had decided to divert the whole convoy to Brisbane, Australia.

I remember I was loaded down with my gear and I almost fell off the gangway when we arrived in Brisbane. I think it was Lieutenant Hard who pulled me back so that I got off the ship safely. We stored our footlockers in a warehouse and marched out to the area where we were going to be bivouacked—the Ascot Race Track. Since we arrived on the 22nd of December, people were inviting us to their homes for Christmas. They didn't know us from Adam, but because we were American troops, they thought that it would be the hospitable thing to do. There were some Chinese families that invited me to their homes, but not having many social graces at that time, I declined. The first time I encountered two Chinese kids speaking English with a British accent as I was wandering around downtown, I almost did a double take. The other memorable things I did while in Brisbane were to buy a Dunhill pipe and to get my fill of milk shakes at the "milk bars."

We stayed in Brisbane until December 28. Then the 2nd Battalion, along with fifty pilots and the 26th Artillery Brigade, were put on the *Bloemfontein*, a Dutch passenger-freighter chartered by the U.S. Navy, and sent to Java to help the Dutch defend the island. We all wondered why we had been picked to go to Java, especially since we were an artillery unit going in alone without any infantry to support. Lieutenant Hard later explained to me that it was like baseball—we were being sacrificed at bat so that the Allies would have a little more time to prepare for war. I never did care for baseball, and *that* just made me dislike it more.

THE BATTLE FOR JAVA

After traveling northward by way of the Great Barrier Reef, we made our way to Darwin as part of the *USS Houston* convoy. From Darwin we headed north toward the Flores Sea around Timor Island and landed safely in Surabaya on January 10. From there we took a train inland to Malang, a mountain resort in East Java, and moved into Camp Singosari, next to an airfield. Colonel Eubanks and the 19th Bombardment Group had been forced out of the Philippines by the Japanese invasion and were in need of help, so we did what we could to help them out: gas up the airplanes, take care of the armament, and load .50–caliber belts and bombs. At the same time, we began preparing for the inevitable Japanese attack. The gun crews were very ingenious. They dug a circular pit with a small cone in the center where the gun carriage could sit, and they dug the pit deep enough so that they would have a steep firing angle to shoot at the aircrafts. Machine guns were also mounted in sandbag emplacements around the airfield.

The first bombing raid occurred on the morning of February 3. A formation of Japanese planes bombed the Singosari airfield, followed by Zeroes that came in low to strafe the area. I remember I was near the guardhouse, and there was a concrete culvert that ran by the side of the road. The first thing I did was to duck into the culvert. And I'll never forget this—Felepe Rios, a pure-blooded Indian from Mexico, was standing up there shooting with this bolt-action Springfield, one shot at a time, and he said, "Eddie, you've got the BAR. Get up here and help me!" I don't know if you have ever heard the term "buck fever," but any hunter knows that the first time anyone sees a buck come snorting at you, you freeze. That's what is called "buck fever," and that's what I had that first time. I don't think I was even scared—I just froze until Felepe yelled at me. Then I suddenly realized that I had a job to do, so I started using my weapon, but I stayed in the culvert.

It was only afterwards that I realized that any bullets fired from the plane would have gone down there like a bowling alley. But at the time, I thought the culvert was the safest place. Although no Americans were killed in the attack, four B-17s and two trucks were destroyed on the ground, and you could see bomb craters all over the camp.

On the second raid, February 9, instead of making the airfield the primary target, they bombed around the camp, because that was where they thought our anti-aircraft guns were. I was out in the cornfield adjacent to the airfield. I had picked a spot that was not yet covered, and I had cleared it with Brody about my mounting a .50–caliber machine gun on the back of a jeep. Most of the other machine gunners had dug a hole and driven the jeep into it so that they were partly hidden, but I decided in the cornfield I was already fairly hidden. So I parked the jeep near an abandoned Dutch house that Brody and I had moved into. When the bombing started, I ducked into the foxhole. You could feel the bombs—boom, boom, boom. And as each bomb fell, the concussion felt closer. Brody saw me and said, "What are you doing?" I said, "They're bombing us." And he said, "Eddie, I don't know how long this war is going to last, but I've trained you to be a machine gunner and a BAR man. You have a job to do, and you can't do it down there in the foxhole." So he coaxed me out like a little puppy. And he said, "Look, Eddie, don't worry about getting killed or even getting hurt. You can't do your job if you're thinking about that. Maybe you'll get hurt, and maybe you won't. The important thing is that you've got to do your job." So I decided, "Okay, the next time they come at us, I'm just going to stand up there and try to hit back."

I was waiting at the gun, and when this Zero started to straighten and run toward me, that was when I started shooting. I thought like a damn fool that I could swing the gun around fast enough that I could get him when he was climbing out the other way. But it doesn't work that way—you're lucky if you can get one shot at him, because he's diving down at you at 180 miles an hour. I don't think I ever shot any of them down, but I shot nose-to-nose whenever I had the chance. Now, Willie Hoover would say anyone in his right mind would duck if he saw someone shooting at him. But I'm a machine gunner—I'm supposed to shoot back. After the bombers flew away, I noticed there were big pieces of shrapnel all over the place. Like a damn fool, I touched a piece, and it was red hot. Then I realized how dangerous shrapnel is because of the jagged edges. I thought, "Holy smoke, that thing could cut your head right off!"

After the first two raids, it seemed like they came at closer intervals. There were at least three more raids in the next ten days before we were ordered to leave Singosari to go defend the west end of the island. Now, Willie Hoover was exaggerating when he said there wasn't any corn left in the field by the time I finished my job.[4] It was usually a combination raid—bombing and strafing. If the escorting Zeroes don't see any threat to the bombers, they will take their time to strafe while the bombers are dropping the bombs. Like Brody said, when soldiers are trained to do something, they just do it.

With news that the Japanese invasion was eminent, Colonel Eubanks received orders from Washington to begin evacuating personnel and equipment and fly out to Australia. He offered to forgo the equipment and fly all the troops out, but Colonel Tharp turned it down because our orders were to stay and defend Java under the command of the Dutch army. Sure enough, on March 1, seven Japanese divisions invaded both sides of the island. We were instructed to go to the west end of the island and provide support for the Australian troops there. The three cities we were told to defend were Batavia (now Jakarta), Bandung, and Surabaya. At all costs we were to stop the Japanese advance at Buitenzorg and hold them at the Leuwiliang River, because once they crossed that river, they would have a clear shot at Batavia, the capital of the East Indies.

I was the machine gunner assigned to protect Lieutenant Stensland, the forward observer for the artillery. It was his job to scout the enemy's position and telephone the information back to our guns. Well, he was so close to the enemy that we were being mortared. I kept trying to tell "the Bear"— that's the nickname we gave him because he was built like one—to move back. He said, "Not yet, not yet! Let me get some more fire in." Our guns were hitting targets on the west side of the river, and the Japanese were replying with mortars and infantry guns. Then we fired back in the direction that we thought the mortars were coming from. We never made intimate contact with the Japanese—it was just firing contact. Pretty soon, he said, "Okay, we got to move back," because the Japanese were coming across the Leuwiliang River.

It was the largest amphibious operation at this point of the war, and the Allied forces on the island were no match. After two days of fighting the Japanese, we began retreating east towards Bandung. That was when we found out that they had landed forces in the middle of the island as well. We were told to move into the mountain country south of Bandung. It was monsoon season and there was heavy rain. I remember we hid in the rubber plantation whenever the Japanese bombed us. Then on March 8, we received news that the Dutch had capitulated, and all troops were ordered to surrender. Judging further resistance useless, the British, Australian, and American forces joined in the formal surrender at Bandung on March 12. We, of course, were disappointed and would rather have fought to the bitter end. But I can understand the attitude of the Dutch: "Let's not destroy any more than we have to, because after the war, we're going to get it back anyway." So that was why Bandung was declared an open city, meaning that the Japanese were not to bomb it. What they didn't know was that FDR had no intention of letting the colonies fall back into the same hands. I remember the general feeling was that we had gotten the short end of the stick. Even though we didn't have anything to do with the decision to surrender, we still had this feeling that we hadn't done a good enough job. And *that* hurt as much as anything else.

Practically speaking, the Allies could *not* have won this battle or held on to the island. The advantage and disadvantage of an island is that you can only run so far before you have to start swimming. We were all put under Dutch command, and that was one of the reasons why we had so much trouble, because communication was lousy and we had never worked together before. Once we found out about the Battle of the Java Sea, when just about the entire Asiatic fleet was damaged or sunk, we knew that we no longer had sea control. Then, of course, we had never had air control to begin with. On top of that, we were running short on equipment and grossly outnumbered. So we knew there was nothing to stop the Japanese unless they decided to bypass Java, which was unlikely, because their plan had always been to take Malaya down to Java and wage a separate campaign in the Philippines.

Again, I was lucky. Out of a battalion of 500–odd people, we lost only four men during the eight days of fighting. That's not bad, especially when compared to the casualties of the *USS Houston*. The ship had been informed by the Dutch that the Sunda Strait was clear and that they could make a run for it. Instead, they met up with the Japanese invasion fleet and got trapped. They lost two-thirds of their complement—643 out of 1,011 men died trying to get through the Sunda Strait. So we realized that the navy didn't always have it so good. Because of my Chinese background, I was anticipating the worst because I had heard about the Rape of Nanking and all the atrocities that the Japanese had committed in China.[5] I knew what the Japanese were capable of, and *that* was what bothered me the most. But all I could do was wait and see.

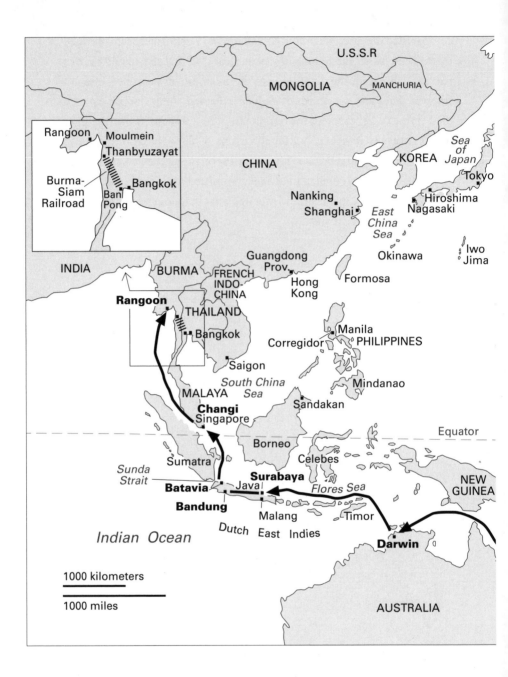

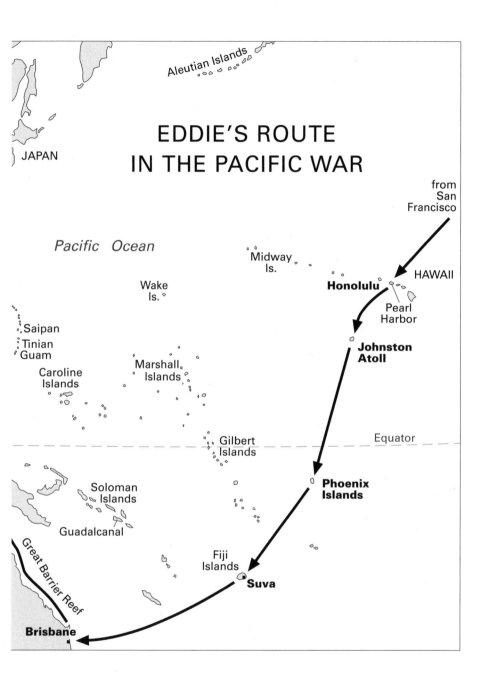

EDDIE'S ROUTE
IN THE PACIFIC WAR

from
San
Francisco

Aleutian Islands

JAPAN

Pacific Ocean

Midway
Is.

Wake
Is.

Saipan
Tinian
Guam

Caroline
Islands

Marshall
Islands

HAWAII

Honolulu

Pearl
Harbor

Johnston
Atoll

Gilbert
Islands

Equator

Soloman
Islands

Guadalcanal

Phoenix
Islands

Great Barrier Reef

Fiji
Islands

Suva

Brisbane

FOUR · A PRISONER OF THE JAPANESE

Becoming a POW survivor is a learning process. When you're taken, you don't know anything about the enemy; you don't know what they are going to do; and what you anticipate may never happen or it may be worse than you could ever imagine. The thing is—there's no way of knowing until you're confronted with it. When things got bad, we used to say to one another, "God, it can't get any worse than this," but then it did. So we got to the point where we said, "Okay, there are no more surprises. It can only get worse." That was when we learned to take it one day at a time.

GAROET RACE TRACK

After the surrender we had orders from the Japanese to move to the Garoet Race Track, an area near Bandung, and we set up a bivouac there. For about three weeks we didn't see a single Japanese. It was almost like being in fantasyland—we had capitulated to an enemy, but we had yet to see them. Some prisoners, wanting to escape, went to Tjilatjap on the southern side of the island, hoping to find a native sailing vessel. There they saw the *Langley*, an old aircraft carrier coming in with some cargo, sunk by the Japanese within sight of land. Even if they could get out to sea, they would have been detected by the Japanese Air Force. We had no air superiority; we had no sea superiority. The closest place to run to was Australia—that's at least 1,200 miles of open sea!

While we waited for further orders from the Japanese, Sergeant Baker told us that we were running low on supplies. He said, "If you should run across any food, we can sure use it." So I decided to go into town and get in touch with some of the Chinese merchants. Even though my Chinese was pretty bad, I made them understand that we were interested in buying any canned goods they wanted to sell. A few merchants got together, filled up a cart, and came out to the racetrack. Baker bought everything they had. I went back the following night because someone wanted to know if they had any phonograph records for the record player we had. The closest thing I could think of calling it was *cheong dip*. But they didn't know what I was talking about, and I didn't see anything resembling one. While I was there, they offered me tea and cookies, and one of them said, "You don't want to be taken by the Japanese. Why don't you let us hide you? Surely one more Chinese in the community wouldn't be noticed." I decided after thinking it over that it wasn't such a good idea because my Chinese wasn't that good, and I didn't speak Dutch or Malayan. I knew instinctively that if push came to shove, these people would probably give me up in order to protect their own family. I certainly would not want to put any family in jeopardy. And if I were going to be in jeopardy, I might as well stay with my own group—people I could trust and relate to.

I'll never forget this incident that happened in Garoet because it actually came in handy later on. This old lady, who was in her sixties and no more than four feet six and eighty pounds, had two heavy baskets on a "yo-ho" pole[1] with things that she wanted to sell. Brody was the first to ask if he could try carrying the load on the "yo-ho" pole. She finally understood what Brody wanted and told him to go ahead. So Brody put the pole on his shoulder and he tried picking up the load. At first, he couldn't find the center point, so the baskets would tip either at the front or back. Finally, he found the right point and he tried picking up the two baskets. He looked at us and he said, "You will not believe how heavy these two baskets are!" So, just to satisfy his own curiosity, he laid the pole down, squatted down, put his hands around one of the baskets, and tried to lift it. He could, but with difficulty. Then we all played around trying to lift the load with the "yo-ho" pole. Meanwhile, this old lady was standing by the side watching us. When we were all through trying, she picked up the pole, put it on her shoulders, shrugged a little just to get comfortable, picked up the load, and went down the road giggling to herself all the way until we couldn't hear her anymore.

TANJONG PRIOK

About three weeks later, the Japanese ordered us to move our camp to Tanjong Priok on the outskirts of Batavia. When we got there, we thought it was pretty primitive. We were housed in open huts, at least 100 people to a hut, so it was very crowded. The entire camp must have had at least a couple of thousand prisoners—British, Dutch, and American. And there were Gurkhas from Nepal, because I remember how gutsy they were. They did not request, they *demanded* wheat flour from the Japanese to make chapati because they would not eat rice. They told the Japanese, "You've got to give us wheat to make chapati." And I thought to myself, "Holy smoke! Everyone else is afraid to speak up at all, and here these guys, because of their religious background, are demanding what they feel is right and due them." And they got it! Also at that camp was a fellow from India who claimed that he spoke twenty-six languages fluently. Anyone who spoke any language at all would try him out, and no one could stump him. To me, that was incredible! It was just an eye-opener, meeting people from all walks of life and all nationalities, including Welsh, Scots, New Zealanders, and South Africans.

Some of the guys at that point still had this mentality: "If it isn't steak and potatoes, it's not a meal." Or they would refuse to eat the rice because rice was associated with coolies. Of course, the British, who were doing the cooking, didn't know how to cook it right. They used fifty-gallon drums, so the rice would be burnt on the bottom, pretty well done in the middle, and completely undone on top. Our basic meal was watery rice with very little meat and mostly vegetables. Others refused to eat what was given out because they still had money to buy canned food. But since I had been raised on a lean diet of rice and vegetables, I didn't have any problems with it. Even so, I decided that I was going to scrounge everything that was possible, whenever possible. When they gave out some cheese that was not completely cured, the guys were going to throw it away. That was when I said,

"If you're going to throw it away, you throw it *here*." I put it on my mosquito netting and just hung it up to dry. Even at that point, I realized that food was going to be the most important thing in my life.

We were put to work on the docks, unloading supplies onto trucks or loading loot bound for Japan. We started out with oil drums. They had to be around sixty gallons or so, much larger than our usual forty-five gallon drums. It was hard work and dangerous, because if the drums got away from you, they could roll over your toes or crush fingers and whatnot. We also unloaded things like 100–kilo bags of sugar and rice. We didn't realize that in the tropics, everything was either bagged in 50 or 100 kilos. When the Japanese said, "One man, one," it just blew our minds. It took four men to put it up on someone's back, but one man was supposed to carry it. Even my big Texan friends, who were used to hard work, were absolutely shocked by the idea of carrying 220 pounds on their backs. But from past experience working on the ranch, I knew that if I just put my mind to it, any job could be done.

When I got my first bag, I literally had to manhandle it up to the warehouse and stack it. Then on the way back, I noticed the Javanese stevedores were not much bigger than me. I thought, "If they can do it, there must be a way I can do it too." So I watched them until I figured it out. On my next load, I tried it, and it worked. I came back and told the fellows what the trick was. They said, "Eddie, it can't be that simple." I said, "I think it is." But they weren't willing to try it. Then on my second, third, and fourth load, I began to refine it. Here's the trick: Remember that incident in Garoet with the old lady and the "yo-ho" pole? Well, she didn't really walk with that load; she shuffled. You see, the "yo-ho" pole is tapered from the center to the end very much like a bow, so there's springiness to it. If there were 100 pounds in each of the two baskets, when you get the load completely on your shoulder, you would be carrying 200 pounds, but you're not, because as soon as you pick it up, it starts to oscillate. The trick is when the oscillation is upward, you step forward; when it's down, you're already set in your step. That's why you see this little shuffle—it's in rhythm with the oscillation—you're basically changing dead weight to live weight. Now, with a 100–kilo bag on your back, what you do is slightly hunch over and find a rhythm to move forward so that it no longer just bears down directly on you. You have to keep moving ahead of the direct load, otherwise the bag will drive you into the ground. I'll never forget at one Lost Battalion reunion, my wife Lois was talking to Captain Wright, who had been our battery commander, and he said, "Mrs. Fung, the first time I ever saw Eddie carrying a sack of rice, it reminded me of a little brown rat with a big load on his back."

Difficult as the work was, we really didn't have much choice but to do it. The first time Lieutenant Ilo Hard went out with the work detail and found out that we were to load and unload Japanese ships, he got up on his hind legs and said, "It's against the Geneva Conventions to do military work." Of course, that didn't matter, because the Japanese government never ratified the Geneva Conventions. The Japanese major, who happened to speak English, told Ilo, "My orders are to load and unload these ships. You're the only help I have. If you won't work, then you're of no use to us." He had two machine guns set up, and he said, "I'll give you five minutes to decide." Ilo decided that it was better to go ahead and do the work than to take the chance of killing off a work detail of 100 men, because it was definitely a threat.

When I was with a large group of people, I didn't stand out as a Chinese. It was only when I went out with the small working parties that a Japanese guard might notice all of a sudden, "My god, there's a Chinese!" There were three ways that the Japanese dealt with me on these work details. One way, they would treat me like any ordinary American soldier. The other way would be mild curiosity—"What are you?" The third way was the one that I came to fear the most—the guy would come up to me and beat the hell out of me. The first time that happened, I was just doing my job when all of a sudden I felt a fist bash into my head. After it was over, I found out from his friend that they had both been in China and apparently he didn't like the Chinese. This other guy wasn't affected the same way, so I never knew how a Japanese was going to react to me. But there was no way to hide myself, so I just tried to stay away from them and to be as inconspicuous as possible. My worst fears—that I would be tortured and killed because I was Chinese—were unfounded. I realized later that as much as the Japanese hated the Chinese, they hated the white man even more for having colonized and taken over parts of Asia. So, out of revenge and to prove their superiority, they took great pleasure in tormenting and bringing their white captives to their knees.

BICYCLE CAMP

In May we moved from Tanjong Priok to Bicycle Camp in the center of Batavia. We had to walk quite a distance with all our gear. It was hot, and my main concern was, "Boy, stay on your feet!" As we trudged along, people started throwing things away to lighten their load, and I would pick them up—shirts, shoes, and things like that. That was the first time I used the technique of psyching myself to keep going. In the beginning, when I started tiring, I would say, "Just another 100 yards before you think about throwing something away." Then as I reached 100 yards, I would psyche myself for another 100 yards. And when 100 yards seemed too great a distance, then I would say 50 yards. I did that for several cycles. Then when that got pretty tiring, I would cut it down to 10 yards. I just kept doing this to pump myself up. Finally, I saw the gates to the camp and I knew we had arrived.

Compared to Tanjong Priok, Bicycle Camp was a Hilton. It had once been a Dutch military compound for the 10th Battalion, a bicycle unit, so the POWs nicknamed it Bicycle Camp. According to Van Waterford's book *Prisoners of the Japanese in World War II*, we received better treatment at this camp because the Japanese wanted to fatten us up before sending us to Japan or Burma to do slave labor. There were over 2,000 British, Dutch, Australian, and American prisoners, and we were kept in segregated quarters, four men to a cubicle. A barbed wire fence enclosed the camp, and there were guards on duty at the guardhouse at all times. So right off the bat we realized that this was going to be somewhat of a formal camp. We had to check in and check out, and all prisoners, regardless of rank, had to salute the guards with a bow whenever we passed the guardhouse.

The most significant event at Bicycle Camp occurred on the Fourth of July, when all the prisoners were forced to sign the oath of allegiance to the Imperial Japanese Army. A couple of weeks before, they had rounded up all the Australian and American officers, interrogated them, and told them that they were going to have to sign the oath. Brigadier Blackburn, the Australian senior officer in charge, said, "There's no way we're going to sign an oath of allegiance to the enemy." After about two weeks of this, the Japanese said, "Either you sign or we start shooting one officer a day." Well, when you think about it, if Blackburn had decided to call their bluff, and the Japanese shot one officer, there would be no turning back on either side. So Blackburn decided to save face. He told the Japanese, "Okay, the enlisted men will sign first. After they sign, then the officers will sign." The word was that he would take full responsibility if there were any repercussions after the war. So our official date of becoming a part of the Imperial Japanese Army was July 4, 1942.

The oath basically said that we had enlisted in their army and that we would obey their rules and promise not to escape. Of course, as Texans, if we say we're going to do something, we're going to do it. So whatever we had been coerced to sign, like it or not, our word had been put down. When people asked us later what that meant, we would jokingly say, "Well, when the Japanese were winning, we went to their side. When they were losing, we came back. We're not crazy—we know which side to be on." Now, whether we would have fought on the Japanese side if they had put guns in our hands cannot be answered easily. Let me give you an example: I have at home what I call a getaway bag. It has can rations for about a week, water, batteries, and a transistor radio. After a good shake one time, my wife said, "Ed, you'll share that getaway bag with me, won't you?" I looked at her and I said, "Lois, the stock answer is, 'Yes, I will share it with you.' But I'll tell you right now, the truth of the matter is, I don't know what I would do. If I were confronted with a situation where we could live together for one week or I could live on the same rations and stretch it to a month, if that's my choice, I can only tell you at the time when I have to make it."

Bicycle Camp was where we first came into contact with the *USS Houston* survivors. The way we marched in with our barrack bags and in uniform, they thought we were going to liberate them! They were housed in barracks across from us, and one of the guys went visiting and found out these guys were almost bare-assed naked. When they had been forced to jump off the sinking ship, they had had on only skivvies (T-shirts), underwear, and a lot of them didn't even have that. Most of us still had a full barracks bag of clothes and shoes, so without anyone telling us what to do, we went over there, found guys our size, and just gave them whatever they needed. We got down to one suit of khakis, two extra pairs of underwear, and two pairs of socks to keep for ourselves. Sam McMaster, who was an old China sailor, and two of the Chinese stewards were about my size, so I just left stuff for them in their cubicle. That was the way it was right from the beginning—no officers were involved; no one had to say a word.

Bicycle Camp was also where I got slapped for the first time. There were five Chinese stewards from the *Houston*—all Northerners who spoke Mandarin, whereas I spoke Cantonese—and I was visiting them one day when a Japanese guard came by. We all stood up and bowed. All of a sudden this guard started working me over something terrible. I couldn't understand a word he was saying and I couldn't understand why he was slapping me around. After he got through, he gave me a contemptuous look and walked away. I was crying; I was mad; and I felt humiliated as hell. Finally, Marco Su, one of the Chinese stewards, told me, "He was trying to be friendly, and he was speaking to you in Mandarin. The more he tried to talk to you, the more you just stood there not saying a word. He thought that you were trying to snub him. So he just got mad and started beating on you, and the more he beat you, the madder he got."

The bruises didn't hurt as much as the feeling of humiliation. To show you how bad I felt, I didn't even draw my food that evening. When Corporal Jack Cellum brought it back to me, I said, "I don't want it, Jack, I'm not up to it." I couldn't reconcile how I was going to handle this—you slap a child, but you don't slap a grown man. Back in the old days, a man might slap you with a glove and you would know that means you're going to have a duel. Or sure, go ahead and punch a guy if you want, but slap a guy? That's not a manly thing to do. That just never made sense to us until we realized that was exactly what they did to each other— corporal punishment was a way of life in the Japanese army.

I should have learned my lesson, but I didn't, because soon after, I got into a fight with one of the guards over a cigarette lighter. I had bought it at the Camp Bowie post exchange and it had the 131st Field Artillery insignia on the side. I think it cost me a buck and a quarter. It was the last of my money and I decided I was going to have something to show for that month's paycheck. Other than that, I had no other sentimental value attached to it. Well, I was lighting my pipe and putting the lighter away when one of the guards walked by and saw me with it. He wanted to see it, so I showed it to him. The typical scenario is: If a Japanese liked something, he would point to his nose and say, "You presento me." I shook my head and said, "No." He almost yelled, "You presento to me!" I said, "No!" The madder he got, the more stubborn I got. I held out my hand for the lighter and he kept saying, "Presento!" I kept saying, "No!" So, finally, he slapped it in my hand and punched me down. He was not trying to kill me; he was just mad. But by that time, I had the lighter clenched in my fist. And I figured, "If you're going to get this, I'm going to be dead and you're going to have to pry open my fingers." The irony of it all was that I got through the camps with the lighter only to have it stolen from me on the plane coming home. I almost laughed when I discovered it was gone, because I had fought with my life to keep it. But by that time, we had been liberated and it didn't matter any more.

The food at Bicycle Camp was good because the Chinese mess stewards were doing the cooking. For instance, instead of having plain rice, we might have fried rice. And they always tried to make things like stew look and taste more palatable. The portions were adequate, and we were still able to purchase food at the canteen—canned goods, eggs, fruit, and so on. Everyone who went out on work parties was given money by the officers to buy food for the camp. The food was put in a storeroom, supposedly to be shared with everyone, but we never got any of it. There were stories about where the money came from. Supposedly, Lieutenant Stensland was on a mission with a quarter of a million dollars from General MacArthur to buy food and charter some vessels for the Philippines. When that became impossible, he decided to attach himself to our unit and turn the money over to a senior officer. There was a special officers' mess and, of course, we knew what they were eating because the Chinese stewards were the cooks. So there was resentment that the officers had money and with the money they were buying extra foodstuff for themselves. Rank has its privileges, but we never agreed with that. We thought that we were supposed to be in this together. As much as possible, we helped each other out in the group, and, despite the resentment, when the officers got into trouble, we helped them out too. But we never got over the fact that they felt they were different and entitled.

We were assigned to go out on work parties. It was hard work, but the hours were reasonable. For instance, we might be put to work mixing cement or building a project by hand. For most of us, just being outside the camp and having the opportunity to scrounge were incentives enough. The guards weren't too strict about our scrounging as long as we weren't too flagrant. That was when I started developing almost a radar about whether I could get away with more or less that day. Most of the Australians wore the bush hats, and they would stuff things under their hats. Then, of course, when we stole things like copper wire, we would wind it around our bodies. It was always food that I was after. There was a term called "crotching"—that was the favorite place to hide things—so you couldn't steal a lot at any one time. If you were really brave, you would bring in two cans on your person. Captain Cates, who was a high school chemistry teacher, said to us one day, "While you guys are out on work details, if you come across any acetic acid, try to get me a small bottle." So we asked him, "Is it dangerous?" He said, "Oh, no. You can make vinegar out of it—two percent solution of acetic acid is vinegar." I remember thinking, "That's like magic!" Once in a while we would get specific requests like that, but usually we just scrounged whatever wasn't nailed down.

There were three or four of us who stood out as being natural scroungers. We got together one day and asked ourselves, "What is it in our background that makes us that way?" We never came up with a satisfactory answer. Take, for instance, "Pack Rat" McCone—that was his nickname, so you can imagine the stuff that he would pick up—he was the son of a senator in Montana. One time he brought in two or three Number Ten cans of fruit and vegetables. And we all asked, "How did you do that, Pack Rat?" To show you how ingenious Pack Rat was: When we got to Changi, where the British had been for decades but still there were no running showers, within the first day Pack Rat had rigged up a hand pump, showerhead, and electric lights. We asked him where he had gotten the stuff. And he said, "Oh, I got it from here somewhere." He was absolutely the best scrounger of the American group. There was universal admiration for Pack Rat because he did it not to benefit himself but everyone else.

Another interesting guy I got to know at Bicycle Camp was John Wisecup, a big marine corporal. He was quite an artist. He used to draw cartoons depicting life in Bicycle Camp, and I'll never forget his signature. He would draw a cup like a wine glass and he would put "Wise" inside it—Wisecup. He was known for his caricatures of army and navy officers. Colonel Searle, who was a senior officer with the army, came all the way over to the navy barracks to see Wisecup one day. People were saying, "Wisecup, you're in big trouble, the colonel's looking for you." Colonel Searle went right up to him and said, "I want to congratulate you on catching my likeness, and may I keep the original?" Wisecup was one of these characters you never forgot.

There were all kinds of activities going on in camp when we weren't out working. Guys were making models of aircrafts and warships like the *Houston*. Preston "P. E." Stone, a truck driver, made a Model A engine with four cylinders, and it actually worked in the sense that you could move the parts around. Jack Kenner, who owned the only portable radio in the American group, was a little more ambitious: He made a Ford V-8 engine. I had a small hand telescope, which I somehow thought would come in handy when I got into the army, and B. D. Fillmore used the lenses to make a microscope. The Australians were very adept at using plastic glass to make things, like watch crystals, and they would hammer out aluminum into all kinds of artistic motifs. Others made jewelry, woven belts, woodcuts, and ashtrays. I made a cribbage board, and I learned to play chess and bridge by watching others play.

The Australians would compete with the Americans to see who could put on the best camp show. That was when we realized what talents we had among us: comedians, singers, musicians, actors, impersonators, and so on. I'll never forget the show that Tom "Tex" McFarland, a marine who later became a water commissioner in Texas, put on. This navy lieutenant by the name of Hamlin recited all of "Dangerous Dan McGrew" from memory. He must have been up there on stage for at least half an hour reciting it—I thought that was pretty amazing! But the highlight of the show was a neon sign that the stage people had rigged up: "When in a fog, light up your wog." To appreciate this, you have to understand that the only tobacco available in the camp was this crude native weed we called "wog," a word used for anything that was native. It may sound like a small thing, but it didn't take much for us to get enjoyment out of it. In fact, one of the worst punishments inflicted on us was when the Japanese camp commandant got upset over some trivial matter and forbade any more camp shows.

Then, in early October, word came down that we were going to leave Bicycle Camp and go to Changi on the island of Singapore. Although we didn't know it then, the Japanese had decided that we were going to be used as labor to help build the Burma-Siam railroad. We were told that we could bring anything we wanted. "You're going to a great area," the Japanese said. Some of us were still optimistic enough to believe that, so we didn't think anything about it. We obediently marched down to the docks and got on the ship, *King Kong Maru*.

HELLSHIPS

Have you ever heard the term "hellship?"[2] I swear, the Japanese can squeeze more men into a confined space than anyone in the world. In our case, 191 of us were squeezed into a ship's hold that measured no more than thirty by thirty feet. We could see right away that we were not going to be able to all sit down at the same time. One of the first things we did was to pile our gear around the edges of the hold, so that we would have as much room as possible. The second thing we did was to set aside an area for the people who were sick. The third thing was to designate a latrine area for those who couldn't make it up to the latrine. Then people decided among themselves who was going to sit down, who was going to lie down, and so on. Then we just took turns.

The Japanese rice they fed us was meager and water was scarce. Fortunately, when we found out that we were going to be on a ship for three days, the camp gave each of us three days of rations and we filled up our canteens. I found out that there were usually steam lines on the ship that leaked water, and what I could do was to hold my canteen under the drip to get more water if I needed it. So I did my reconnaissance work as soon as we got on board the ship. As I was looking around for steam pipes, I spotted a pile of Bermuda onions in the passageway, so I took several. At that point, food wasn't the foremost thing since we had rations with us. On the other hand, onions were fresh vegetables, and these were the sweet variety. I remember eating them like apples, even though I wouldn't think of doing that now. But the worst was yet to come.

After a brief stay in Changi, we were put on another ship—the

FIG. 18. AND 19.
*Front and back of
the only postcard
Eddie was able to
send home from
Changi in 1942.
Prisoners were
allowed to write no
more than twenty-
five words.*

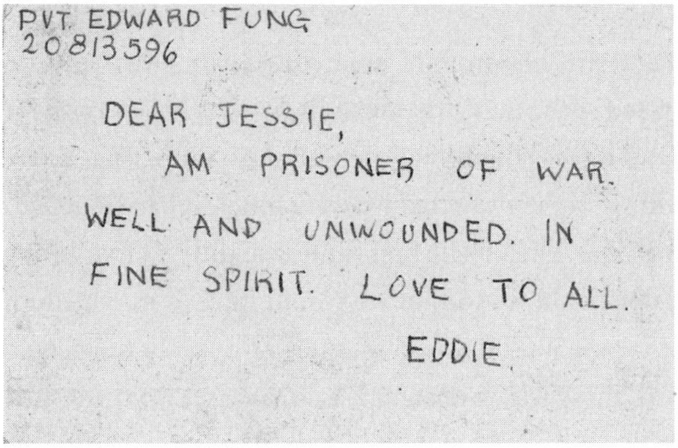

Mayebassi—and I will never forget this. We were in the hold of that ship for three whole days without moving. I don't remember how hot the temperatures got, but the humidity had to be 200 percent! We were below the waterline, toward the stern end of the ship, and there was no wind chute to bring in any ventilation. The hold had hauled horses previously, because there was horse manure all over. The load before that had to be rice, because there was fermented rice below the horse manure. There we were—damn near 200 of us—stuffed in that hold. The feeling of claustrophobia and heat was intense. We were sweating until we were dry and dehydrated. Water was in short supply, and I broke out in a heat rash. I swore to God if I ever got out of there, I would never complain about heat again! Of course, it was all due to bureaucratic thinking. They thought that they would be underway anytime, so why unload and reload? What the hell, we're only prisoners!

Once we got underway and we could feel some air, it was a blessing. We didn't care where we were going as long as we were moving. The rest of the trip was rather uneventful, except that more people came down with dysentery. The latrine was about three decks up, so they couldn't make it up there in the first place, and if they did, they would have had to stand in line to use the outdoor facilities that had been rigged up for us. It was basically a "three holer" plank hung over the side of the ship. The hold was filthy beyond description. Lucky for me, I was constipated the whole time and never had to use the latrine.

MOULMEIN PRISON

When we got to Rangoon, they trans-shipped us on a barge to get to Moulmein. At that point I got scared, because I had heard stories about how the Japanese had tied a bunch of Chinese together with barbed wire, transported them out to sea on barges, and just literally dumped them overboard. I was thinking to myself, "My god, they're putting us on barges! What's going to happen next?" As it turned out, nothing happened. Rather, it was the most pleasant part of the trip, because we were on an open barge that had gravel on top of it, and we were allowed to lie on top of the gravel. It was fairly clean and dry, and the Japanese gave us little packets of sweet cookies and hard candy. We thought that was pretty darn good, almost like having a picnic. I couldn't help but think of Kipling's poem "Road to Mandalay": "By the Moulmein pagoda, looking eastward to the sea."

When we arrived at Moulmein prison—a real "gaol," as the Brits called it—they put us in a large cell. We could hear prisoners being worked over—they were screaming day and night—but we weren't subjected to any torture. We later found out we were in the leper ward. Being that Chinese and leprosy have never been on good terms, for the next ten years I sweated it out because Lois told me the incubation period was that long. The way we found out was through a sailor by the name of Donald Brain. I was amazed when I found out that he could speak Farsi, Burmese, and all kinds of languages. I said, "Donald, where did you learn to speak Burmese?" He said, "Well, before I went into the navy, my family were oil-field workers, and they worked all over Saudi Arabia and the Orient. And everywhere we went, I would pick up some street language." Donald also found out about the railroad from the native inmates, because the Japanese were starting to round up men to help build it. That was the first time we heard there was going to be a railroad.

From Moulmein, we marched down to the railroad station to take the train to Thanbyuzayat, and there I encountered an experience of humanity that I'll never forget. The Japanese had occupied Burma. They were the victors, and, as far as anyone could see, they were going to take it all. But here, many Burmese and a few white nuns from a convent close by were lined up along our route, and they were tossing us cigarettes, bananas, candy, and all sorts of things. The Japanese were shooing them away, but they kept throwing it at us. I've never seen grown men break down and cry, but I saw it then. Up to that time, no native had ever displayed any sign of what the Japanese would consider disloyalty. They weren't being defiant; they were just trying to show us that they felt sorry for us. By the time we got down to the train station, all of us had something that they had given us. Even I, who rarely cry, was moved to tears.

THANBYUZAYAT

Thanbyuzayat was a pretty big camp—about 6,000 people at the time. We were there for no more than four or five days of indoctrination. Upon arrival, we were herded into an open field and lined up in front of a raised wooden platform. From there Colonel Nagatomo gave his welcoming speech about what we were going to be doing under the supervision of the Japanese. He said that as prisoners we would basically have to work for our keep; that we weren't allowed to loaf; and that the railroad was an important project that we were privileged to be involved in. He spoke through an interpreter, although we heard rumors that he could speak English. I remember him saying, "Be cheerful in your work," and "Work is good for you," and that sort of thing. At the time, it didn't seem that comical, nor cynical. We thought, "Okay, he's just giving us his sales pitch."

The speech was fairly long—about half an hour—and it was the first time we had officially heard about the railroad. We had no idea that it would stretch 262 miles through the tropical jungles and that we would be required to complete it in twelve months' time, although the Japanese engi-

FIG. 20. *A Japanese guard at the entrance of Thanbyuzayat camp, 1943. Courtesy Australian War Memorial, 045258.*

neers had originally said that even a single line of track would take two to five years to build. Nothing was said by the Japanese about how critical it was to have this rail link between Rangoon and Bangkok in order to get equipment and supplies to the Burma front. As it stood, supply ships from Singapore had to sail some 1,300 miles through the Malacca straits and north across the Indian Ocean to Rangoon—exposed the entire distance to Allied submarines and bombers. The railroad was thus crucial to their taking India next and ultimately winning the war. I later learned that a total of 61,000 Allied prisoners and 250,000 civilians, including Malaysians, Indians, Thais, and Burmese, were used to build the railroad, which was completed in a record sixteen months at the cost of 12,500 POW and 70,000 Asian lives.

The next morning when we got up, before dawn, we heard what sounded like chanting. So, out of curiosity, we went towards the sound and, from a distance, we could see four Japanese soldiers holding a telephone post above their heads, and they were double-timing and running around in a circle. When I found out that this was punishment for coming back drunk and a little late, I thought, "Holy smoke, if this is punishment for just being drunk, what do they do when you do something really bad?" Of course, by this time, we were beginning to see how the Japanese treated their own troops and why they behaved the way they did towards us. You don't sympathize with it; you don't empathize with it; you just come to a gradual understanding that's the way they are.

WORKING ON THE RAILROAD

Between 10,000 to 11,000 prisoners worked on the Burma side of the railroad, as compared to 50,000 on the Thailand side. The Japanese organized the work force on both sides into sections. The Burmese side was divided into two sections, and prisoner groups No. 3 and No. 5 were allocated to them and put under the supervision of the 5th Railway Regiment of the Japanese Imperial Army. Four other groups of prisoners were assigned to the Thailand side under the 9th Railway Regiment. We were known as the Fitzsimmons group (under Captain Fitzsimmons) and made a part of group No. 3. Because there were only 191 of us, they decided the best way to use us was as a mobile force or advance party to help set up facilities for the groups that would follow us. Most of the time, they combined us with the Australians as part of the Black Force, which was a good thing, because Australians and Texans got along famously.[3] We were lucky that we had the easier stretch of the road at the north end, because work at the south end was horrible. Then again, we were lucky because when the other American group, consisting of 478 men under Colonel Tharp, came up after us and joined group No. 5 on the Burma side, they were bombed and sustained casualties. They also came up during the tail end of the rainy season when working conditions got worse. The unluckiest group was the thirteen American POWs who were assigned to work at Hellfire Pass on the Thailand side, cutting a passageway through a granite hillside as high as eighty feet in one section.

As a mobile force, we worked out of many camps, which were named

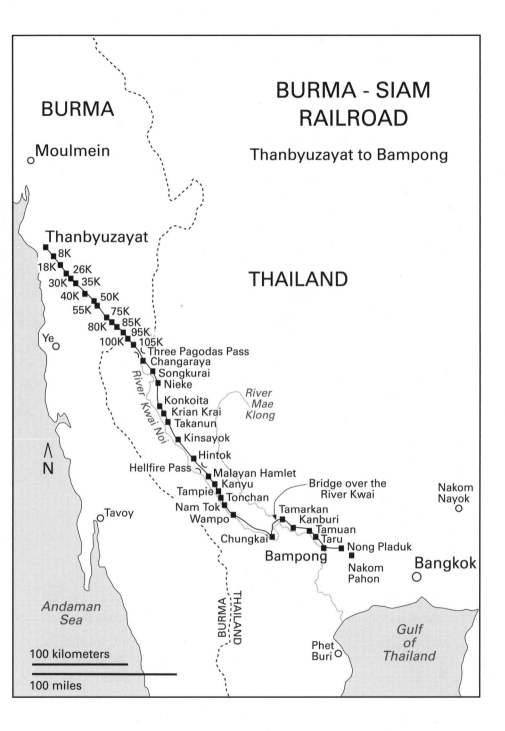

according to their distance by kilometers from Thanbyuzayat, such as 25 Kilo, 40 Kilo, and so on. During the fifteen months we were working on the railroad, I remember at least six major moves: 40, 25, 30, 45, 85, and 105 Kilo camps. The reason we started out at 40 Kilo was because some track had already been laid as far as 25 Kilo. We were to clear the ground from 40 Kilo going backwards toward Thanbyuzayat as well as forward toward 45 Kilo. This Japanese idea of "hopscotching" was not a bad idea. It's quite simple: If you set up camp at 55 Kilo, you could work backwards for 10 kilometers to 45 Kilo, or you could work forward 10 kilometers to 65 Kilo. Then once everything is done at 65, you could jump to 80, set up camp there, and work back to 65. That way, you only have to "commute" a certain distance to work. Of course, there were other groups working behind us, and groups did not all move at the same time; all of the moves and jumps had to be coordinated by the Japanese. Each time we moved camp, everything went with us—the sick, the kitchen gear, the whole works. We marched to the next camp and, hopefully, the supply trains would catch up with us.

As soon as we got to 40 Kilo, we had to set up camp. The natives who were doing the right-of-way work had preceded us, but their camps were usually slapdash and disorganized. We would line up the bamboo huts with intervals in between. There was an aisleway down the middle of the hut, and wide platforms made of bamboo slats on each side for sleeping. Each hut was roughly 50 feet wide and 150 feet long, and each person was allotted one yard width of space. The roof was made of *atap* (palm leaves) and the sides were open-ended, which meant there was little protection from the wind and rains. To make more space, we would sometimes build bunk beds.

Basic sanitation, no matter how crummy, was important to us. When we set up a camp, we would designate an area for the kitchen, an area for the hospital, an area for the latrine, and so on. We took care of the simple things that would contribute to our hygiene. This was something that the natives just didn't do, so in that regard, the Allied troops were more organized, disciplined, and clean. Usually, the Japanese railroad people would tell the camp commander almost as soon as we arrived, "We want X number of people for work tomorrow morning." If he said 300, that would mean 700 people in a camp of 1,000 would stay behind and help organize the

FIG. 21. *The interior of a typical atap-roofed hut at a POW camp, 1943. Courtesy Australian War Memorial, 157878.*

camp while the other guys were away at work. Every day they would do more, until the camp was really set up. As we moved up and down the railroad, if the camp had been organized by one of the Allied groups, even if the natives had moved in, the basic structure would be there and all we would have to do was clean up and repair.

As it turned out, we only stayed at 40 Kilo for a matter of two or three weeks, because the well that we dug ran dry. Because we didn't have an adequate water supply, we had to back off to 25 Kilo. That was the only time we made a backward move. But we did go out on some cut-and-fill work parties, so we got a general idea of what the work was going to be like. The right-of-way had been cleared by the natives, so what we had to do was start building the railroad track, keeping it as level as possible, because rail engines can only run up a certain grade. Putting it in simple terms, if you had a hill and a valley and a hill, and the railroad runs across the middle, you would have to cut off the top of the two hills and fill it into the valley. The Japanese engineers decided our allotment. They didn't care whether it was mud, dirt, sand, or rock. They would measure out X number of meters—how wide and how deep—and we had to finish that work allotment before we could quit for the day.

The first time we went out on a cut-and-fill job, the Japanese engineer had laid out the work so that we were kind of working on top of each other. He probably thought that would make it easier for the guards to keep an eye on us. So Lieutenant Stensland, who had been a civil engineer in peacetime, tried to get across to the engineer that he could see by the pegs and the flags where the railroad was to go. He tried to convince the Japanese engineer that if he laid this work allotment in a long stretch, we wouldn't be working on top of each other, but he wasn't getting through to him. Finally, I walked up to them and I wrote the Chinese word *tung,* meaning "the same." What the Bear was trying to show him was: Whether you dug a trench that was one foot deep and one foot wide by three feet long or a trench that was three feet deep by one foot square, it's the same amount of dirt. So the Japanese engineer went, "Oh! Wakaru, wakaru—I understand." Then all of a sudden he looked at me and said, "You Chinese?" I said, "Yes, American." I wrote down *fu mo* for "father and mother" to tell him they were Chinese, and then I wrote down that I was born in Mei Gwok, meaning America. Then he said, "Okay, okay." I didn't realize then that I should not get involved as a "go-between," because, aside from possibly displeasing one side or the other, I was calling attention to myself. But the Bear was a good officer—he was the only officer who went out to work with us and who stuck up for us—and I wanted to help him out.

So, after a while, whenever we went out to work in the morning, the Japanese engineer would say good morning to the Bear—"Ohayo." Then he would point more or less in the direction that he wanted us to work. He would tell the Bear, "Seventy-five meters," and he would say how many men. If he said 100, that would mean each man had to dig and carry .75 cubic meters of dirt to the places that required the fill. He would let the Bear lay out the work, because they could see that we were trying to be efficient. For instance, if we had a stretch of hill to cut down and the dirt had to be hand-carried away, we would start working in levels—a top, middle, and lower level—and it would be stair-stepped. Naturally, you shovel dirt downhill—that's common sense—whereas if the Japanese had their way, they would have you dig a hole first. Our way was to dig the hole from the top, undercut the ledges, and then use crowbars to dig behind and bring five or six cubic meters down at one time, instead of literally digging it out one shovelful at a time. The first time we did that, the Japanese engineer literally clapped. That was the only time we ever got any praise from the Japanese. So any time the Americans were out there working, we had very little trouble with the Japanese engineers.

At the beginning, it was relatively easy work, because it was soft dirt and dry; the rainy season had not started yet. So for the first few days, we would get out there at four or five o'clock in the morning and be through by noon. We would be marching home and passing the Aussies, and we would joke with them, "You guys need any help?" They would tell us, "Yanks, you're crazy! They're going to move it up!" Sure enough, they kicked the load up to 1.2 meters, which was almost a 50 percent increase. We were still doing it with ease. But the Australians kept telling us, "Take all day to do it. Don't do it in the shortest time possible, because they'll just keep adding it on." But being naturally competitive, we wanted to be the first one off the job, and at this stage, we were still in top shape, and the picks, spades, and *chunkels* (native hoes) were still pretty good. But in carrying away the dirt, we suddenly came face-to-face with the primitiveness of the equipment we had to work with. Everyone was naturally looking for wheelbarrows, but all we had was a big rice sack with two poles—like a stretcher with one person at each end. It was just something we had to learn to work with.

Once the right-of-way was ready, we learned to lay down the cross ties and rails on each side. Then we started drilling holes for the spikes. Next, we pounded in the spikes. Then the Japanese engineer had to measure the track to make sure the alignment and spacing were correct. Then we would make little rocks from big ones for ballast—that was what held the cross ties in place. The Japanese never got used to the way we worked. The first time we had to unload a bunch of rails that were about thirty feet long and seventy pounds to a foot, they were screaming at us to hurry. The engineers would not bother to learn English, because once they got the work laid out, they were gone. It was the Korean guards who made sure we didn't loaf on the job.

Cut-and-fill work was pretty routine and there wasn't much ingenuity involved. But when we started building bridges—that was when we marveled at the ingenuity of the Japanese engineers. First, we had to cut down the trees to make the piles, which were usually thirty-five or forty feet long. The Japanese engineers would sharpen one end of the pile and nail in a steel strap so that it would not split when we began the pile driving. Next, we had to build a temporary scaffold with timber to hold a row of five piles upright. Instead of wires, the Japanese used what were called "dogs" (a wrought-iron piece of rod) to tie the scaffold together. Then we drove the five piles supported by the scaffold into the ground about a foot and a half deep in order to lock them into position. Once we had the first row of piles loosely in place, we would build the next temporary scaffold and lock in another row of piles, then tie it to the first row and continue until we were all the way across to the other end of the bridge.

Now we were ready for the pile driving. On the top of each pile, we would drill a hole. Into that hole went a metal lead pole about twenty-five feet long and an inch in diameter, upon which the rammer, weighing some 1,000 pounds, could be hoisted. We then attached what we called "spider ropes" to the weight, basically to pulleys so that a bunch of guys at the end of the ropes could raise the weight and drop it. Someone would start chanting "Ichi, ni, no, san, yo." When we got to "yo," the guys would let the ropes go, and the weight would drop. Inch by inch, we drove that piling in, until the Japanese engineer decided it wasn't going to go another eighth of an inch. On a good day, we might drive three sets of piles, and usually each set was five across and about five feet apart. So if the bridge were sixty feet long, we would need twelve sets of piles. After we drove all the piles in, we would dismantle the scaffolding and start putting in the cross braces and the final bridge. That involved trimming the top of the piles, putting planks across the top to make the roadbed, and laying down the cross ties and rails. It was hard work, but, on the other hand, it was more interesting than just digging and carrying dirt away.[4]

One of the toughest jobs we had to do was clearing a bamboo grove that was in the path of the right-of-way. You have no idea how bamboo can interlace underneath the ground and how much digging it takes to get to the root system, cut it loose, and then manhandle the whole thing

FIG. 22. *POWs laying track on the Burma-Siam railway, 1943. Courtesy Australian War Memorial, P00406.034.*

FIG. 23. *An example of bridge building at Tamarkan, Thailand, 1943. Courtesy Australian War Memorial, 118879.*

over the side. Elephants were put to work, trying to break up the root system, and they couldn't do it. We had seen elephants do heavy work, like rolling logs, lifting them, and so on. We had seen them obey orders no matter who gave them, but apparently the Japanese thought they could drive them to greater effort, and they didn't respond to that well. The elephants got so mad that they went on a rampage. That was scary, because we could hear them making that eerie trumpet sound. Then we could hear them charging through the brush, but the bamboo thickets were so heavy that we couldn't tell from which direction the animals were coming. That was when we came up with this old bit, "One hundred men equals one elephant," because it took that many of us to loosen up and roll the root system aside. Then we still had to fill the hole back in. It was like digging a grave, except this one had to be at least fifty feet long, twenty-five feet wide, and six feet deep. If we were lucky, we could probably clear a medium-size bamboo grove in a day or two. Over the course of the whole time that we were on the railroad, we must have cleared out as many as eight groves. But it was the big ones that we remembered, because it took so much time and so many men to do the job.

The Aussies were right—when the Japanese saw that we were doing the job with ease, that was when they decided we could handle more. As the workload increased, we got weaker and weaker. Overall, I don't think our workday was ever shorter than twelve hours. We got up at four in the morning because the Japanese army worked on Tokyo time, and we never got home much earlier than four or five in the afternoon. We worked ten days, then got one day off. We were paid ten cents a day, including the day off. So, even though you didn't work, you would still get some money. And we got one holiday on the emperor's birthday—April 29. No matter how rushed the work was on the railroad, we always got that day off. Noncoms were paid fifteen cents, and officers were paid according to rank in Japanese equivalents. But a strange thing happened on the way to the bank, and each officer only got twenty dollars. The Japanese explained to them that they were being charged room and board and that money was being set aside for them in Japanese banks so that the officers would have money to restart their lives after the war. This was particularly funny, considering that we were all being paid in occupational money, which would become worthless after the war. The first time we were paid, Colonel Black set the example of putting aside ten dollars for the Red Cross fund to buy food and supplies for the sick. The other officers decided, "Okay, that sounds like a good idea," and followed suit. So, you can see, we were always looking out for the sick.

OUR MEAGER RATIONS

Our basic ration was 500 grams or about one pound of rice per working-man per day, but only those working were issued rations. So if the Japanese engineers asked for only 300 men in a camp of 1,000 men, we would immediately be on one-third rations. Everyone shared; it was a perfect socialist state. Even half a pound of raw rice would be pretty filling if we had that all the way through, because later, as we moved up the railroad to 105 Kilo, more of the men got weak and sick, and we were lucky if we could send out 20 percent of the men as a workforce. That meant we were at one-fifth rations—barely a bowlful of rice per man when cooked. So you can see why our diet, which was meager to begin with, became worse as time went on.

Aside from rice, we got vegetables—usually winter melon, pumpkin, and yam. Sometimes we would get things like eggplants, cucumbers, onions, jicama, and mung beans, and everything would go into the stew pot. Every once in a while there would be some meat. The Japanese would slaughter an ox and take the lion's share, and we would add what they gave us to the stew pot. The cook would cut up the meat in small bits and it was "catch as catch can" whether you got a piece of meat or not. But at least the stew would have a stock flavor and a little protein. Or, if we were near a river, we might get fish. One of the big hauls that the guys got one time was a python. It had just swallowed some small animal and was feeling very lethargic. So one of the guys shot it with the guard's rifle (since the guard kept missing it), and we put the snake in the stew pot.

For breakfast, all we got was *jook* (rice gruel), and, if we were lucky, a little ginger and sugar added to it. At midday, the rice and stew would be brought out to us by two men who were considered "light sick." These same two men would also be what we called "tea tenders." They would keep a pot of water boiling, and even though we didn't have any tea to put in, we still called them "tea centers." There was no scheduled tea break, but if anyone needed a drink of water, he could go ahead as long as he didn't linger. We would say to ourselves, "I'm going to have a cup of tea." Psychologically, you can fool yourself into almost anything! I remember there was an Englishman who had a teabag that he used over and over again. There couldn't have been any flavor left, but he kept dipping that thing in hot water. As far as he was concerned, he was having tea.

Our main meal was in the evening whenever we got back from work. In the beginning, we had people arguing and fighting about the unequal portions until we found someone who could be the official food dispenser. That person turned out to be Preston "P. E." Stone. He just had a knack for dishing out the rations evenly and stirring the pot so that no one got more solids than another person. If there were any leftovers, we would utilize the British system called *leggi*, a Malayan term for "seconds." We were each given a number, and if P. E. Stone thought that he might have enough for six *leggis*, then number one through six would line up for seconds. If it turned out there was only enough for five, then we all knew that the next *leggi* number would start with six, and so on. In other words, everyone knew that eventually, unless he died, he would have a chance at seconds. Of course, we could supplement the poor diet by buying food at the canteen set up by the Japanese at most of the camps. They sold things like toothpaste, tobacco, tomatoes, sugar, and salt. An egg cost fifty cents—that was five days of wages. So if you were smart, you would not spend your money at the canteen, but wait for an opportunity to trade with the natives and get a better bargain.

When we were first issued woks by the Japanese, the cooks didn't even know what they were, but they soon learned how to use them. One of the problems our cook, Vince Carey, an Australian, always had with them was cleaning the wok afterwards. I was there one day and he was cursing up a storm as he soaked and scraped the wok. Well, in the summertime when my father used to take me to the potato farm in Stockton, I remembered how they cooked the rice in the wok. So I said to Vince, "Here's the way you cook rice." The first thing I had to do was to show him how to wash the rice until it was pretty clean, because although the rice was not bad, it was still pretty dirty. It took a while to convince him that washing the rice did not wash away all the vitamins, and that it would make the rice more palatable. Next, I had to show him how to determine the right amount of water to add to the washed rice—the water should come up to the first knuckle of the middle finger touching the rice. "Now," I said, "it's going to vary because each crop of rice is different. You're going to have to play around with it. But this is the general rule of thumb." The wok had a wooden cover, so I had him scrounge up some clean cloths to make a cloth rope to put around the cover so that the steam didn't all escape.

I told Vince, "Look, you don't have to cook the whole ration of rice. Let's cook a quarter ration—just something so that you can see what needs to be done." So he said, "Let's try about a third ration." Well, I had learned at the ranch helping the cooks how much wood to stack to burn down to the coals. So we built up the fire, using bamboo, of course—a quick fire. When it got to steaming, I said, "Whatever you do, do *not* lift the lid to look at it." Then the fire burned down and I told him not to disturb it— "Just leave the coals alone." After the steaming had almost stopped, I said, "Now you can spread your coals around so that the heat gets to as much of the wok as possible." When the rice was done, I said, "Okay, take the big wooden paddle and scoop the rice out." And he said, "What do I do with the crud at the bottom?" I said, "Leave the cover off. Now watch what happens." After the crust started to break away from the side of the wok, I just lifted out the whole thing. I said, "That's how you cook rice." He said, "But what should we do with the crust?" I said, "That's a treat. When we were kids, my mom would fold in a little piece of ham or just shake a little salt on it—that's all that's needed." And I said, "Just give it to the hospital. It's tough on the gums, tough on the teeth, tough on the digestion, but it's a treat." Vince later taught the other Australians how to cook rice properly in a wok. Like him, they too thought it was magic.

It began to dawn on me that all these little things that I had learned through the years could be put to good use in the jungles. For example, when we got our first cow from the Japanese, Ray King was butchering it and throwing out all the entrails, liver, kidneys, and lungs. So I said, "Ray, are you going to throw those out?" He said, "Yeah, there's no use for them." I said, "Okay, may I have them?" So I took the liver and the kidneys and I told Ray—except that it wasn't the right time yet because we weren't hungry enough—I said, "You know that you can clean out the tripe and the intestines? It's a lot of work, but they're eatable. Even when you slaughter the cow, if you drain the blood, that's got nutrients." He said, "What do you do with the blood?" I said, "You can make blood pudding by steaming it. It tastes like hell, but it's got nutritional value." Well, after that, they started at least saving the liver and the kidneys and so on. I said, "If nothing else, give it to the hospital." Eventually we got to the point where if we got anything like a cow again, the kitchen staff would go to the extent of taking the guts, the tripe, and everything down to the stream and washing the intestines inside out, and they would throw everything except the skin into the stew. They learned to utilize every bit of food that the Japanese gave us.

When I think back to my childhood, it was almost as if I had been preparing all my life to be a prisoner of the Japanese because the rice diet was compatible to me, and I was familiar with most of the foods we were given to eat, like *dung gwa* (winter melon) and *faan goot* (jicama). One time I came back with a mess kit full of *fu gwa* (bitter melon) cooked with chicken livers. I had been working at the Japanese headquarters and one of the cooks had given some to me. When I got back and opened it up, Paul Leatherwood, one of the Jacksboro boys, said, "What is that, Ed?" I said, "It's bitter melon—a unique Chinese vegetable." So I gave him half a slice to try, and I said, "If you spit this out, it's okay, but I'll warn you right now, it's bitter." So he tasted it and said, "Oh, god!" He spat it out and he said, "You're right. It's bitter. How can you eat that stuff?" I said, "It's a delicacy and an acquired taste." And he said, "You can have it, Eddie!" Another time, when we were near a river, the guys were horrified when I cooked up a batch of snails and ate them. To sum it up, Leonard Drake, who bunked near me, once said to me, "Eddie, you mean to tell me that you had to eat all this stuff at home?" I said, "Yup." And he said, "I don't know how you did it." I jokingly said, "Well, why do you think I left home, Leonard?"

CONDITIONS IN THE JUNGLE

When we first became prisoners, I had the basics—a mess kit, a canteen, a blanket, and a mosquito net. Clotheswise, I had two suits of suntans (khaki shirt and pants), four sets of underwear, some socks, two pairs of shoes, and a raincoat. Some I gave away to the *Houston* survivors. Within a few months, the rest of the clothes were all gone, because the humidity and mildew in the tropics just chewed up the threads that held the clothes and shoes together. So, early on in the game, we realized that we weren't going to be able to keep our clothes in repair. Gradually, we all adopted what we called the "G-string" as the uniform of the day. We got the idea of making the G-strings from the Japanese. Their military underwear was a very simple piece of apparel. It was about ten inches wide and thirty-odd inches long, and on one end it had a string that was to go around the waist. You put the flap behind you, you draw it up and tuck it under the string, you let it hang over, and that's what we called a G-string. We had two issues of it that I can remember. The last one was really sexy—it was black. Anyway, we saw how simple it was because there was no upkeep; there were no seams to fall apart. We could use it as a sweat cloth, and it was easy to wash. I think it was the Brimhall boys from Jacksboro who made the first G-strings, and we thought it was funny as hell. Then people started making their own. From the legs of a pair of pants, you could easily make two G-strings. We couldn't do anything about the shoes, and the Japanese didn't issue us any, so we were going around barefooted early on.

With the kind of work we were doing and without proper tools, protective clothing, and shoes, it was inevitable that work casualties would happen. We were always on the lookout for scorpions, tarantulas, and snakes. The biggest danger on the bridges was falling off the scaffolding or having the ropes break and the logs fall on top of you. Then, when we were breaking up rocks to make ballast, our eyes and legs would be exposed to flying chips. But that was the work environment, and we just had to get used to it. I got my first ulcer when I slipped and fell in the rainy weather and got scratched by a bamboo stake. I didn't think anything of it, but when I got back to camp, someone said, "You better have that thing looked at, Eddie." I said, "It's only a scratch." He said, "You still better go up and see the doc." And Doctor Hekking told me at the time, "Eddie, you've got to be very careful. These things can turn into tropical ulcers."

What he was talking about were germs getting into the open wound and infection setting in. This particular bacteria was like a spirochete—it dug inward. In severe cases, it would eat completely around the shinbone of the leg. In the average cases, a good-sized ulcer would be about two to four inches long and about an inch to two wide on the leg area. Wounds of this size would still have a chance of healing. Guys would try putting their legs in the water, hoping that the fish would nibble away the dead flesh. Some guys were desperate enough to plant maggots in the wound, because maggots were known to eat only dead flesh. The trick there is to be sure you pull out the same number of maggots that you put in. We found out that the most effective way was for the doctor to scrape away the rotted flesh with a sharpened spoon, although that hurt like hell. Then it was a matter of keeping the wound clean long enough so that it didn't become re-infected. Putting sulfanilamide or iodoform on it would have helped, except that the Japanese didn't provide us with any medicine. When even scraping was not going to help, the doctors would amputate. They got very good at it, considering that there was no anesthesia nor surgical tools. They would use a meat saw from the kitchen, and the amazing thing was, there was never a shortage of blood donors, despite everyone's poor state of health. Dr. Hekking never believed in cutting unless it was absolutely the last resort. I was lucky the first time. Apparently, my immune system was still working, so the ulcer healed without any infection setting in.

We were lucky to get Doctor Henri Hekking as our camp doctor, because he helped keep our losses down. Our group lost only 13 out of 191 people in the year and a half that we were in the jungles. The other American group of 478 people lost 120. In fact, our group had the lowest death rate among all sixty-odd railroad camps. Doctor Hekking was born and raised in Java, and he went to medical school in the Netherlands. But as far as the British were concerned, he was not a qualified medical officer. So here he was at Thanbyuzayat—just surplus. Captain Fitzsimmons was going back and forth to base camp almost every month to get the pay for our group, and he found out there were surplus doctors there. Fitzsimmons contributed his wristwatch, and Lieutenant Lattimore, a pocket watch, and they used the watches as a bribe to the Japanese to get Doctor Hekking. He turned out to be a godsend because he already knew quite a bit about how to survive in the tropics. His grandmother had taught him about herbs, and he had learned tropical medicine while stationed for five years in the Celebes, an island northeast of Java. He told us right from the start, "Once we use up everything in our medical bags, the Japanese will not give us anything more, so I will try to help you heal yourselves. I'll tell you what kind of medicinal and eatable plants to look for in the jungle; I'll tell you how not to get into trouble; and I'll tell you how to keep your wounds from being re-infected."

We always thought Doctor Hekking was magic. At 25 Kilo, when we were still able to buy eggs at the canteen, he told us, "Now, when you boil your egg or when you fry your egg, will you bring me the shell?" No one could figure out what the hell he wanted with the shells. And he said, "Please wash the outside of the egg before you break it or soft boil it." So we did as we were told, and everyone took their shells to Doctor Hekking. We asked him, "What are you going to do with that, Doc?" He said, "I'll show you." He got out a frying pan and he crushed the eggshells. He toasted it until he could grind it into a powder. Then he said, "That's calcium." And he said, "At this stage, you're really not experiencing hunger yet, but you must learn to eat everything that is eatable. Don't throw anything away." Doc wasn't just a medical doctor; he was a witch doctor. He knew how to psyche you out. For example, he would say to you, "Here's the magic potion that will get you well. You're *absolutely* going to get well, because I reserved this *just* for you." And what he would do is basically give you a shot of saline, but you're going to believe it's a magic potion. He was just one of these guys who could sell refrigerators to Eskimos. He didn't lie to us. What he did was to get us in a very receptive mood to heal ourselves. What's that joke— nature heals and the physician collects the fee? So the doc knew, given enough time, we were going to make it if he could just keep us alive long enough. After the war, we used to kid him about being a witch doctor, and he would say, "Yeah, but I kept you alive."

JAPANESE BRUTALITY, KOREAN SADISM

To simplify assembly and for security reasons, the Japanese organized us into what they called *kumi*—groupings of 100 men. Since we had less than 200 men, they threw in some Australians to make up the difference, and automatically we began nicknaming them "Tex." We were warned that if anyone should escape, ten men from his *kumi* would die. At first, we

FIG. 24. *Dr. Henri Hekking. Courtesy Lost Battalion Room, Decatur, Texas.*

thought, "Well, if that's going to happen, let's try to escape with the entire *kumi.*" But the Japanese had an answer to that—*kumis* on each side of that *kumi* would be killed. In other words, it didn't matter whether one escaped or ten escaped, somebody was going to pay the price.

Even knowing this, the officers would teach us the rudiments of how to survive outside the camp should we be able to escape. We were given lessons in star reading—how to find directions at night—and what to take in our escape kits: a compass, a pocketknife, a map, food, etc. There were never any formal escape committees like in Germany, where the British were nuts about formality. That was fine and dandy if you were operating under the Geneva Conventions, but the Japanese didn't play by those rules. The first time anyone tried to escape was a group of three Australians. The leader of the group had worked in Burma and he spoke Burmese. Even knowing the country, they were captured within fifteen miles, because the natives were not willing to help them. Actually, within the first five miles one of the guys fell ill—he had appendicitis. So they left him behind by common consent. The other two got another ten miles before they were captured. They were all brought back, and this was when we started shaking our heads and wondering if we would ever figure out the Japanese: The guy with the appendicitis was taken care of medically—his appendix was taken out. They waited until he had recovered, then they blindfolded them, tied them to stakes, and shot them in a public execution. It was supposed to be an object lesson: Anyone who tries to escape will wind up like this. You have to hand it to the Aussies because they yelled out to their Brigadier before they were shot, "Don't worry, it's not your fault. We gave it a try."

Further proof that the *kumi* system worked: One time I was mistaken for a native, and they refused to let me back into camp after work. At the time I didn't know what was going on, because I kept trying to stay with my group, but this Korean guard kept cutting me out as if he was cutting out a horse or a cow. So I decided, "Okay, whatever your problem is, I'll just have to go along with it." Finally, when we got to the guardhouse and they took a count, they found out they were missing one man. That's when it finally dawned on this Korean guard, "My god, this guy actually belongs here!"

We got slapped and knocked around on a routine basis, sometimes for no reason at all. It might have been because the Japanese had gotten some bad news about how the war was going; or it might have been because the Korean guards had gotten up on the wrong side of the bed that day. Regardless of the reason, they would usually take it out on us. When it was done by a Japanese soldier to humiliate us, I didn't hate him for it because I figured he was just doing his job. But the Korean guards, instead of just slapping us, would try to hit us with a closed fist or a rifle butt, and they would do it with such pleasure—that was the reason I could never forgive them. I know it was because they had been colonized by the Japanese and not allowed to keep their Korean names or even speak Korean. And they were the lowest men in the Japanese military hierarchy; they weren't even allowed the privilege of being fighting men. So they took it out on anyone who was beneath them, namely us. Even though I understood all of this, I still could not help but feel intense hatred for the Korean guards and their sadistic actions.

I had relatively few acts of corporal punishment visited upon me, probably because I was an ordinary ant worker who always managed to remain inconspicuous. But for no reason at all, one day coming back from work, this Korean guard took offense with me. He took a roundhouse swing and hit me right in my left ear. It was so unexpected that I didn't slide with the punch and as a result, I took a direct hit and lost partial hearing in that ear.

To this day, I don't know what caused him to hit me that way. I didn't have any illegal goods on me; I hadn't given him a hard look. I just couldn't figure out why he singled me out. Another time, one of the Korean guards grabbed my favorite pipe and started chewing on it. I kept trying to get it back from him, and "Slug" Wright,[5] who had been beaten up pretty badly by them before, yelled at me, "Eddie, don't fight him!" I decided, "No, that's my pipe." After a while, I finally got it back and he quit tousling me. I didn't put that pipe into my mouth again until I had the bit replaced after the war. To me, it was never clean enough.

We gave all the Korean guards nicknames. When we were liberated, we were asked which Korean guards gave us the most trouble, and we could only identify them by their nicknames. Somehow, the war tribunal was able to figure out their real names and some of them were punished for their war crimes. "The Undertaker" got his name because he had the gaunt look of a mortician. The other implication, of course, was that he put a lot of people under, or, shall we say, he made them candidates for the undertaker. He was a very vicious person and he was at least six feet tall. Most of the short Korean guards would have to find higher ground to stand on so that they could hit a taller prisoner more easily. If necessary, they would make the prisoner stand in a hole. A gentler name was "Hollywood," because this Korean guard thought he was the debonair type. He was always asking people if they were from Hollywood. Of course, if you wanted to get on the good side of him, you would say, "Oh, yeah! I lived right near there." Then you could start making up stories and carry on a conversation with him for an hour or two to avoid working. Unfortunately, when you're not working, someone else has to do your work. On the other hand, the guard is being distracted, so he's not going to be hitting anyone. So we didn't really mind.

Most of the other names would either be comical or descriptive—like "Liver Lips"—that's almost self-explanatory. Another was called "B. B.," and the initials stood for "Boy Bastard." His friend was called "B. B. C.," which stood for "Boy Bastard's Cobber"—the Australian term for a mate or buddy. One day he heard that, and he said, "What does that mean?" And we said, "Oh, it means British Broadcasting Company—a very famous radio station in England." There was "Donald Duck," because of the way he walked, but he was a vicious son of a gun. Then there was "Christian

George," who never hit anyone. He was never cut out to be a soldier any-where, anytime. He spoke some English because he had been to mission-ary school. One of the most comical things that ever happened to him was during Japanese guard inspection. His rifle was dirty by military standards and he was told by the sergeant to clean his rifle. So he took the rifle down to the creek where there was running water, got some soap and a brush, and cleaned his rifle. Then he put it back together and took it to the ser-geant for inspection. The sergeant just went completely gaga, and that evening George was seen standing in our chow line with his mess kit. Another time George caught one of the prisoners trading with a native, and he was trying to tell him "*dame dame*," which meant "bad" in Japa-nese. He didn't want to hit the prisoner, he didn't want to hit the trader, so he ended up hitting the oxen that was pulling the cart. It was a form of comic relief and something that we would talk about for months when-ever we got into a down situation. Anyone who has ever been in military service knows someone like that—he's got two left feet and he can never march in formation. They are called "sad sacks." We never expected to run across one in the jungles. It was a good happenstance, because running across one decent person was almost enough to make up for 100 bad ones.

There was a distinction between just the everyday slap or fist thrown at you and real punishment for some infraction or another. I fortunately was never caught and punished for anything, but I saw and heard plenty. Take the case of this Dutchman. I can't even remember what he did wrong, but he had to kneel on a piece of bamboo for two and a half hours with a small bamboo rod about an inch and a half in diameter behind his knees. What this did was to dislocate the knees. When he was finally released by the guard, they had to carry him in that position to the medical hut. It took Dr. Hekking at least three days to get him straightened out. As soon as he felt the blood circulating, he started screaming. That triggered my memory of stories about Chinese women who had bound feet, and how they must have suffered when they tried to unbind their feet so that they would be natural again. Fortu-nately, the knees weren't completely separated, and the Dutchman even-tually recovered.

A common form of punishment was being made to stand in front of the guardhouse holding up a "fishplate" (a thirty-pound piece of metal used to connect two rails) for hours. Well, Corporal Jack Cellum got caught doing something, and he had to hold it out in front of him for twenty-four hours. Every time his arms dropped, there was someone there to bash him with a bamboo rod, which only made it worse. There was this other big guy by the name of Herman Scroggins. He had done something to displease one of the guards, and he had to hold the fishplate above his head—straight up—for twenty-four hours. I don't know how he did it, but he was one tough fellow. He was determined not to give the Japanese the satisfaction of humiliating him and breaking his spirit. It was not just a matter of physical strength but intestinal fortitude and controlled defiance.

One of the worst cases of punishment involved an interpreter who was literally put into a cesspool until he drowned because they were not happy with the way he had interpreted. We're talking about a latrine full of human waste. They didn't have to push him down. They just waited until he was so tired his legs would no longer hold him up. The camp commander tried to reason with the Japanese commander, hoping that they would lift him out after a few hours. But apparently that was never their intention. They had planned to kill him right from the start. You might think, "Gee, there were enough of you guys to revolt." We always knew that we could overpower the Japanese and Korean guards, but then what? We couldn't go anywhere, and they would just send in more Japanese guards to punish us and really make an impression. No, the best thing we could do was hope that the guy was strong enough to get through his punishment.

However, there was one prank we played on the Japanese that we almost got away with at 70 Kilo. The Japanese were making a propaganda movie and they wanted to show us marching out of camp. They had filmed the canteen to show what nice things were available to the prisoners, and they even issued us clothing to make sure we looked presentable. We were to march by the camera and sing at the top of our voices the song, "Bless Them All." It went like this: "Bless them all, bless them all, the long and the short and the tall. There will be no promotions this side of the ocean, bless them all." Except that instead of "Bless them all," we sang "Fuck them all." After the Japanese developed the film, someone caught that, and they came back and made us do it all over again. But the Japanese director made sure we didn't do any more singing.

SCROUNGING

While in the jungles, I continued developing my skills as a scrounger even though I knew what the consequences would be if I were ever caught. Fortunately, that never happened. You see, to be a good thief, you have to use good judgment. If the opportunity is ripe, you take it, but you don't want to do it too often because you can stretch your luck. You have to work on instinct almost. The other thing is, you can steal, but what are you going to do with it? You can't eat it all, you're not always able to give it away, and you can't keep it, because the Japanese conducted snap searches. So you steal when you have the need and the opportunity and you find ways to get rid of the evidence. The first time I stole, I happened to be with John Owens—this big guy who weighed 225 pounds. We saw this basket of cigarettes. He looked at me, and I looked at him, and without saying anything, we each took a handle. We were at a railway station area, and there was no one around, but we decided to play it safe. We pushed it under one of the buildings so that if they found it missing, they might think someone misplaced it or maybe the natives did it. The next day we went back and it was still there, so we took it back to camp. We knew we couldn't keep it, so everyone had a great day of smoking. John and I didn't even know each other, and neither of us smoked cigarettes, but we both had the same thought at the same time.

Most of the time, I scrounged for food, and my best source was the Japanese kitchen. Slug Wright, who was working there, warned me, "Watch out, Eddie, they mined the kitchen because they've been losing too much stuff." I decided, "No, it doesn't matter, because they have to have a safe way in and out. All I have to figure out is where they walk." Then I decided, "No, there's an easier way." So what I did was, at nighttime—what we called "moonlight reconnaissance"—I untied enough of the vines that held the bamboo walls together so that I could remove part of the wall and sneak in. One of the things I saw was this 100–pound sack of sugar. The trick about scrounging is that you have to get in and get out quickly—you don't fool around. So I dragged the 100 pounds out and put the wall back together again. The first thing I thought of was Dr. Hekking and the sick people in the hospital—what a treat this would be for them. So I divided it between

Dr. Hekking and the kitchen. That way, at least everyone would get a taste of it. It wasn't always about food. Once when Paul Leatherwood was laid up and he couldn't go to work, he told me he knew how to barber. "But," he said, "I don't have any tools. I don't even have any scissors." It took me about a week before I located what he needed at Japanese headquarters. This enabled him to earn extra money cutting hair at ten cents per head.

I remember my closest call was the time I tried to steal a bucket of lard. The Japanese kitchen had slaughtered a hog and rendered out a bucket of lard. It hadn't cooled down enough to be hard yet, and I could smell the rendering. I waited until about 1:00 or 2:00 in the morning, when I knew that most people would be asleep. I went into the Japanese kitchen and I was just about to pick up the bucket handle when a Japanese guard walked through the kitchen on his way to the latrine. Before he got to the latrine, he saw me, and he started talking to me. And with both of his hands, he was touching me all over. I couldn't understand a word he was saying, but he was speaking in a soft, soothing tone, so I knew he wasn't angry. The only thing I could think of was that he was making advances at me. If I nodded or shook my head at the wrong time, it could be disastrous, so I decided to just freeze and not do anything. Then, after about ten minutes of this, the urgency of his trip to the latrine took over. As soon as he went for the latrine, I took off with the bucket. The following morning, I noticed that the grease had shrunk down to about three-quarters, and I thought, "Holy smoke, maybe someone had scrounged from me!" Then I realized that the oil had shrunk in volume because it had cooled down. That gave me the idea of heating the bucket back up so that the volume would increase and I would have more to sell. Even charging a dollar per cupful, I had no trouble finding customers, because lard is basically a source of protein. If nothing else, people could use it to make fried rice or they could mix the rice with the grease to make it a little more palatable. I got rid of at least 90 percent of it. Then I took the rest over to the hospital and gave it to Dr. Hekking.

The other way I could get rid of stolen goods and at the same time get things that the camp needed was by trading with the natives. Donald Brain took me out on my first trading trip. Since he knew Burmese, he did all the talking. When he wasn't around, I would trade on my own. I learned that if two people want to communicate, they can always find a way. The trader knows you have something to trade and they know you basically want goods or money. They either show you the amount of money or show you the goods. You shake your head or nod your head—it's that simple. Since they were being paid in occupational money, which wasn't of much value to them, they wanted to convert the money into anything of material value— like clothes, wristwatches, or cameras. I think some of the guys even had guns and hand grenades to sell them, and they usually had shag tobacco and *shindegar* (dark sugar) to sell us.

OUR DAYS OFF

On our one day off, we would just lounge around, relax, and catch up on sleep. Or we would clean up the area and take care of personal things— like washing our clothes and repairing things. As much as possible, we tried to keep our living quarters swept up and orderly. The only filthy area was the latrine. We had to walk through (without exaggeration) an inch-thick pile of maggots because there was nothing other than ashes from the kitchen to sprinkle on top of the human waste. The flies were always breeding, and after a while, when we had no more footwear, we just had to walk bare-footed over the pile of maggots. Of course, during the rainy season it got worse. But we always kept our living area fairly clean. The same was true about our personal hygiene. The Australians and the Americans, no matter how bad the conditions were, would always try to find some stream or puddle of water to wash out the dirt before we got back to camp. But the British soldiers did not always go to the same extent and they developed all kinds of lice. The first time I saw lice crawling all over their torsos, it literally turned my stomach. It was just plain common sense to keep yourself clean if at all possible because you're in filth all day. But they didn't seem to care, and we couldn't understand that. The Dutch were very hygienic and they were clean in all respects—the body and their living quarters. They had the lowest death rate of all because they were used to the tropics and they basically took good care of themselves. They also knew how to get away with the least amount of work, whereas we Americans took pride in finishing any workload assigned to us.

I took advantage of the day off to keep my mosquito net in good repair—that's probably why I didn't catch malaria as early as the other guys—and to make pots and pans from discarded steel drums. I was not a tinsmith, but I had learned the fundamentals in junior high school and I used to watch these guys in the hardware store next to my father's shop make atomizers out of tin. Unfortunately, working with steel drums was a lot more difficult, especially without tools, but I managed to cut out the shape I wanted with a chisel and a hammer that I had scrounged from the Japanese. Buckets were more difficult to make than frying pans because of the oblong piece of material that I had to cut and fold into a cylinder. No matter how good I made the bucket, it was bound to leak. So what I did was to scrounge some rice from the kitchen, put it in the bucket with a little water, let the rice get really soft, and then hope that the rice would fill any leaks. The frying pans were easier to make—all I had to do was cut out a big circle with a handle on it and then shape the sides of the pan. I gave the pots and pans to anyone who needed a container to boil water or a frying pan to make things like fried rice. Each time we moved from camp to camp, I would swear to myself, "I'm not going to carry chunks of iron, hammers, and chisels around anymore." But then I would decide that as long as I could make it to the next camp, I would keep making them. It gave me something to do, and I knew that whoever needed a bucket would appreciate it.

On one of our rest days at 25 Kilo, Colonel Black got permission to set up what was called Melbourne Cup Day—the Australian version of our Kentucky Derby. We planned for several weeks to make it a festive occasion. We had guys dressed up like ladies at the races, and someone even set up a pari-mutuel type of machine. For the race, we had little wooden horses—a piece of log with four legs sticking down—and the rider would straddle it and race around the track. We had bookmakers to set up the odds, and even the Japanese sergeants and Korean guards enjoyed the show. In the three-and-a-half years, that Melbourne Cup Day was something that would live on in our memories. An Australian by the name of Robert Farrands won the "tin cup" for first prize, and he was on a ship to Japan when the ship was sunk. Would you believe, when he was rescued by a U.S. submarine, he was holding on to that cup? He was determined to bring it home with him.

CAMARADERIE

We were a small group of 191 made up of navy, marines, and army people. Regardless of how we kidded each other about the various services we had joined, there was one thing we had in common—we were an American unit and we knew we had to pull together. Some pulled harder, but we all tried to do our best. For instance, I was a better scrounger than others, while someone else might be better at physical labor. But as long as we did our best and we looked after each other, *that* was what mattered. I can't really think of any person in our group who was a slacker or anyone who was a contentious kind of person, so I considered myself lucky in that respect. But there was one big fight that happened between John Owens and Sergeant Homero Martinez, the only noncom in our group. Homero was a Mexican American and well educated, and John resented having to take orders from him. It was bare knuckles, and John outweighed Homero by eighty pounds. They fought until they were exhausted. Afterwards, they came to a grudging respect for each other because they had stood up to each other. Other than that one time, everyone got along fine. As we soon learned, no one had any physical or emotional energy to waste over trivial matters, and to survive, we had to watch out for one another. No one had to tell us this—we just knew. In retrospect, I think this had a lot to do with the way most of the guys from Texas had been brought up. They didn't even think of it in terms of survival at the beginning. It was just natural for them to help each other out. These guys, without knowing it, laid the groundwork for our survival.

Right from the beginning, we formed small tribal groups of two, three, or four men to look after one another. If three guys were in a group and one of them got sick and couldn't boil his own water, the other two guys would do it for him. When it was time to pick up rations, they would pick his up too. It was a buddy system. If the illness was not too debilitating, he could stay in camp and look after little things like boiling water, straightening up the sleeping area, or making sure no one stole anything from them. Now, if two people got down, it was still possible for one person to help the other two, and in the direst circumstances, if all three were down, then some other group would look after them. There was no written contract, and no one kept scores. We all did it willingly, because "there but for the grace of God go I." Being the only Chinatown kid and a loner all my life, I guess I was the exception to the rule in not belonging to a tribe. I was still immature and I just didn't trust myself enough to get close to anyone. As much as possible, I was determined to make it on my own, although I knew that if I became completely incapacitated, someone would help me out. I would literally bet my life on that; comradeship was that strong among us. In the final analysis, I believe *that* saved us as much as Dr. Hekking's medical skills and what little luck we had.

When I first read *King Rat* by James Clavell, I knew he must have been a prisoner at one time. There was a scene in which he wrote about two people who were a group or a tribe sharing a can of condensed milk. They boiled the water in the can to extract the last bit. No one but a prisoner would do that. Then he wrote about how one guy, when he had done King Rat a favor, got a cigarette, and he looked over at his buddy, and they knew that they were going to share that later on. There were things in the novel that didn't take more than one sentence, but it was enough to tell me that this author hadn't just researched the subject—he had lived through it. I would have bet my life on it without looking it up, but, quick like a bunny, I went down to the public library to check out his biographical background. I was right— Clavell had been a prisoner of war of the Japanese. I later found out his wife had suggested that he write *King Rat* because he was having a mental block when he tried to do anything else. She told him, "You've got to get those prison camp days behind you. Write about it and get it out of your system." So he wrote *King Rat*. It rang true because he understood the important role camaraderie plays in any POW's effort to survive captivity.

FIVE · A POW SURVIVOR

After we had been in the jungle for six months, the Japanese became anxious about completing the railroad, and the speedo period began. Then it became a matter of plain survival, and, hopefully, survival with a little dignity left at the end. By that, I mean you haven't stolen food from a comrade, you haven't cheated a friend, and you haven't shirked your duty. That was about the best any of us could hope for.

SPEEDO!

Speedo started in May of '43, after we had moved from 25 Kilo to 30 Kilo. The tide of war had begun to turn against Japan, and the Japanese were desperate to finish the railroad. Nagatomo was given one year to complete the railroad, and he could see that it was not going to be finished in that time. He was said to have told Brigadier General Varley that he would have to commit hara-kiri if they didn't finish on time. So the Japanese figured, "Okay, let's speed everything up!" There were no more days off, and even the sick were put to work. The workload went up—from 1.5 cubic meters to 2.2, then to 2.8 and 3.2. They just kept increasing the workload. May was also the beginning of the monsoon season, when we could get as much as 250 inches of rain in a month. It was like being under Niagara Falls! It was bad enough carrying dirt the way we did, but carrying waterlogged dirt just added to the load. Of course, by this time most people had no shoes, so carrying even fifty pounds on slippery ground was almost an impossibility. It was the general overwork, constant exposure to weather, and reduced rations that finally took its toll on us. Everybody was under pressure. The Japanese and the Koreans started a reign of terror. They would bash us for no apparent reason except that they thought it would help speed up the work.

By then, our favorite expression to describe a workday was "from can't see to can't see," meaning we worked from before dawn to after sunset—basically sixteen, eighteen hours a day. There was no such thing as hoping that we wouldn't finish the job and they would send us home. We stayed out there until the work was done. The first time we were assigned 3.2 cubic meters, we said to ourselves, "There's no way in the world that we can do this in one day." But we always found a way to get the job done. During one of the Allied bombing raids, the bombers took out part of the bridge at Tamarkan. To get the freight across the damaged bridge, we had to unload it, walk it over a wooden bridge, and reload it onto boxcars on the other side of the river. We worked like that for five days and five nights continuously—without stopping to sleep. Up to that time, we would have never thought that possible, but we soon found out that as far as the human body is concerned, anything is possible. So it's true that a POW never says "That's my limit," because for him, there is no limit.

As we got further up the railroad, the country changed from level to hilly. The work was basically still cut and fill, breaking up rocks for ballast, building bridges, cutting timber, and so on. But we were on shorter rations and the elements were beginning to get to us—the constant condition of being soaked and chilled. The humidity was enough to kill you. By then, we had started to employ tricks—not to sabotage but to cut the workload down. For example, when we built a bridge, the piling usually started with a hole that was dug about a foot deep, and the Japanese would mark the pole to the depth that they wanted it to go. If we had the opportunity, we would change the mark so that instead of driving it in ten feet, we would try to get away with five feet.

Rations got shorter for two reasons. One, the supply line from Thanbyuzayat was longer, and pilfering along the way depleted what was being brought up. And two, the men were getting sicker and fewer people were going out on working parties, so our rations were being cut all the time. I found out later that we were being weighed periodically because the Japanese had this idea that the less a person weighed, the less rations he needed. So we're talking about a vicious cycle now. Assuming that you could stay fairly healthy, you're still going to lose weight from the hard work and the fact that you're on reduced rations. I was just amazed that *that* was why we were being weighed. Even the scrounging got harder, because the Japanese were on pretty thin rations themselves. Toward the end of the railroad, we got boxes of rotten meat. It had been sent up from base camp, and by the time it got to us, it was completely rotten and there was nothing we could do about it. Without opening the cases, we knew what would happen—maggots would be crawling out, besides the stink of the rotten meat. We had no choice but to bury the cases.

MENTAL TORTURE

When we sat around in groups after work, the subject was always food. We not only talked about food that we had had; we talked about food that we were going to have; and we talked about how we would prepare it or what we would order. This was usually after a meal; otherwise, it would literally drive us up the wall, because our gastric juices would be operating without anything to encourage it. There were times like the emperor's birthday, when they would give us a day off and extras—a whole hog for the camp and maybe a little sake. I remember it was on one of those occasions that Sergeant Powell impressed me all to hell. He was born in India and had chosen to become a Muslim, and, as such, he didn't eat pork. That day, he even refused to eat the gravy that the cook had made from the pork. He took his ration of gravy and swapped it with four other men for rice so that he wouldn't take all of one man's rations. So they all had extra gravy and he had extra rice. Here was a British soldier in the middle of nowhere. There was no one to monitor him; yet he remained true to his belief. If there was anything that he thought was tainted with pork, he would not eat it, which was pretty darn hard to do.

Anyhow, on days like that, when we had had a relatively satisfying meal, we would sit around and talk about food. Then the next thing would be family. You would think that a bunch of men would talk about sex, but that was so far down the line it almost never came up. People would just talk to get their minds off the situation they were in, because we all knew we weren't going to be going home any day soon. We knew everything there was to know about someone's life—whether he liked his cousins or not, whether he had problems with his siblings or parents—there were no secrets. I would listen, but I didn't feel the need to share anything about myself. For one thing, my background was so different that I wasn't sure they would understand. How do you explain to someone that you were only allowed to live in twelve square blocks of a city? Secondly, I really didn't know that much about my own family, except the obvious things, like their graduating from Lowell High and going on to UC Berkeley. So that was why I never got started on my family. You could always tell when Thanksgiving or Christmas came around. Guys would be down in the dumps because they were thinking of their families and the holidays. Coming from a different cultural background, I was fortunate not to have these bouts of depression. As far as Chinese New Year was concerned, I didn't know when it was going to happen anyhow, so that didn't bother me.[1]

But, as I soon learned, being Chinese did have its disadvantages. One time I was tortured by the Japanese, another time by two Chinese boatmen, and it was only because I was Chinese. The first time was at 55 Kilo. The Japanese had used hand grenades to dynamite and gather a whole bunch of fish, and they were making fish cakes. They even had tangerine peels! I didn't know where they had gotten them, but I knew exactly what they were going to do with them. They had five or six Japanese filleting and chopping, and the other one was cooking the fish stock. They had a big mosquito net so that the bones wouldn't fall into the soup, and there was nothing I could scrounge! The fish heads, the carcasses, everything was going into the fish stock. There was one guy making *fu jook* (dried bean curd). I had never seen it done before, but I knew exactly what it was. He had a big kettle, and as the soybean was forming a skin on the top, he would take a little stick and roll it out. Then he would hang them on bamboo poles to dry. Because I was Chinese, I knew it was *fu jook*, and I knew what the fish cakes were going to taste like with tangerine peels and everything in it.

The second time it happened was when we were working near the bridge

FIG. 25. *Three water-stained photos that Eddie carried with him through the war: sister Jessie with her daughter Karen; niece Karen on a walker; and sisters Mary (left) and Jessie (right) with their mother and sister Mints at graduation from UC Berkeley.*

on the River Kwai. One day, I smelled *sawn jue ow see* (garlic and black bean sauce)—any Cantonese Chinese knows what that means. These two Chinese boatmen were taking a little break. They had a jug of whiskey and they were cooking some spare ribs with *sawn jue ow see*. And it drove me nuts! I knew what they were cooking; I could smell what they were cooking. I didn't care about the whiskey, but I couldn't go up to them and beg for some spareribs. What people call torture is always a picture of physical torture, but mental torture is worse!

TROPICAL DISEASES

It was during the speedo period that Dr. Hekking saved my life twice. The first time was when I had two ulcers, one on each leg—right and left shinbones—and they were getting to be about two square inches in size. That was when he told me, "I've got to scrape all the dead flesh away." And he said, "You've got to help me by *letting* me do this." This meant that either I bear the pain or someone would have to hold me down. An ulcer of that size took the doc about ten minutes each, and I was able to put my leg up so that he could hold it with one hand and scrape with the other. All he had to do was scrape it until blood showed, because blood was considered an antiseptic. That was the worst pain I had ever felt. There was no disinfectant, so what I had to do was sterilize a piece of cloth in boiling water, place it on top of the wound, and hold it in place with a bandage. As a rule, you didn't go back to work until after it had started to scab. I was out for about a week. Up to then, I had never wanted to go on sick call because, one, I was afraid it would be too hard for me to pick up the load again; two, I knew that they couldn't do anything for me in the hospital; and three, as long as I could report to work, I knew there would be one more full ration. But Dr. Hekking convinced me that I shouldn't take any chances on the ulcers.

The second time Dr. Hekking saved my life was when I had malaria and dysentery. The medic did the usual thing—he gave me quinine. It turned out that I was allergic to quinine, and Dr. Hekking had to pull me out of that. He basically shocked me out of the allergy. Then he told me, "Eddie, you can't take quinine—it's poisonous to your system. So from now on when you get malaria, all you can do is cover up and sweat it out." That was the sickest I ever got. I was down to sixty pounds and basically skin and bones. You can't imagine how awful it is to be hit by malaria and dysentery at the same time. Malaria gives you chills and fevers, and you're thirsty as hell, so you have to keep drinking; otherwise, you're going to get dehydrated. With dysentery, it's a natural method of dehydrating, so it's a double whammy. There's only so much you can do about hydrating yourself when water is all you have. So I kept boiling and drinking water. The other thing I had to do was force myself to eat even though I didn't have any appetite, because if I didn't, it would just make my condition worse. I was laid up for two weeks, and I basically stayed in bed except to go to the latrine.

Dysentery was usually spread by flies in the food or in the rations somewhere along the line. It was so common that 99 percent of the POWs got it. After we came back to the States, the doctors at Walter Reed Hospital used to ask us, "How did you know what kind of dysentery you had?" (There were two kinds: amoebic and bacillus.) "Did you have a lab test?" We all used to laugh, "Where do you think we were, Doc?" "Then how did you know?" Well, with amoebic, you might have to go fifteen, thirty times a day, and with bacillus, you might go seventy-five, one hundred times a day, but it doesn't reoccur, so that's how you know. The same way, we knew what kind of malaria we had—you can tell from the cycles of fever and chills. The doctors at Walter Reed would say, "That's not very scientific." And we would reply, "Well, that's the best we can do."

I happened to have the bacillus type, which meant I was forever sitting in the *benjo* (toilet). When I got there, I would put a palm leaf under my butt and hopefully see mucus and not blood, because blood would mean that I was hemorrhaging inside. After that main bout, I never got dysentery again. With malaria, we found out there were many kinds, and the worst kind to get was cerebral—it literally cooked the brain. I just remember shaking a lot when I had the chills, and burning up when I had the fever. The first bout lasted about four weeks, although I forced myself to go back to work after two weeks. Later, I was able to fight it off in a matter of a week or so. They say you don't build up immunity to it, but for some reason my body was able to fight it off.

That was the worst physical point in my captivity. I had never had a death wish before, but I was debating, "Do I want to fight this or do I want to just let go and forget the whole thing?" Adding up the pros and cons, the only thing that tipped the balance was my curious nature. I wanted to see what the next day would bring; whether it was good, bad, or indifferent, I just wanted to know. So I hung in there. Of course, I could have been worse off than that. A lot of the other fellows got beriberi, pellagra, and dengue fever.[2] We were just lucky we didn't catch cholera from the natives. When I heard that people were dying wholesale, it horrified me because of what my mother had always warned me about cholera. People would vomit and excrete, as if they were dying at both ends. You could literally see them melt in front of you and fade away. After cholera broke out in one of the British camps, you could smell that camp for miles. And before they cleared out of the camp, they had to burn people who were not quite dead yet. But they had to leave, and they couldn't take any chances. There was only one other time that I lived in mortal fear of my life: I had run out of water when I was out on a working party and I came across a running brook. Remembering my Boy Scout training, I figured this had to be purified water because it had been running for miles. I took a drink, and from that moment on, I lived in apprehension for days, worrying that I might get cholera. I swore from then on, every drop of water was going to be boiled—never again!

MOUNTING CASUALTIES AT 105 KILO

Things got worse and worse until we got to 105 Kilo—that was absolutely the bottom of the pit. It was high up in the mountains, and we experienced our first cold spell. We were still in the monsoon season and supplies were short. I even had to scrounge rice and basic camp supplies. The work was no different, but people were dying every day from disease and malnutrition. Some just found it easier to give up than to endure the suffering. The classic case was this little Dutchman. He had said if he were not free by a certain date that he would kill himself. And he did. Other people would start thinking about how depressing the conditions were, what it was like at home, and how great it would be to be home again, not realizing that they had to get through this period of hell first. Somewhere in between, they just didn't make it.

The closest person to me to die was W. F. Mattfeld. He was from Oakland, and the fact that he was from across the Bay made us feel almost like relatives. Mattie died of beriberi and cardiac arrest. We had just come back from work, and he told his buddy, "Red, I feel a little tired. I think I'll take a little nap before dinner." So Charles "Red" Oosting said, "Don't worry, Matt, I'll go get your chow. You just relax." After Red came back with the food and had finished eating, he noticed, "Gee, Mattie's food is getting cold." So he shook Mattie—no response. It suddenly dawned on Red that Mattie had died, but he looked so peaceful that no one could believe he was dead. He just lay down, and that was it. My first thought was, "I hope I can go that easily when it's my turn." Now, Mattie had a billfold with a two-dollar bill in it, and he had asked Red, "If I don't make it through, would you take this back to my mother?" Red had said, "Sure, don't worry, you can take it back yourself." So with Mattie gone, Red was now in charge of the billfold and the two-dollar bill. He could have spent that two dollars to help himself and replaced it later, but he didn't. Mattie wanted that billfold and that two dollars to go to his mother, and that was what happened. I have to admire people like that. I don't care what he's done or what he might become. For nothing else, I respect him for that one act alone.

There was one other example of brotherly love in the face of death that I will never forget. We called them Mutt and Jeff, although Clifford England's nickname was Pee Wee and R. L. Eckland's name was Swede. But in our minds, they were Mutt and Jeff, because Swede was six feet two and Pee Wee was small like me. Somehow, the Swede went out of his mind, and for some reason, the Japanese never bothered with anyone who was crazy. As he walked from his bed to the railroad station with all his belongings—his blanket, his canteen, his mess kit, everything—he started to give his things away. Pee Wee, following right behind him, would explain to people that the Swede was out of his mind and would they please give the stuff back. Everyone understood and returned the stuff, and Pee Wee would carry it. When they got to the guard shack, the Swede just sat there by the railway track. Pee Wee tried to explain to the Japanese that he was crazy and that he was waiting for a train to take him home. They just left both of them alone. After a while the Swede got hungry and thirsty and he decided he wanted a drink. Pee Wee had his canteen, but he didn't give him a drink. Instead, he said, "Let's go back to camp and we'll get a drink and maybe something to eat." So he got him back to camp, and the Swede died during the evening hours. Pee Wee took it pretty hard because they had been through thick and thin together. Of course, by that time we were on our last legs. We were weak physically, but on the other hand, mentally we knew the railroad was almost done, and sooner or later things would get better. Pee Wee had hoped that maybe the Swede would make it, but he didn't.

We didn't have a morgue as such, so we put the Swede near the latrine area until he could be buried the next day. And that night, because we were up in the high hill country and it seemed to affect our kidneys, we were going to the latrine quite frequently. As we passed him, we could see that the Swede was going through the various stages of rigor mortis. One time his knees would be drawn up; another time his legs would be sticking out. So each time we went by, we would try to put him back into repose. Of course, it didn't work, because rigor mortis takes its own course. It was touching and almost humorous in that we were treating the Swede as if he was still around. He was, but he was dead.

In general, when a person died, he was taken to an area of the hospital, which served as the morgue, to be prepared for burial the next day. In the beginning, we tried to give each man a decent burial—a coffin and an honor guard. But toward the end of the railroad, a man was lucky if he had a rice sack for a shroud, and, depending on the weather conditions, if we could dig a hole to cover him up. We would bury him, say a few words, and make a simple cross with his name and the pertinent data—unit, rank, serial number, date of birth, and date of death. Within our group someone always recorded the information and the exact location of the burial site. All of this came in handy after the war, because the military decided to disinter all 133 American bodies and bring them back to the States. Some were reburied at Punchbowl in Hawaii; most were brought back to their hometowns. Although the cemeteries in Kanburi (Kanchaniburi), Thanbyuzayat, and Chungkai were all well tended, we didn't want to leave one American behind.

COMPLETION OF THE RAILROAD

The railroad was officially finished on October 17, 1943, when the two stretches of rail—one snaking down from Thanbyuzayat and the other up from Bampong—were linked at Konkoita. But we didn't know this until we heard it from someone who was passing through on his way to the base hospital at 85 Kilo. What he told us didn't mean anything, because we were still working. I remember distinctly that we were doing ballast work. And we kept working until the train came to take us to Kanburi on the Thailand side of the border in January. Other than an inspection by Nagatomo and General Varley, we had no inkling that the railroad was completed. That was the second time I saw Nagatomo—the first time had been at the beginning of the railroad. We were standing at attention, and he was checking the troops to see how we were faring. And just as he got in front of me, I fainted dead away. What happened was that I forgot to wiggle my toes. (When you are standing at attention, absolutely stock-still, you need to do something like wiggle your toes to keep your blood circulating; otherwise, the blood will pool to your feet.) Fortunately for me, Nagatomo chose to ignore me and just continued on with his inspection.

I remember they were using one of these hand-pumped trolleys to make sure that the railroad was really passable. Up to then, the only things that had traveled on the railroad were these diesel trucks with a set of rail wheels that could be raised and lowered. They would drive these trucks right over the train tracks, lower these sets of wheels, raise it until the tires were off the ground, and then it became a locomotive. As much as we hated the Japanese, there were times when we really had to admire them for their ingenuity. The nice thing about the diesel truck was that if it derailed, all the engineer had to do was scream for a bunch of POWs to lift it back up. None of us ever got a hernia; we always managed to muscle it back up on the tracks. But when it came to derailed steam engines, we tried, but we could never do it. The Japanese always thought that if they could just get enough men on a job, anything was possible. No way! It didn't matter how small the steam train was, it was still a massive, inert piece of metal!

So for us, 105 Kilo was *it* as far as railroad building was concerned. We packed up and took everything with us on the train ride to Kanburi—the camp cooks took their woks, and the doctors took all their medical supplies. It turned out to be a forty-two-hour train ride, and we made it in one fell swoop. That was when we had our first look at the railway south of 105 Kilo. The terrain we passed kept getting rougher and more mountainous, until we were almost on the side of the mountain. As we looked down, we could see the long distance that we would fall should the train derail. The train took it ver-r-y slowly over some of those tracks. And we were thinking, "Holy smoke, hope all these rickety structures hold up," because if the Brits had sabotaged it, we would go right over the side of the mountain. Seeing the Thailand side of the railroad for the first time, we suddenly realized how horrendous their work had been compared to ours. We passed through the stretch called Hellfire Pass that was complete granite, and POWs had had to somehow dynamite through it. There were also hilly sections where they had had to build viaducts that were eighty feet high—literally tiers of wooden structures that didn't look very safe. That was when we realized how darn lucky we had been, working the northern stretch that we had.

LAND OF MILK AND HONEY

Compared to where we had been, Kanburi was a land of milk and honey. The work was reasonable, we had enough to eat, and we could even buy things if we had any money. We went out on work details pretty much like before, loading and unloading supplies, but we weren't under the gun as we had been on the railroad. And when we got back from work, we were even able to take a shower. The guys had rigged up a four-man water pump. That was a godsend because the temperature in Thailand was around 85 to 90 degrees, day and night. Four guys took turns pumping the water, because no one could pump continuously for more than a half hour at a time. To show you that the camp was now a formal POW camp, the officers would shower first!

The rations were fairly decent. We each had at least two bowls of rice twice a day, and the cooks, with access to a little seasoning, were able to make the stew more palatable. Every once in a while, we got fish. The first time it happened, I said, "Oh, boy, they're giving us a whole fried fish."

After I got mine, I noticed some of the fellows were eating it and putting the head, spine, and tail aside. I said, "Are you guys going to throw that away?" And they said, "You want this, Eddie?" So I got all the fish heads, all the bones, and all the tails together, and boiled it into a broth. After I strained it, I mixed in a little ginger and a little sugar, and pounded up some rice to thicken it. Then, at the next meal, I stood at the end of the line where they were dishing it out and gave everyone a little spoon of gravy to go on top of their rice. And the guys said appreciatively, "Oh, you *can* do something with the fish heads."

We could also buy things at the canteen for reasonable prices. Eggs cost ten cents, bananas were five cents apiece, and a jigger full of peanuts was a nickel. We had gone from ten cents a day for enlisted men to fifteen cents a day, so, assuming that we worked thirty days, that would make it $4.50. That amount didn't buy you much; what you had to do was figure a way to earn more money. There was one guy we called "Ma" Ballew, because he took in laundry from the officers. Others would mend people's clothes— like a tailor. How I made my money was in scrounging and then selling what I scrounged to the native traders.

EXTRA CASH

The best haul I ever made was a case of quinine. I was working in Japanese headquarters, and there was a medical officer who kept his supplies there. Dr. Hekking said to me one day, "When you're out on the working party, see if you can scrounge some quinine—I'm almost out." And he added, "Do what you can, but don't get into any trouble." The first day, I found out where the medical supplies were, and there were four cases of quinine. I cased the place for two days and found a way in through the back by untying the matting. What I should have done was to steal the quinine, sell it to a native trader, take the money, and give it to the doc to buy quinine. Instead of that, I stole the whole case of quinine. I took it out bottle by bottle—twenty-four bottles in a wooden crate with straw. Then I got the case back in order, put the top back on, and put the empty case on the bottom. I figured it would take some time before the Japanese medic got to the bottom case, and by then I would be gone.

I was in charge of the food baskets that day, and my instinct was, "They're not going to search me today." The question was, "Do I bring back four, five bottles at a time, or try to take the whole thing in?" My instinct said, "Do it once—if you're caught, you're caught. If you take back six bottles at a time, you take four times the chance." There was an Australian who was helping me carry the pole at one end of the load. He said, "Eddie, you're going to get us killed." I said, "No, they're not going to search us." So I put some bananas on top of the baskets, and I said, "I'll give you half for help-ing me carry it in." He said, "What are you going to do with it?" I said, "Give it to the doc for the hospital." "Now," he said, "if you're going to do that, I'll help you carry it in." We got it in. So I told the Australian, "You can take half to your doctor if you want." He said, "Let's see what your doctor wants first. If he's a good bloke, he'll share it with us." And that was what Doc did—he shared it with all the other doctors. Doc saved my life twice, so I will always be beholden to him. He knew he could count on me whenever he needed anything. In fact, I asked him before I got the quinine, "You want a microscope? They got a microscope in there, and a nice wooden case too." He said in exasperation, "Eddie, I would love that microscope, but where am I going to hide it?"

After I requisitioned the quinine for Dr. Hekking, I decided every opportunity I had to work at Japanese headquarters, I would make arrange-ments to do some trading. There was this food vendor who was Thai, but he looked Chinese, and it got to the point where anytime I was working at Japanese headquarters, he would fill my mess kit with *chow fun* (a Chinese pasta dish). I started feeling him out to see if he knew any traders, because I never saw him doing any trading. He said, "Well, let me look around, and the next time you're here, we can talk about it." So the next time I was there, I asked him, "Did you have any luck?" He said, "Yeah, I found someone." He pointed to a spot and said, "He'll be right over that fence. All you have to do is throw whatever you want to sell over the fence and he will pay you the money through the fence." No negotiations; it was whatever he was willing to give me. Once I threw it over the fence, he could walk away. Luck-ily, I was never cheated. When you're trading, you have to find someone trustworthy.

There were established traders in the camp who would take things out to sell to the natives for a commission, but I didn't want to play that middleman role. If a friend said he would like to get ten dollars for something, and I couldn't get ten dollars for it, I would feel bad. If I got twenty dollars for the article, then I would be in a dilemma—should I give him the extra ten dollars or keep it? Usually, the trader got a 10–percent commission for the sale. But when you think about it, a 10–percent commission on twenty dollars is only two dollars. Why should I fuss about two dollars when I could just take stuff from Japanese headquarters and get full value, and no one else would be involved except the native trader on the other side of the fence? If I got caught, I would be the only one. I was very lucky that I never got caught because if I had, besides beating me up, they would have turned me over to the *kempetai*, the Japanese equivalent of the Gestapo.

When I had accumulated $200, I decided it was time to give myself a birthday party. I had actually turned twenty-one a year earlier, and before I left home, Mom had told me, "That's going to be an important day in your life—you will become a man." I had not been able to fulfill my mom's wish to celebrate at the time, because we were too deep into the speedo cycle, and I was pretty sick besides. And there had been nothing to have a birthday party with, not even for myself, so I decided now was the time. There was a Chinese merchant who often came to the camp commissary. I told him, "I would like you to bring me some food for my twenty-first birthday party, however much food $200 can buy." And I said, "We have a couple of hundred Americans here, and I would like to give them a good Chinese meal. I'll leave it up to you." He brought in four dishes—pork, duck, chicken, and fish. At mealtime, I set all the food at the end of the chow line. Everyone got the regular food and then a spoonful of each of the four dishes. I don't think that merchant cheated me, because I know I got my money's worth. And being Chinese, he understood what I was trying to do.

I left my money with Captain Fitzsimmons for safe keeping, and George Reis, who was master sergeant of Headquarters Battery, approached Captain Fitzsimmons and said, "Would you ask Eddie if he would be willing to lend me 100 ticals, and I will pay him four American dollars for every tical when we are freed and I get home?" So Captain Fitzsimmons asked me, and I said, "Well, I feel I'm exploiting the situation. Four to one sounds pretty outrageous." The captain said, "He was the one who made the offer. You didn't ask for it. If he's willing to pay you four for one, that's what he's willing to pay." I said, "You don't think I'm being a shark?" He said, "No, you're not trying to set the rates. He's only asking if you're willing to accept the rates." The three of us got together, and George said, "Do you want me to write a note for you, Ed?" And I said, "No, George, that's not necessary. You've given me your word. Let's take the two possibilities. If I don't make it through, I will suspect you would be willing to send the $400 to my family. If you don't make it through, I'm not going to ask your family for 100 ticals and add to their misery of finding out their son didn't make it." So I said, "If we can accept those terms, there's no need for a piece of paper. We don't even need Captain Fitzsimmons as the witness. As far as I'm concerned, I'm willing to take your word for it." Sure enough, by the time I got back to San Francisco from Walter Reed Hospital, there was a letter with a Park Avenue address, and inside was a check for $400 and an invitation to George's wedding. I remember thinking, "Wouldn't it be great if all human relationships were this above board?"

LEARNING FROM OTHERS

We used to sit around and talk about how much back pay we had coming. That was when George Reis, who had graduated from Cornell in '35, gave us our first lesson in economics. He told us, "Assuming that you're paid $30 a month, in twelve months you have $360, and in three years, you'll have over $1,000." So we said, "Gee, George, back in the days of Camp Bowie, you could buy a brand new car for $600." And he said, "Yeah, but what makes you think that the price of the car, assuming you can get one, is still $600?" That was when he taught us about inflation. "You remember when we first got into Burma? A catty of sugar was $2.50. By the time we got to 85 Kilo, it was $25. For the trader to come all the way up to 85 Kilo takes him more time. So even though he can still buy a catty of sugar for a dollar, now he's got to sell it for more in order to make his trip worthwhile." Then he said, "Now, the same thing is happening in the United States. You're still thinking in terms of 1940, but it's now 1944. In the first place, they're probably not making automobiles, because all production is going towards the war." We were thinking that with $1,000 back pay, we would be able to go into a store and buy a suit and dicker for a discount because there would be thirty or fifty of us. But George told us that the fact that we could go in there as a group would not make any difference because, most likely, stores wouldn't have any goods to sell us. And we kept thinking, "He's crazy, how could there not be consumer goods?" As it turned out, he was right, and as Rip Van Winkles frozen in the time frame of 1941, we were in for a rude awakening.

There were other people at Kanburi from whom I learned things. Charlie Mott had been with the Flying Tigers and been shot down in Burma. He was a terrific chess player. We found out that he was the junior champion of Southern California at one time. One day he set up a simultaneous chess match where he played ten people all at once, one after the other. We asked him, "Charlie, aren't you chewing a lot more than you can swallow?" He said, "Oh no, duck soup. If you got any money at all, bet on me and get the best odds you can." And he said, "I'll take at least eight out of ten, and with any luck at all, I'll take all ten." So we decided, "Okay, we don't know you from Adam, but if you say you're that good, we'll bet on you." Sure enough, he took all ten; not even one draw. Afterwards, we asked him how he could play ten guys simultaneously and keep track of each game. He said, "That's the beauty of playing simultaneous chess—you act spontaneously. You look at the board, make your play in no more than thirty seconds, and move on to the next game. It's not as difficult as you think. If you really want to get difficult, try blindfolded chess." He explained that in blindfolded chess, the opponent tells you the move that he has made and you memorize it in your mind's eye. "To an outsider," he said, "it seems very difficult. But to a chess player, if he concentrates, he can do it." So I learned from people like Charlie. It may seem trivial or it may not even be profitable for me to know things like this, but I learned what people were capable of.

On a personal level, it was Dr. Hekking who helped me come to terms with my ethnic identity as a Chinese American. I remember when I first arrived in the jungle, Captain Fitzsimmons called me in one day and said, "Eddie, I can change your service record so it reads that you're half Chinese." And I said, "Why would we do that, Captain?" He said, "They may not be as rough on a half Chinese." I told Captain Fitzsimmons, "My father would turn over in his grave if I did that. Let's just take our chances and leave it the way it is." That was when I realized that I was Chinese culturally and philosophically. There was nothing I could do to change that. I wasn't extra proud of it; I wasn't ashamed of it; I just knew that was the reality of it—I am Chinese, period.

Dr. Hekking reinforced this when he gave me a copy of Lin Yutang's *Importance of Living* to read. I think from our past conversations, he could sense my ambivalence about being Chinese. I told him I had left home twice, and he probably wondered, "What are you running from? After all, at sixteen years old, you haven't even gotten your education yet." Since he was born in Indonesia and had dealt with a lot of natives, he probably could see how the natives had suffered under the Dutch restrictions that were imposed on them. Maybe that was what he saw as the analogy to the restricted life I had experienced in San Francisco Chinatown, and the explanation as to why I felt almost ashamed of being Chinese. I think he gave me Lin Yutang's book because he wanted me to learn about China's rich culture and history. I read *The Importance of Living* a number of times, but it wasn't until years later, after I had married Lois, that it made an impact on my sense of ethnic pride.

THE JAPANESE WAY OF THINKING

We got our first and only Red Cross package when we were in Kanburi. There was a card with each package that we had to sign, and it went back to the Red Cross, acknowledging the receipt of said package. The Japanese told us it was six men to a package, but we each had to sign a card. In other words, they kept the other five packages. We didn't argue about who was going to get what. The evaporated milk went to the hospital—that was the one thing that we all agreed on. After that, everything was split among the six men. Cigarettes were the most difficult because there were ten. That meant we each got one cigarette. With the remaining four, the guys would light one up and each person would take a draw. Since I was the pipe smoker, the guys gave me all the pipe tobacco, which I thought was pretty generous of them. We found out after the war that there were books and athletic equipment from the Red Cross locked up in the Japanese warehouses, and we hated them not so much for keeping back the athletic equipment—but the reading material, we could have used that. Same thing with our mail—they kept saying they needed time to censor it. When we offered to help, they said, "No, no, we'll do it ourselves." After the war, there were sacks and sacks of mail waiting to be delivered.

The Japanese did not want us getting any news except from them. Gus Forsman, a sailor, and Captain Parker were incarcerated by the *kempetai* for trying to smuggle in a Thai newspaper written in English. For that, they were sentenced to seven years in prison. Of course, we thought it was funny as hell—you're a prisoner of war and you're being sentenced! They were tortured too because the Japanese wanted to know who else was implicated, but the men stuck to their story. The Japanese would tell us these stories about the fantastic deeds of Japanese soldiers and airmen. One guy on a bombing raid got all shot up, but he managed to fly his plane back to the base. It turned out that he had been dead for hours! Another guy in a fighter plane was strafing a ship and ran out of ammunition. So he flew at deck level, drew a samurai sword, and cut off the captain's head! It was amazing to us that they could print such childish propaganda in newspapers like the *Rangoon Times* and expect people to believe it.

We just never understood the Japanese way of thinking. At times, it almost seemed comical. For example, toward the end of the war, they decided that maybe our prayers were helping us win the war. So they told us, "No more church services" and "No more chaplains to give services," as if a person could not pray by himself. We thought, "This is really funny if they think this is going to help them win the war." As another example: We had been plagued by flies since the beginning. They were big and thick and everywhere—on our food and in the latrines—and we really couldn't do anything about it. But at Kanburi, the Japanese decided, "There are too many flies in this camp." So every man had to catch a quota of 100 flies every day and take them to the guardhouse to be counted. They kept it up for a couple of weeks before they realized that it wasn't making the slightest dent in the fly population. Of course, there were guys who took advantage of the fact that the Japanese wanted the flies, so they would start breeding flies or they would cut the big flies into halves. There were all sorts of ways we would try to cheat the Japanese. Sometimes we got away with it and sometimes we didn't. Later, when I applied for a job at Livermore Lab and one section of the application form said "List all the jobs that you've been paid for," I put down "fly catching" just as a joke, because we had been paid a penny for 100 flies. Would you believe I got called in for a job dealing with small animals and environmental studies!

The Japanese got a laugh out of me one day. We were working near the kitchen at Japanese headquarters and the cook called us over with that Oriental hand gesture—palm down. He had put out two buckets of food for us—one with rice and one with some stew. The guys were scrambling to get their mess kits. What I did was grab one of those big palm leaves, wipe it off, and fold it as I would a corner for *joong* (glutinous rice wrapped in bamboo leaves). Then I broke off two twigs for chopsticks. I was the first one there, and the cook looked at me and he laughed. He gave me a big scoop of rice and put some stew on top. I walked aside and began eating with my makeshift chopsticks—and he was still laughing. Meanwhile, these other guys were still trying to scrounge up mess kits. So you never know what to expect from a Japanese. Some will treat you like a human being, but most of them will treat you like a dog. But you always remember the ones who treated you like a human being. It was rare, but we did meet some.

ALLIED BOMBINGS

Beginning in '44, the Allied bombing raids came pretty regularly at Kanburi and Tamarkan. The first time we were bombed was in Kanburi. They were bombing the Japanese headquarters area and the bombs were coming out of the bomb bays like a farmer pitching hay. It was the first time we had seen B-24s. I said to myself, "That's got to be it; that's got to be the bomb load!" They were using the smokestack of the paper mill that was about two miles from our camp as the "initial point" or landmark. Slug Wright had an empty peach can practically fall on his head. Some guy in the crew had eaten peaches, and Slug swore there was still syrup in the can that he could wipe off and taste. The second time they came over, they were trying to hit the bridge at Tamarkan, and the Japanese were foolish enough to open up fire. Unfortunately, some of the bombs hit the base camp and killed some POWs. When we heard that, we started cursing the bombers. We had just gotten out of the jungles, and now our own people were after us. Thanbyuzayat was bombed twice. The first time, twelve people were killed and thirty-two wounded. The second time, seventeen people were killed and about forty wounded. Colonel Black was in the foxhole when a 500–pound bomb hit nearby. He suffered internal injuries and was deaf for months afterwards. He also got shot with a .50–caliber in his arm and he carried that wound until the day he died. He used to show it to people and say, "That wasn't by a Nip; that was by an American!" We thought, "Good god, what kind of intelligence do these people have?" After the war, the Air Force said that they thought it was a supply depot and that there were no Red Cross markings on the grounds or the huts.

The Japanese didn't like it one bit, and to boost their morale, they took it out on us. So now we were being hit from both sides. Then, too, whenever the bombers hit the railroad or knocked out a bridge, we would have to work overtime to repair them. If the damage was extensive and we couldn't repair it right away, we would have to carry everything across the river and trans-ship it to another boxcar. It just made a lot of extra work for us. I remember one time we were working in the Tamarkan area when we were bombed. We could hear the planes starting to come over and there we were, coming home over the bridge. So the first thing we did was run like hell to get off the bridge, then head into the jungles and find any cover we could. Since then, whenever I hear an airplane engine—and I don't care if it's a jet or a propeller—I want to know exactly where that airplane is, because throughout the war, a plane always meant danger to us, whether it belonged to the Japanese or the Allies.

There were many times when we wondered whether this might not become the most dangerous part of our captivity. Of course, we were beginning to hear rumors that there might be a wholesale slaughter if the Japanese lost the war. With their attitude of not taking prisoners and not becoming prisoners, some credence was put upon that rumor. When they had us dig a large moat all around the whole camp, we started thinking, "Holy smoke, this could be the death trap!" It was a ditch about nine feet

FIG. 26. The "bridge on the River Kwai" in Tamarkan, Thailand, after an Allied bombing raid in 1945. Eddie was there at the beginning of the bombing raids in November 1944. Courtesy Australian War Memorial, 122329.

wide at the top, tapering down to four-and-a-half feet at the bottom, and it had to be at least eight feet deep. We imagined that we would all be forced into the moat, and with four machine guns—one at each corner—there would be no way to escape. We decided that if worse comes to worst, we would try to pole vault over the ditch or overtake the guards. We weren't going to just sit there and be slaughtered like sheep.

Soon after, the officers and the men were separated, and we figured they were trying to get to the point where they could say that they had lived up to the Geneva Conventions. The scuttlebutt was that negotiations were going on, so we thought that maybe we were getting close to the end of the war. We found out later that the Japanese actually destroyed all the plans and correspondence regarding the railroad, as if the physical presence of the railroad would not testify to the fact that it had been built! After the war, we also found out about the "annihilation order." There were similar orders for all the camps, which basically called for the final disposal of all prisoners in case we got in the way of the last-ditch fight. So there has never been any doubt in my mind that had the U.S. not dropped the atom bomb and forced Japan to surrender, we would have all been killed.

LIBERATION

Each group of POWs had a different liberation date. Ours was August 19, 1945. We were working at our last camp in Nakhon Nayok, digging caves and building roads, because this was supposed to be "Custer's Last Stand" for the Japanese. A few days before the war ended, we were scheduled to go out on a work party. We had been issued our lunches and we were ready to go to work, but it was called off. The following day, we were called for another work detail, but again we didn't go out. At first we didn't think anything of it, because there were always things to catch up on in camp— I remember I got a haircut. By the third day, we started wondering if some-

FIG. 27. *The plaque on the memorial honoring F Battery in Jacksboro, Texas. Eddie's name is second in the middle column.*

thing wasn't going on. Then around ten o'clock, we heard the British bugler sounding assembly. All of a sudden, in the pit of my stomach, I had this feeling, "Something really big is going to happen."

They had us all line up at the parade ground—all 3,000 people—and Warrant Officer Stimson, who was in charge of the camp, said to us, "Gentlemen, this is the happiest moment of my life. The Japanese commandant has asked me to inform you that the war has ended." There was absolute silence for about a minute. Then one of the British soldiers went, "Hip-hip-hurrah!" Right after that, there was a race to see who would put up the first flag. Then the second race was to see who would have the tallest flagstaff. I was thinking, "Holy smoke, here we go again—same old rat race!" The Americans had to make a flag because we didn't have one. That was the only time we ever regretted that we weren't thirteen colonies anymore, because we had to cut out and sew on forty-eight stars. As it turned out, the Dutch flag was the first to go up, but our flag was the highest. I had always had doubts about whether I would make it through. I remember just feeling relieved: "Okay, you're still here, you've made it through."

I think throughout my ordeal as a POW of the Japanese, my worst moment had to be in May '45. I had finally come to terms with my past and I was looking forward to going home and telling my mother face to face, "Okay Mom, I understand what you and Pop have been trying to get through to me—about what it means to be Chinese—and I'm going to try and live up to it." But as it turned out, my mother died in May of '45. It's strange, but I knew exactly when she died, because May was the beginning of the rainy season, and it was then that I had this strong premonition, "I'm not going to see her again." There was never a time when I was more down, even when I had the dysentery and malaria at the same time in '43. So I've lived with the fact that I was an unfilial son and a disappointment to my parents. There are two ways that I can put it: If there is an afterlife, then wherever they are, my parents will know that I'm trying to live the life they taught me to live. If there isn't an afterlife, I will know that I'm trying to live the way they taught me to live. So either way it will all work out.

SIX · LEARNING TO LIVE WITH MYSELF

When I ran away from home and was bumming around in my teens, I never expe-rienced any hardships. I was just out for adventure. I knew that if some bad things should happen, that was all part of the adventure. It was only after the prison camp days that I realized what hard times really meant. I knew that it was going to shape my life whether I liked it or not. The only control I had was in the shaping it was going to take—whether it was going to make me a better or lesser person.

GETTING OUT OF CAMP

I think it was the Australians who started it. They didn't go by the guard shack to get out of camp. Instead, they climbed over the fence and went to town to get liquored up. Most of the Americans were pretty well behaved. We had been notified by the Allies to stay put and wait for some-one to come get us. The first couple of days, we busied ourselves with house-keeping chores, like cleaning up the hut and cleaning out the bedbugs. We found a clear space on the parade ground where we could build little bonfires. Then we untied the bamboo slats of our beds, took them over to the fire, and shook out the bedbugs. Even though we were leaving, we weren't going to put up with these critters anymore. Besides, we didn't know how long it was going to be before anyone would come get us.

The Korean guards had been dismissed, and we only had the Japanese guards, who told us they were there to protect us! There was no talk about how we were going to beat up on them or seek some kind of revenge. It just didn't seem like it would benefit any of us to start the vicious cycle all over again. It wasn't that we would ever forget what the Japanese did to us, but there was no point in behaving as they had, simply because we could. Later, we heard that some of the guys who had gone outside the camp met up with some of the Korean guards, who were moaning and groaning to the prisoners they met, "How are we going to get home?" A week before, we probably would have beaten them senseless. But it was so pathetic, the guys just told them, "Go find the Red Cross and they will help you, because there's nothing we can do for you."

A week later, the trucks came by to take us to Bangkok, which was about eighty miles away. We took everything that we had, as if we were moving to another camp. I had my rucksack, a hatchet, my wooden clogs, G-string, and wooden dog tag. I didn't throw anything away until we got to Calcutta. We stayed in Bangkok no more than three days to get cleaned up and to get a new uniform so that we would look presentable again. When the British found out that the U.S. was sending in planes to get the Americans out, they demanded that the British officers go first. We later heard that the American pilots told them, "Our orders are to take the Americans first, and your rank doesn't mean beans to us." We got a good laugh over that because we had never gotten along with the British officers. For them to carry on for three and a half years as if they were still in a regular army just didn't make any sense to us. We got on one of four C-47s in Bangkok, and our pilot flew about twelve hundred feet over the railroad. He wanted us to see where we had been, and we told him, "We know where we've been." And I said, "We also know what you guys did to the railroad."

On the way to Rangoon, the plane developed engine problems, and the pilot sent the copilot back to say, "No worries—lots of emergency airstrips around here." So they dropped us down on an airstrip and radioed in to Calcutta for another replacement aircraft. While we were on the ground waiting for the aircraft, the pilot got us some Number Ten cans of pineapple grapefruit juice to drink. Then the pilot said to the crew chief, "Have we still got some of those ten-in-one rations?" And the crew chief said, "Oh, we got lots of those." We didn't know what they were, because when we went over we had C-rations, and they were cans of things like stew. So we opened up these little cardboard boxes and found little cans of potted meat and scrambled eggs, some instant coffee, cigarettes, and a small package of toilet paper. (The reason they called it "ten in one" was because it was ten days of rations for one person or ten people could have one day's rations.) It was quite palatable, and we were eating these things as if we were eating steak and eggs. The pilot said, "You guys like this stuff?" And we said, "Yeah, it's pretty tasty." And he said, "I think we got *more* of them if you want." We must have eaten everything they had on the plane, and they couldn't get over the fact that we liked the food so much.

When we got to Rangoon, there was a reception committee there—a group of English ladies to serve us tea and sandwiches. We were so shy that we just reached out and grabbed a sandwich off the tray and stepped back six feet. We had been using the "F" word so often that we were afraid to open our mouths even to say "Thank you." It suddenly occurred to us that we were going to be meeting women again, and we had better start learning how to behave as civilized people in mixed society. That was why it was a relief for us when we arrived at the 142nd General Army Hospital in Calcutta. We were back in the army again. Even though the army nurses were women too, they were officers, and, as enlisted men, we knew how to behave toward them.

The nurses proved to be as tough as any officer could be when we got out of line. The first night we slept over, a nurse found us all sleeping on the concrete floor when she came in the next morning. She looked at us and she said, "If this ward is not shipshape in five minutes, all of you are going to be on report." We got all the mattresses back on the cots, made up the beds, and she didn't say another word. A few days later, we heard that the nurse complained to the head doctor about how unruly we were. Essentially, the doctor told the nurses to give us some slack: "Check them out at bedtime, then taps and lights out. If they're in bed, they're in bed." So we caught on. As soon as the lights were out and the nurse went back to her desk, we slept on the floor, and before reveille, all the beds were made up. I'm not sure if the nurses ever understood why we couldn't sleep on a soft bed. We appreciated the clean sheets and everything, but for the longest time, we just couldn't sleep on anything unless it was absolutely hard and flat.

We had gotten into Calcutta late at night, and the mess sergeant had been very nice to us. He gave us each macaroni and cheese, half a pint of milk, and fruit salad. And he said, "This is all I can do for you tonight, but I'll set you up with a breakfast tomorrow that you'll never forget." Next morning, we got ham, bacon, sausage, eggs any style, all kinds of fruit, coffee, and milk. We took our regular ranch-hand breakfast and we couldn't eat one tenth of what we took. When the doctors made the rounds, we asked them, "How come we can't eat?" And the doctor said, "Your stomach is the size of a fist or smaller. If you eat too much greasy food, you're going to have the runs. Just get used to it gradually." I remember I had my first cup of coffee in three and a half years. I practically inhaled it before sitting down and savoring at least five or six cups of it. At the time, even army coffee smelled and tasted good.

We were there for about three weeks to be fattened up. They served us lots of food cafeteria style, but our chow line was for ex-prisoners only. I guess even the cooks and the doctors had a lot to learn from that first breakfast. They had tried to be real nice to us, but our stomachs couldn't take it. We were allowed to go to town. The first place I looked for was a Chinese restaurant. I found one and I had chow mein— curried flavor chow mein. I didn't know why it was that I had spent most of my life escaping Chinatown, and the first chance I had, I would try to get in touch with anything Chinese. I just knew I felt homesick for Chinese food. I walked around town, enjoying the sights, and blew my first paycheck on a blue sapphire ring for my mother. Once I got used to the idea that cows were sacred in India, I wasn't even bothered by all the cows wandering in the streets. Other than going to town, I frequented the PX on the hospital grounds. The word was that ex-prisoners could walk into the PX anytime and order anything they wanted, and they were not to be charged. So we had milk shakes and Coca–Colas galore—the exact thing that the doctors had warned us against. My main thing was milk shakes. I had two at a time and I paid for it afterwards with the runs, but I didn't care.

BACK IN THE U.S.A.

The route of the plane ride from Calcutta to Washington, DC, was Karachi to Tripoli, Tripoli to Casablanca, Casablanca to the Azores, Azores to Newfoundland, and then Newfoundland to Washington, DC. That was because of the limited range of the two-engine DC-3 aircraft we were on. The plan was to get us on a four-engine aircraft in Casablanca. We had a four-hour layover in Casablanca, and they gave us the same prime-rib dinner that Churchill and Roosevelt had had at their big meeting in 1943. Prior to our flying out, they took us through ditching procedures, in case the plane had to come down at sea. That was when we began wondering whether we couldn't find some other way to get home. When we passed New York, I remember that the pilot circled the Statue of Liberty three times after he found out that we had been away from the country for so long. That was when it hit us—that we were actually home and back in the good old U.S.A.

By the time we got to Walter Reed Hospital, we were all somewhat presentable. My weight was up to 100 pounds, from my lowest weight of 60 pounds. That was because we had been recuperating from the time we left the jungle in January of '44—twenty months earlier. At Walter Reed, we were basically on duty every day from 8:00 to 5:00 in the sense that we were at the beck and call of all the doctors. They took our history about malaria, dysentery, and so on. We had proctology examinations to see what damage had been done to the rectum. Back in those days, they didn't have things like endoscopes with fiber optics. Instead, they inserted a tube that was close to three-fourths of an inch in diameter, and you had to be positioned in a certain way so that your rectum was lined up with the sigmoid. That was the worst examination we had. The one that was most perplexing was the psychological examination. We had to go through several locked doors to get to the "nut ward." From some of the questions that the psychiatrists asked us, we thought they were nuts: "How do you feel about girls?" We told them that we hadn't had a chance to really find out yet. "Do you have a normal sex drive?" We said that we thought we did. It went on in this vein, and we just could not understand, "Where is all this getting to?"

The other bad thing we had happen to us was the de-worming session. We evidently all had tapeworms inside our stomach linings from walking barefoot in the jungles. They gave us a pill that had to be the size of a golf ball. I'll never forget the army nurse, Captain Adams, who administered it to us. The pill had chloroform that was supposed to kill the tapeworm, and after we swallowed it, it would help expel the worm. So we said to her, "Is this to kill the worms or us?" And she said, "You guys don't shut up, I'll feed you another one." Of course, the doctors could never figure it out— here we were on a starvation diet and then we had worms on top of that! As I said, they would ask us how we knew what kind of malaria we had, what kind of dysentery we had, and so on. And when we told them about the beriberi, pellagra, and the other tropical diseases, a lot of them really did not know what we were talking about. All of these exams took over a week. With the army, it was always "Hurry up and wait."

HOMECOMING

I didn't call home until we had arrived safely at Walter Reed. I could have cabled from Calcutta, but I decided that there was still a lot of ground to cover before I got home. There was always the possibility of a plane crash. After all, I had never flown before, and I wasn't sure when I was going to get in. When I did call home on September 21, a cousin of ours was at the house and he answered the phone. Since he only spoke Chinese, I had to ask in Chinese to speak to my mother. I said, "This is Man Quong." He hesitated and said, "Your mother *gwo hau*," meaning "she has passed away." I thought he said, "*Gwo fow*," meaning "out of town." I assumed he meant she was at the butcher shop in Lodi. I asked, "When is she coming back?" At that point, he turned the phone over to Myra Lee, who had gone to school with me. I heard her voice and said, "What are you doing at the house?" She said, "I'm married to your brother Bill." So that took me off the track. Even before I got home from Walter Reed, the word must have gone around: "Ed is a little crazy—he thinks his mommy's going to come back."

When I finally got home, it was late in the evening, and I found Ah So and Myra home. Ah So wanted to get some firecrackers and shoot them off, and I said, "Don't do that—it'll wake up the whole neighborhood." Then when I got it straight from Myra about Mom being dead and I started to walk out of the house, Ah So said, "You're not going to do anything fool-ish, are you, Eddie?" I said, "Don't be silly. I'm just going out for some fresh air, just want to be by myself for a while." I remember I was feeling disappointed that I didn't get a chance to talk to Mom at least one more time. But by that time I was pretty used to things not turning out the way

I had anticipated. I decided there was nothing to hang around San Francisco for, so I headed down to Santa Barbara for "R and R."

My "R and R" was spent at the Biltmore Hotel, which was nearest my home town. We had been told that after sixty days, we would be given an automatic extension of "R and R" if we requested it. We could invite guests to come stay at the Biltmore and there would be no charge. So a lot of the guys invited their girlfriends, or, in Donald "Pineapple" Johnson's case, he invited his parents from Nebraska to come stay with him. The only people I knew to invite were my sisters. Jess was in Bakersfield, but she couldn't come because she had children to take care of. Mints and Grace were working as waitresses in Hollywood at the time, so they each came and stayed one night. After two weeks, I was bored out of my skull. I just couldn't take the inactivity or fill up time with empty activities. I didn't drink and I didn't know how to jitterbug. There were organized field trips to the missions and that kind of thing, but I wasn't interested. I went horseback riding once, but it didn't seem as enjoyable as before. Since I wasn't due to report at Camp Beale for another month, I decided to go visit my sister in Bakersfield.

REENLISTMENT

When I finally got to Camp Beale in Marysville, that was when they asked me if I wanted to stay in the army or not. At that time, you could retire on 50 percent of your pay after twenty years. I had never given any thought about staying anyplace for twenty years, because growing up in Chinatown, no one had a steady job; no one thought in terms of staying with a company, getting a pension, and so on. In fact, when I first got back, I looked into becoming a plumber. I went to this guy, Rosenbaum, who had a plumbing shop in Chinatown, and I asked him, "How do I go about learning to be a plumber so I can start my own shop?" He said, "I can teach you everything I know, but you'll never become a journeyman because you will never be admitted into the union. And unless you're in the union, you will never be able to open your own shop." I asked him why that was, and he said, "Because you're Chinese." Then he asked me, "Why do you want to become a plumber?" And I said, "I notice there aren't any Chinese plumbers." And he said, "Now you know why." That was when I first became

aware of racial discrimination in the job market. The other reason I considered reenlisting was that I had no desire to stay home now that Mom was gone. I also did not want to go back to Texas and be a cowboy. I thought, "It was okay when you were a snotty-nosed kid, but I don't think you want to do that for the rest of your life." I had grown up, but maturity didn't come until at least thirty years later. I decided the easiest thing to do was to just stay in the army until I knew what I wanted to do with the rest of my life.

The next question was whether I wanted to stay with the artillery or the infantry, because the 36th Division was basically an infantry division. I decided I wanted to give the Air Corps a try, because to any foot soldier on the ground, an airman looks like he has an easier job: "Those guys can fly their mission, go home, and have a nice soft bed to sleep in." Never mind that the pilot has to fly through flak-infested skies with fighters trying to knock him down, and that he has to fly in formation slow, straight, and steady while everybody is gunning for him. I just knew I didn't want to be a foot soldier anymore, and the Air Corps seemed the next best thing to do. So they said, "Okay, if you want to try the Air Corps, we'll send you to the Replacement Depot in Wichita Falls, and they can decide what they want to do with you."

I got to Shepherd Field in Wichita Falls on a Friday evening, and right away, they told me I was in charge of quarters, since I was now a corporal. I was just getting settled in when one of the new draftees came back from town and said, "Corporal, there's a big parade downtown, and there's a bunch of geezers with stripes just like yours." He was referring to my seven stripes—each bar represented six months overseas. He showed me the newspaper, and I realized the parade was for my group. It mentioned the hotel where they were going to have the reception that evening. So I went up there, and as I walked into this big ballroom, I noticed the officers were sitting at the front table. Seeing Colonel Tharp, I went up and saluted him. Then the guys started yelling, "Hey, Eddie!" And when they saw my uniform, they yelled, "You dirty traitor, going over to the Air Corps!" It was weird in a way because we had gone through three and a half years practically bare naked, and here we were in full uniform, and I swear to God I had a tough time recognizing some of them. With a big crowd like that, it was pretty confusing. Before I had a chance to say hello, someone else would grab me. But it was also a joyous occasion, especially for the Fitzsimmons group, because we had been such a tight group through thick and thin.

The Air Corps decided to send me to Lowry Air Force Base, near Denver, to be trained as a clerk-typist, although my first choice had been cryptography school. While at Lowry, I went on an eating binge. They were serving pork chops one evening, and the military, when they give you a pork chop, we're talking about an inch thick. The normal portion was two chops, and the motto over any mess hall was "Take all you want, but eat all you take." I ate my first portion of pork chops with my vegetables and so on. I went back and I said to the server, "Why don't you save us both a lot of trouble and let me have four more?" He said, "Sure, corporal, any number you want. Just remember the sign—take all you want but eat all you take." So I ate the four pork chops and I went back and said, "How about another four?" He called the mess sergeant, and the mess sergeant said, "What's the problem?" He said, "The corporal wants another four pork chops, and he's already had six." He said, "Is he eating the pork chops?" He said, "Yeah, he has an empty tray." "So give him what he wants." So I said, "While you're at it, make it six. Then I won't have to come back."

The mess sergeant got a cup of coffee and sat down by me, and he said, "Don't worry corporal, I'm just taking a break." We got to talking, and he finally said, "I understand why you're stuffing yourself, but I don't know where you're putting it!" I said, "I don't know either, but I'm going to be full when I'm finished." He said, "Do you do this all the time?" I said, "No, just once in a while. If something looks appealing or appetizing, it just triggers something in me." So he said, "You know that you can eat all you want any time you want. As a mess sergeant, I enjoy seeing a man eat." Every once in a while, I would go on binges like that, and that was how I got to be 125 pounds at my discharge point.

After six weeks of training, I was told to report to my duty station, Andrews Air Force Base in Aberdeen, Maryland. On my way there, I decided to stop off in Missouri for a haircut. As I walked into this barbershop that had five or six people in there, all the conversation suddenly stopped. So I waited until it was my turn and the shop was empty, and I said, "If you don't mind my asking, was it because of me that the conversation stopped?" The barber said, "Those people probably thought you were Japanese." So I said, "What difference would that make? I've seen Japanese Americans in uniform." He looked at my stripes and he said, "How long have you been away?" I said, "We've been overseas for forty-six months." And he said, "You don't know about the internment?" I said, "What internment?" So he told me briefly about how thousands of Japanese Americans on the West Coast had been locked up in internment camps during the war.[1] And I said, "That happened?" And he said, "Yes, it happened. These people probably thought you were Japanese. I've seen Chinese, so I know the difference." I said, "How in hell can a thing like that happen in the U.S.?" He said, "Well, you have to have been here. People were in a state of hysteria, thinking that the Japs were going to land in the West Coast any minute, and they were probably looking to lock up Germans on the East Coast."

It was at that point when I realized there were people who might not know the difference between a Chinese and Japanese and I would just have to make allowances for that. I told the barber, "It's ironic that I'm being mistaken for a Japanese when I've been a guest of the Japanese for three and a half years." And he said, "God, you're not pulling my leg, are you? The next time those guys come in, I'm going to tell them." So I said, "No, tell them not to be too fast on the trigger, that's all. Give someone the benefit of the doubt. That's all we ask." I walked away thinking, "I wish people could learn what we had learned without having to go through all the brutality and the suffering, but I guess it doesn't work that way."

When I got to Andrews Air Force Base, I was assigned to work under Sergeant Major John Costello, who apparently knew every trick in the book. He told me, "Eddie, normally I would have to discharge you after six years in the service, but I've got a little gimmick up my sleeve. If you sign up for six more months, I can give you your reenlistment bonus, which is $50 for each year you've served. So right away, that's $300." He added, "Before I sign you up, I'm going to discharge you and send you home and then bring you back to your place of enlistment. You're not actually going to leave; it's all on paper. So there's another X number of dollars." He knew all the ways to generate dollars, and he said, "But I got to sign you up for a minimum of six months to do this." And he said, "If nothing else, it will give you some more time to decide whether you want to make the army your career or not." So I followed his advice and signed up for six more months.

I turned out to be a lousy clerk-typist. The first assignment I was given was to type up an order for a person to do something. It took me all day to type up a simple paragraph, and I still didn't have it right. John Costello came by and said, "Having a little trouble, Eddie?" I said, "John, I'm just not cut out to be a clerk-typist." So he took the form that I was supposed to type out, went to his desk, got out three sheets of paper, put the carbon paper in between, tapped the paper evenly, slipped it into his typewriter, and within thirty seconds, he had the order typed out. And he said, "Eddie, it's going to take you a while, because I'm one of the best typists in the army." He told me that he gave demonstrations and that he could type rhythm on a typewriter. "They won't allow me on the teletype because I jam it up—

I type too fast." And he said, "Don't worry about it. You'll get the hang of it." I said, "John, I don't think so. I'm all thumbs."

Before I decided to quit the air force, I said to John, "If I asked to go to another school or train for something else, do you think I would get it?" He replied, "If you sign up for a three-year enlistment, I'll almost guarantee it. Did you have something in mind?" I said, "No, I'm not sure there's anything I can really do for the Air Corps that someone else can't do." I decided that I had better take my discharge at that point and be done with it. I knew by then that if I stayed in the army, it would have been for the wrong reason—that it was a safe cocoon—and that was not the way I wanted to live my life.

WORK AND SCHOOLING IN BAKERSFIELD

After I was discharged, I wasn't sure what I wanted to do next, so I went home. But for some reason, San Francisco seemed awfully cold to me. At first I thought it was because my body was still in the tropics. But then, even in Aberdeen, where it snowed, I had not felt cold. That was when Jess suggested I come down to Bakersfield, where it was a little warmer, so that I could get my thermostat readjusted. I knew I couldn't live in San Francisco anymore. With my mother gone, the city just didn't hold any special attraction for me. She was the main reason, the only reason I had wanted to come back.

When I got to Bakersfield, I decided right away that I couldn't stay idle. So Jessie introduced me to Jack Quan, a wholesale meat jobber, and she told him that I knew something about meat cutting. Jack said, "You want a job?" And I said, "I have to tell you, I barely got started on learning the meat-cutting trade. I haven't touched any tools since I was fourteen years old." "Oh," he said, "I'll teach you everything you need to know." He was desperate for help, so that was how I got started working as a meat cutter again.

What Jack did was to sell cut-up meat to small grocery stores and restaurants. Basically, he would buy the beef halves and we would cut it up for steaks, and the rest would be used for hamburger. We would make pork sausage and prepare trays of pork chops cut for display. All that the small-grocery owner had to do was to put them in his display case. Occasionally, we would fill orders for veal chops, rib steaks, or T-bone steaks—whatever they thought would sell in their neighborhood stores. Then there were always the special demands of the restaurants from day to day, depending on their menus. I worked eight hours a day and I was paid sixty dollars a month at the beginning. After a year, it was kicked up to eighty dollars. That was pretty good, considering that Jack had to teach me everything. The work wasn't hard—all I had to do was take the orders in the morning, deal with the orders, and then deliver them.

Since I had a little spare time in the evenings, I decided to take some night courses at the high school nearby—courses like algebra and geometry that I had never had. It was Jess who told me that there was a JC (junior college) in Bakersfield. I said to her, "Jess, I'm a dropout from the junior year of high school. I don't think I'm ready to go to junior college yet." So she said, "Well, what you can do is go talk to a counselor and see whether you should take night courses or try to matriculate at a JC." So I went there and found out about the GED test that could qualify me for a high school diploma. I didn't want to jump into it right away, so I waited a year before I took the four-hour exam covering math, history, English, and so on. A couple of months later, I got word that I had passed the test. The counselor jokingly said, "Now that you're going to get your GED diploma, what high school do you want it from?" I had already decided that I was going to major in chemistry because of Captain Cates. He was the officer who asked us to be on the lookout for acetic acid in Java. At that time, I thought it was magic and something I would like to learn more about.

When I found out how little books and tuition would cost, I decided to save the GI Bill for later, because I still had three and a half years of back pay to cover it all. I also had all the war bonds that my mother had bought in my name with the pay that the army had sent her while I was a POW. So in terms of finances, I could quit my job and just concentrate on school. The counselor had warned me that I was going to have to make up all these courses I had not taken in high school, and they would be accelerated courses and probably hard for me. The first semester I took twenty-three units, and when Jessie found out, she said, "Ed, for God's sake, you're just starting off and if you fail, it's just going to knock you back. Take the normal load—

fifteen, sixteen units. If you want to stretch it, maybe eighteen, but definitely not more." So I decided, "Okay, that's probably good advice," and I cut back to sixteen units. Then, at the end of the semester, she read in the junior college paper that I had made the honor roll. I said, "What's that?" And she said, "That means you hold a certain grade point average." I didn't think it was any big deal because, after all, I was just taking preliminary courses. Then the second semester of my freshman year, she said, "Ed, you're on the honor roll again!" I said, "I'm not paying attention to grades. I'm just pounding the books." I guess like everything else I have ever tried, I always put my heart and soul into it. For two years in a row, I made the honor roll, and Jess was more amazed than I was—that I could actually make good grades and finish JC in two years.

One of the best teachers I had at the junior college was Mr. Van Ewert, who taught history and philosophy. He had been an intelligence officer in the navy. One day we were just gassing, and he said, "You people have the wrong idea about my being an intelligence officer. I was in intelligence because I have a history background. A lot of what is called 'intelligence' is just basic research." Up to that point, I had studied history in school but had never been able to relate to it. Right from the beginning, Mr. Van Ewert told us, "I know some of you people don't want to be here, but you have to be here. The first thing I will tell you is that you're not required to memorize any dates, because you can always look that up in the almanac. What I want you to do is to be able to see history as a continuous, evolving story of mankind." And he added, "You people who have been through World War II do not think of yourself as being part of history. Twenty years from now, you will begin to see that you were part of history. No matter how small a part you played, you were there."

I remember I would get really engrossed in the papers I had to do for his class. One day, as he was handing me back my paper, he asked me, "Ed, what's your major?" I said, "Chemistry." And he said, "You really should think about history as your major. I can tell from the paper you wrote that you love it." I said, "I love it in the sense that you have piqued my interest by making history a living thing, but I can't change my major, because I'm Chinese." He seemed puzzled, "What does that have to do with your changing your major?" I said, "Well, being practical, I have to think about making a living." He said, "Don't worry about making a living. Do what you enjoy, and the living part will take care of itself." And I said, "No, I'm sorry Mr. Van Ewert, we're brought up to be more practical than that." It's the kind of advice that older people give to young people, who don't have the perspective yet to see how right the advice is. Later, I learned about the Chinese saying, "Get a job you love and you'll never work a day in your life." So maybe he was right, and I was too practical. But that's water over the dam now, except that I do think about it often. I think about how people like Mr. Van Ewert can influence a person's life, even in the short time that I knew him.

MY FIRST MARRIAGE

Jess thought that I should get to know people and have a normal life of dating, so she suggested the Chinese church might be a good place to start. That was where I got acquainted with my first wife. Apparently, no one had ever seriously dated her because—to put it kindly—she was a very naive person. We're talking about a person who in her early twenties still did not know how to take the streetcar by herself. She was overly protected. In a way, I married her for all the wrong reasons. I saw this helpless person, and I couldn't see any reason for it. I thought I could help bring her out of her shell. For her part, she wanted to get away from her parents and try being married. But that didn't work, because we stayed in the same town. I won't say it was all her fault, because at that time my libido was overriding a lot of things. I remember these old-timers in Bakersfield used to tell me, "Ed, right now, your sex drive is almost dictating to you. The most peaceful time of your life will be when your sex drive is down." I thought, "Gee, must be sour grapes." Only in retrospect could I see the wisdom of what they were saying. To make matters worse, we got married shortly after I had started junior college. To take on two major events in my life at the same time was just not a good idea.

She was so protected that she didn't know what life was all about, and that was partly the reason why we got divorced two years later. When we got married, her mother wanted to buy her a mink coat. I said, "Mrs. Lee, I can't even afford to put that thing in storage, much less have her wear it."

Then when her mother found out that I was going to transfer to Stanford, she started talking about buying a house up in Palo Alto so that she and her husband could move up there. (I found out later that my wife had been adopted, and her adoptive parents made a big deal about revealing this to her when she became twenty-one years old. My feeling was that they should tell her only if and when she expressed interest in knowing.) What happened was that right before I finished my second year of JC, she had a nervous breakdown. I was just getting ready for my finals and I probably wasn't paying her as much attention as I should have. Of course, instead of getting her the professional care that she needed, her parents were saying, "She was never like this before she got married to you." I said, "I'm perfectly willing to take any and all blame. The important thing now is to get her professional help."

We decided to put her in a psychiatric clinic in Los Angeles, where she underwent insulin shock. Insulin shock was supposed to be more benign than electrical shock, but shock is shock—to overload anyone's system with insulin is inhumane. When I visited her at the clinic, she begged me to take her home, but I couldn't because I had to follow the best medical advice I could get at that time. My brother-in-law Jim, who was a psychologist, kept telling me, "If you weaken at this stage and take her home, she'll never get well, and it may get worse. You've got to gut it through, Ed." Then after she was out of the hospital, the dilemma became: "Does she stay with me or go back to her parents?" She decided she was more comfortable with her parents. I didn't dispute it. I decided, "This is at least one decision you are going to make on your own."

By the time I transferred to Stanford, the divorce was in interlocutory. The next time I saw her, she was attending San Jose State College and living in a sorority house. I asked her how she was doing, and she said, "Fine." I said, "Look like you'll finish?" And she said, "Oh, no problem." I said, "You're getting on with your life? You're seeing other people?" And she said, "Oh, yeah." I wanted her to know that I was still concerned about her, and that was about the extent of it. I didn't feel that an apology would do any good—it would almost be like crocodile tears. I never got over the fact that I had meddled in her life and in the process caused her to have a mental breakdown. If I had not married her, or if I had been more attentive to her needs, it might not have happened. Other than killing someone, I don't think there is any greater offense you can do to another person than to hurt them. And, as I had been brought up to believe that every wrongdoing has its price, I decided not to take a degree from Stanford, even though I had completed all the requirements for graduation. That was the price I chose to pay for contributing to my wife's breakdown.

GOING TO STANFORD

My JC teacher, Miss Horn, had advised me to apply to Stanford, UC Berkeley, and Reed College when it was time for me to move on to upper-division work. I was accepted at all three, but I chose Stanford because the advisor at Reed was not very encouraging and I didn't want to go to Cal since everyone else in my family had gone there—I wanted to maintain my reputation as the "black sheep" of the family. As it turned out, that may not have been the best move for me, because I had to switch from a semester to a quarter system, and the atmosphere at Stanford was quite different. The classes were much larger and more impersonal, and I saw more of the TA's than the professors. Then, just before finals in my junior year, I picked up a case of poison oak. I had a car, and I used to go out into the hills to study. Coming back, I drove through some smoke, and immediately I felt the itch. Somebody had been burning some brush and it had poison oak in it. Before that night was over, I had broken out all over. The people in the infirmary offered, "We can tell the professors that you should put off your finals." But I didn't want to ask for any special favors, so I took the finals without having time to cram for them. I passed with C's, and that set me back. I didn't do much better in my senior year. It wasn't that the work was hard; I just found it hard adjusting to Stanford. And my feeling guilty over the divorce didn't help matters.

While at Stanford, I lived in the Stanford Village dorms with eight other vets. The janitors told us the dorms had previously been the psych wards for the Veterans Administration, and we thought that was pretty apropos. I asked for and got a room all to myself, because privacy was something I had never had in Chinatown, at the ranch, in the army, and certainly not in the camps. But I hung out with the other vets more than anyone else. We never

FIG. 29. *Eddie (right) with his nephew Herbie (left) in San Francisco while on summer break from Stanford, 1951.*

talked about our war experiences; it was just that we felt we had more in common. For instance, the first time I ever tried to stop smoking was with Eugene "Rip" Rypka. I had picked up the habit after the war. Rip was going for his PhD and he lived in the dorm next to me. We were studying for a chemistry exam, and it was two o'clock in the morning when we suddenly realized we were both out of cigarettes. Without saying a word, we both started ripping apart cigarette butts and putting the tobacco in one pile. Then Rip looked up and said, "What are we going to do for paper, Ed?" And I said, "Rip, this is good old U.S. of A. If nothing else, there's toilet paper, there's newspaper, and even our textbooks are made out of paper. Don't worry about paper." So we got some tissue paper, rolled the cigarettes, lit up, and took a deep draw. Then we looked at each other, and I said, "It's kind of silly for two grown men to act like this—let's quit!" Of course, that didn't last long, and it wasn't until after I married Lois that I gave up smoking for good.

In my senior year, they teamed me up with a Japanese American by the name of Seiji Kami. He had been interned at Heart Mountain during the war. Toward the end of the war, someone came by his camp and asked if anyone wanted to learn how to be a mechanic. Wanting to get out of the internment camp, Seiji volunteered. So that was how Seiji learned to become a master mechanic. During spring break of our senior year, my '41

Chevy started to sound sick, and Seiji offered to overhaul the engine for me at his uncle's home in San Mateo. After we pulled the car into the garage, he looked at me and said, "I know you guys in the army always brag about how you can strip any weapon that you use blindfolded. I'm going to show you I can strip an engine down blindfolded." I said, "Oh, Seiji, I'm not going to fall for that." And he said, "You watch." First thing we did, we drained the oil out of the engine crankcase. Then the next morning, Seiji laid out newspapers all over the garage, and he started stripping that engine blindfolded and putting the parts exactly where he wanted them. In a matter of a day and a half, he had overhauled the engine completely and it was running like a Swiss watch. And he said, "That's what I was taught—to be a master mechanic."

So if he was a master mechanic, what was he doing in college? Well, he was going with a girl who was a schoolteacher. Amy knew that Seiji could make a good living being a master mechanic, but she said, "I'm not going to marry you unless you have a college degree." So Seiji decided, "Okay, closest thing to that would be mechanical engineering." He eventually graduated and got married. I said, "Gee, Seiji, I don't know, I think I would have looked for another girl." He said, "Oh, no. Amy and I are meant for each other. And if that's what she wants, I'll be a mechanical engineer." I have to hand it to him, because he was willing to sacrifice four years of his life to get that degree for her.

One other time Seiji walked into our room with a Japanese fellow, and I figured, "It's probably just someone he knows." And he said, "Ed, I want to introduce you to so-and-so." This guy bowed to me, and I bowed to him, and Seiji was off to the side laughing. I said, "What's the joke, Seiji?" He said, "This man was with the Java invasion forces." I said, "Oh, no!" And the fellow said, "Oh, don't worry, I wasn't a fighting man. Back then I was with supplies. But I was part of the invasion force." It turned out that he was over here for an advanced degree in economics. All I could think of was how small the world was getting to be.

Overall, I didn't have a bad time at Stanford. It was just that I was still getting over my divorce. I tried going to the VA (Veterans Administration) Hospital in San Francisco for psychiatric advice. But after a year of one-to-one therapy, I stopped going because nothing good came of it—my guilt never felt less. I pretty much isolated myself; I didn't go to any of the big games or join any clubs. Anyone who needed an extra ticket for a girlfriend or parent knew I was a soft touch. I didn't even go on any dates, except once, and that one time earned me a bad reputation with one of the sororities. I had taken June Wong out for coffee, and what happened was that I didn't have my car at the time. So we walked to a coffee shop in Palo Alto. It was about a mile and a quarter away, and I didn't think anything of it. We had our coffee and walked back. The following day, one of her sorority sisters said, "You took June out for coffee, right?" I said, "Yes." She said, "When she got home, she plopped down on the bed and went to sleep immediately with all her clothes on—she was so pooped." She said everyone got a laugh out of it. And that was the last time I saw June or went out on a date until I met Lois in 1955.

A METALLURGIST AT WESTERN GEAR

Near the end of my senior year I went to the employment office at Stanford, and I said, "What does it look like for a chem lab technician around here?" They looked up some data and they said, "Western Gear is looking for a lab technician." So I went there and was interviewed by the personnel manager. He took me out to see the metallurgist, who was George Leghorn, and George said, "Here's what I need you to do, that's what the job requirements are." And I said, "That's simple. I think any first year chem student could do that." He said, "If you want the job, you can have it." And that was how I got started at Western Gear in Belmont, a little town located thirty miles south of San Francisco.

What they had there was a lot of plating solutions associated with the heat-treating plant. All the chemicals in the various tanks had to be kept to a certain standard. My job was to check them daily and make the adjustments necessary to bring them up to the required standards. I found out that even if I did my job conscientiously, I still had about four hours left in the day, so I spent the time observing what the other half of the plant was doing and reading up on the lab work. After a while, I told George, "I'm only working about four hours a day on the plating report. If there's anything I can do to help you, let me know." So he started to give me little jobs, which had nothing to do with chemistry. Pretty soon I was spending as much time with metallurgy as I was with chemistry. And that was how I got into metallurgy. Nowadays, they call it "material science." (That's the technology they use to come up with the new aluminum skis and stiff but springy tennis rackets.) After I had been working a year, George said, "I put in for an assistant. If you want the job, I'll give you a try." I said, "George, you can hire any four-year degree man for $400 a month." But he said, "I know that, Ed, but I think you're a natural. What you don't know or can't learn from books, I'll teach you." So that was how I got hired on as an assistant metallurgist.

Six months later, the plant manager, Bill Heard, called me in and he said, "Ed, we're going to give you a raise of seventy-five dollars." I said, "Okay, thanks. Is that all, sir? I want to get back to work." Six months later, he called me in again and he told me, "You got another raise coming, Ed." I said, "Mr. Heard, it would save us both a lot of time if you didn't call me in. I'll notice on my paycheck if you gave me a raise. I can be doing my work instead of getting the details from you first hand." Then the word got around the plant that I was abrupt with the plant manager. You see, when I get involved with work or a job, I always throw myself completely at it. It was that way when I started delivering papers when I was eleven and again when I worked at the ranch. There's no other way I know how to do a job.

The plant ran twenty-four hours a day, and I put in whatever hours were necessary to do my job. I remember early on in '53, I went through a year of insomnia. So during that time, when I couldn't sleep, I thought I might as well work. So there was another rumor that went around the plant about me: "Ed doesn't sleep." One day, Thelma, the bookkeeper, came over to the plant, and she said, "Ed, there's a mistake in your time card." I said, "How so? I'm almost positive I filled it in correctly." She said, "Well, according to your time sheet, you came in on Monday and you didn't check out until Friday." I said, "I was here." And she said, "What did you do about meals?" I said, "I just called on the phone and had them delivered." She said, "You mean you never left the plant physically?" I said, "No." Thelma said, "I never heard of such a thing." I said, "You can check with the journeymen if you want. I was here all the time." And she said, "I believe you, but I've never encountered it before." And I said, "You better stand by for a lot more, because I'm unpredictable." It wasn't a matter of paying me overtime, because I was paid the same amount each month regardless of how many hours I put in. It was just that at the time, I was having insomnia and I was really into my new job.

PTSD HITS

After my discharge I noticed I had this shortness of temper. I just couldn't put up with people who whined about things—like shortages after the war—or people who were basically selfish about getting their way. One time, I was crossing the street, and some guy in a car started beeping at another car and yelling something about the ineptness of the driver. I felt like punching him out simply because he wasn't giving any allowances for other people's shortcomings. He was only concerned about his getting somewhere, and I was thinking, "Even if you get there in a hurry, chances are it's going to be just like the army, and you're going to have to wait." I think things like that put me into a state of rage because we had gotten so used to helping each other out in the camps. I always wondered, "How come other people can't do that? Do they have to be put in a situation like ours before they can learn to treat each other as human beings?" This went on for at least three, four years after the war. I had to watch myself because I was afraid I might strike out. Rather than solve anything, it would have just created more problems.

It was at that point that I went to the VA Hospital in San Francisco and told them, "I have these uncontrollable urges to punch people out for practically no reason at all." Well, the first thing he did was reach into the drawer and offer me some pills. I told him, "No, I don't want to take pills. I want to find out why I'm having these uncontrollable periods of anger." He said, "Well, that's all we have to offer you." I said, "If that's the best you can do, then I'll have to try and resolve it myself." I finally figured out that I had a very low tolerance for people's selfish behaviors, and that the best thing for me to do was stay away from people, period. That didn't solve the problem, but at least I could distance myself from the problem. That wasn't hard to do, because I was basically a loner anyway.

What was it that the author Gavan Daws said? "Memories are buried in a very shallow grave." In other words, they can surface almost anytime, sparked by the backfire of a car, sudden noises, or airplanes. They are suppressed so that we can get on with our normal lives. That's why, as POW survivors, we all had phobias, except that ours were so bizarre that people probably wondered why. To this day, many of us still refuse to eat anything that looks orangey, that reminds us of pumpkin or yam. Pee Wee England had two giant freezers full of food. I used to hoard twenty pounds of coffee in the house and drink thirty cups a day. At one time, some of the guys drank as if distilleries were going out of business, and they smoked like chimneys. The year after we got back from the war, I heard that one of the guys committed suicide. I could never understand how anyone could have gone through what we did and then commit suicide. But I guess we all resolved our problems in our own way. That was why some of the wives almost had to be saints to put up with us in the early stages after the war. A couple of times early on in my marriage to Lois, I had nightmares. She would tell me the following morning that I had cried out or flailed out during the night, and I wasn't even aware of it.

I didn't think about my fits of anger and insomnia in terms of post-traumatic stress disorder until thirty-five years later, when the VA called me in because they had started a PTSD clinic. Actually, the Vietnam veterans got it started—they were the ones who made enough noise that someone finally listened. One of the nurses at the VA Hospital once told me that they could always tell the World War II from the Vietnam vets. The World War II vets will sit there all day and wait for their names to be called. The Vietnam people will come up every ten minutes and demand, "When am I going to be called?" Maybe we're too laid back, because nothing was ever done for us until the Vietnam vets started raising hell. Anyhow, all the POWs in California were called in because they felt that the trauma of being a prisoner was just as severe as that of being in actual combat.

I think all of us felt guilty when we came back because we were being treated as heroes just for having survived. But we never thought of ourselves as heroes. On the contrary, we thought that it was because we hadn't done enough to fight the Japanese that we had become prisoners. Looking at it rationally, there wasn't anything we could have done except die, and that won't have helped matters. It won't have changed the war; it won't have stopped the Japanese; it won't have changed the course of history one bit. But it would have made us feel better—that we had done our level best by paying the ultimate price of dying. The sense of guilt for us didn't surface until later—that's why they call it "posttraumatic." Any psychiatrist will tell you that you shouldn't feel guilty about surviving—that never eases your situation. Brody, my sergeant, was ten times the man I could ever be, and yet he died.[2] You know there's no point in beating yourself over the head because you survived and someone else didn't, but you can't help wondering why. I don't think you ever find an answer to questions like that. For me, I was working at a new job, so that usually took my mind off of anything that bothered me. As long as I kept busy, that was my solution to almost everything.

MY MARRIAGE TO LOIS

After I started my job at Western Gear, I buried myself in work, and my sisters were getting concerned about the fact that I had no social life. My sister Mints had a friend by the name of Emma who knew Lois. They had grown up together in Reno and they happened to be working in the same lab. Mints was saying, "I have a brother that's perfect for Lois," and Emma was saying, "And Lois is probably perfect for him, except how do we get these two people together? They don't go to church, they don't go to nightclubs, they don't really socialize." Then Emma found out that Lois had signed up for a class in social dancing at the YWCA in Berkeley, so Mints enrolled me in the same class. She called me on the phone and said, "I've enrolled you already. You ought to at least give it a try and learn how to dance." And I said, "Well, if you've gone to all that trouble, I'll try it out." So that was how I first got to meet Lois.

We were the only two Chinese in the class, and we started talking about our respective jobs. She worked as a microbiologist for the Water Sanitation Department in Berkeley. I remember saying, "I almost started to work there because I took the test for a chemistry position. If I had taken a job there, I would probably be your subordinate." We made light talk, but neither one of us was very good at it. She was more amused by my intense concentration when the instructor showed us the basic steps. She told me later, "I have never seen such intensity in a person, and all we were doing was learning dance steps." And I said, "Well, you're going to find out that when I start to learn anything new, I get very intense about it." There was no instant chemistry; there was no instant attraction. But a month later, when my birthday came around, I decided to use that as an excuse to ask her for a date, to help me celebrate my birthday. After dinner, she said, "Would you like to have coffee at my place?" When I hesitated, she said, "Don't worry, I live with my father. We'll be well chaperoned." When we got to her flat, lo and behold, she had a birthday cake! She set out the candles and she said, "Happy birthday, Ed." It turned out that she had baked the cake herself, and if there's any way you can get to me, it's through my stomach.

A couple of weeks later, I called her up and asked her to go out to dinner. She said, "Ed, do you really enjoy going out to dinner? We can have dinner at home." And she said, "Do you like Chinese food?" I said, "I love Chinese food." From then on, it was almost a natural evolution, because we found out that we both liked Chinese food, and I found out that she could cook almost any kind of Chinese food for any occasion. Her father had run a restaurant with his wife in Reno for many years, so the whole family knew something about cooking. Then we found out that we were not church-going people, but we were moral—we had standards. We both thought of God as female, as Mother Nature, as a gentler force than the vindictive God who burned down Sodom and Gomorrah for some infraction or another. Politically, we were both Democrats, not that it mattered that much, but it made things a lot easier. And she could read and write Chinese with proficiency.

After I got to know her, I said, "How many years of Chinese school did you have?" She said, "Only about three years." And I said, "How in the world did you learn so much Chinese in such a short time?" She answered, "Well, when I was a little girl, my father would hold me in his arms while he was reading the Chinese paper, and pretty soon he would start reading aloud, and his finger would follow what he was reading." And she said, "I'm not sure that you can learn Chinese that way, but from the time I was two or three years, I remember doing that." Unlike me, she said she had no trouble learning Chinese at all. The family had gone back to China at least two times before the war in the 1930s, and each time they had stayed a few months. That probably helped her become more proficient in Chinese as well.

As far as courting was concerned, we're not talking about flowers and candy and that sort of thing. It was more of getting to know each other, what our likes and dislikes were. We would go window-shopping or to the light opera, even though I wasn't too crazy about either, or we would sit home and listen to classical music. Then I found out that she was an avid bridge player, and that was when I found out there was an absolutely other side to this person—she was a card shark. But cooking was the main thing we both loved, and I learned a lot more about Chinese cooking from her. The other thing I noticed about her: Whenever we came back to Chinatown from a walk downtown, as soon as we crossed California Street (into Chinatown)—and we might have been holding hands or arm in arm—she would sweep away, about a foot apart. I instinctively knew that was the proper thing to do, but it took me a while to figure that one out. In those days, outward display of affection was just not done as far as the Chinese were concerned, and we both knew to observe what was proper. The highest compliment I could pay her would be, "I think if my mom could have picked out a wife for me, she would have approved of you." That was because we were both Chinese in our cultural and philosophical outlooks. Even though we both worked outside, where we were in daily contact with *sai yun* (Westerners), as far as our personal lives were concerned, it was dictated by our Chinese background.

As I soon found out, Lois was a very quiet person, but she had this nice, soft-spoken kind of humor that kind of knocks you over like a steamroller when it hits. We were sitting down one time when we were still courting, and I said to her, "Lois, I'm going to ask your father for your hand." She looked at me and she said, "Is that all you want?" That was when I knew, "She's the one; she's absolutely the one!" We made an agreement right from the beginning. She was thirty-six, and I was thirty-four when we got married, and we said we were not going to try to have children. We both said, "If it happens, it happens; if it doesn't, it doesn't." As it turned out, we did not have children. So one time when we were at a POW reunion, one of the ladies asked Lois if we had any children, and she answered, "We don't have any, but I have one." "Oh," the lady said, "from a previous marriage?" Lois said, "Oh, no, this is my first marriage." Then she pointed at me and said, "That's my kid."

After a couple of months, we were pretty sure that we wanted to get married. I knew she was apprehensive at first because she had heard stories about my divorce. All I could tell her was, "What you see is what you get. That's all there is." I had to also take into consideration that she was living with her father, and I wanted to make sure that it was okay with him. I wanted him to know that I was gaining a father-in-law and he was gaining a son-in-law, and he was welcome to live with us as long as he wanted. We got married in church, not because either one of us was a churchgoer, but because we didn't want something as cold as a civil ceremony at City Hall. And we picked the Unitarian Church because it was nondenominational. My brother Bill was the best man, and Emma was the matron of honor. Then we invited the immediate family to a Chinese banquet at the Far East Café in Chinatown.

We went on a month-long camping trip to Canada for our honeymoon. Lois didn't like it at all, because when I go camping, it's just a sleeping bag and a tent, although on this trip, I found a campground with hot water for showers. The first morning, there was a solid mass of horseflies on the screen door. The next night, it was mosquitoes. She asked me at that point, "How can you enjoy this?" I said, "Sometimes, there are things which get in the way of enjoyment, but most of the time, you don't have these aggravations." We went camping every year for the next eight years. Lois was willing to put up with it because she knew I enjoyed it, but the other reason was for us to do some shopping for her father. When he found out that we were going to Canada, he made a shopping list—Chinese herbs. Back in those days, it was illegal to bring it in because the U.S. had broken off diplomatic relations with Communist China in 1949. We would buy all this stuff from this store in Vancouver, and after we had camped for about three weeks, we would head east and return via Montana or some out-of-the-way place to avoid detection. Her daddy was *so* happy—it was like Christmas for him. Almost every day, he would open the packages and look at them to make sure they weren't getting wormy, or he would put them out in the sun so there was less chance of them getting wormy. So every year that we went

up to Vancouver, he was like a little kid. He would write out his Christmas list, and since he got so much enjoyment out of it, we just went ahead and did it. Lois asked me, "Aren't you worried about bringing illegal stuff in?" I said, "No, no, I just look upon it like trying to run the guard shack when the Japanese were in charge. The only difference is, we have the U.S. in charge. Otherwise, the basic principle is the same. They're the antagonists and we're the protagonists." After her father passed away, we stopped going. It was less fun, and there really wasn't that much that we wanted from Canada. By then Lois had started attending the annual reunions in Texas with me, and we were starting to take longer trips to Asia.

Lois was the kind of person I had been looking for all my life. Six years after our marriage, Dr. Hekking came over from the Netherlands with his family for a visit. They were in the States to check out a son-in-law—that was how old fashioned they were. He called me from Fisherman's Wharf, and before Doc arrived, I told Lois, "Whatever we have which is mine belongs to that man. If I find that he needs anything, I'll freely give it to him, but not what is yours, what is communal property." Without knowing anything about Dr. Hekking, she agreed. She was a very understanding person. Whenever I go out to eat, I usually eat everything that is in front of me, including the garnish. So one time she said, "Ed, can you at least leave the garnish?" "Gee, Lois," I said, "I'm sorry, I didn't mean to embarrass you. I just cannot waste food." She said, "I understand, but you can make adjustments."

Lois was the one who taught me that being Chinese wasn't just about being born Chinese and looking Chinese. There were things you did that made you Chinese, like being part of a family and celebrating the holidays. Of course, her customs and foods were particular to Toishan people, and my folks were from Enping District. For instance, on Chinese New Year's Eve, she would put a pair of tangerines, preferably with leaves on them, to show that they're flourishing, in each room. And she would cook a pot of rice that could feed an army, because we had to have plenty of leftover rice

FIG. 30. *Lois and Eddie on their wedding day, July 8, 1956.*

FIG. 31. *Eddie with his siblings on his wedding day. Left to right, front row: Grace, Jessie, Mints, and Mary; back row: Al, Pee Wee, Eddie, and Bill.*

to start off the new year with. She would leave the lights on to greet the new year, and, of course, clean the house beforehand. It was not just the fact that she knew all about the Chinese customs; she actually lived them. She would tell me about these sayings that her mother had taught her for different situations. And for every occasion, whether it was New Year's, Dragon Boat Festival, Moon Festival, Ching Ming, or whatever, she would tell me what the appropriate foods were and the stories behind them. She had an enormous store of knowledge that she was willing to pass on to me, and that just made Chinese culture come alive for me. In essence, Lois helped me develop as a Chinese person. It was kind of like the old trite saying about how the criminal always returns to the scene of the crime. So here I was, running like mad from Chinatown, and I was back and enjoying it. As she said, "The fact that you don't speak Chinese should not preclude you from being Chinese." Of course, all my siblings were amused that I had become so Chinese compared to them.

MOVING FROM WESTERN GEAR TO LIVERMORE LAB

I had been working at Western Gear for eight or nine years when this new plant manager took over, and he decided he was going to cut costs. We had been producing gear parts for tanks for over ten years, and each set of gears had to be certified to military specifications. He called me into the office one day, and he said, "Ed, how long have we been making gears?" I said, "Well, as far back as I can remember, and before that probably." He said, "Have we ever failed a certification?" I said, "No, sir. We've been audited, and they've checked all our samples, and they're satisfied we're telling them the truth." "Well," he said, "Why don't you just go ahead and sign the certifications and not perform the test?" And I said, "I can't do that. If I put my name on a piece of paper, it means it's been done." "But," he said, "think of all the money we'll save." So I told him, "There's a very simple way that we can do this. You can sign the certifications; I won't do it." A friend of mine heard about it, and he said, "Ed, what you got to do is start writing letters to protect yourself." I said, "Carter, I work for Western Gear. If I have to protect myself from Western Gear, what am I doing here?" That was when I told Lois that I was going to have to quit. "There's no way in the world I can work with that person from this point on. He'll never forget it, and neither will I."

By then I had become buddies with Bill Watson, who had been captured in the Philippines. I overheard him talking to another foreman during our lunch break about the things that he had had to eat, and I turned around and said, "Bill, you must have been taken in the Philippines." He looked at me and said, "Yeah, how did you know?" I said, "I was also a guest of the Japanese." So Watson asked me, "Where were you taken?" I said, "Java." And he said, "I didn't know we had troops in Java." I said, "It's not generally known, but there was one battalion of artillery there." He said, "What in the hell was the artillery doing there with no infantry?" I said, "Who knows? We just went because we were ordered to go." Then he found out I had wound up going up to Burma to work on the railroad, and he said, "Oh, you guys had it rough." I said, "Well, from what I can gather, it was no picnic being in Japan with the severe winters they have. At least in the tropics, weather is fairly temperate the year round." And he said, "Yeah, there's that to be said about it." Right away, he and I bonded. So one of the other reasons I decided to quit Western Gear was that they had fired Watson for no particular reason at all. I protested and said that was no way to treat a good foreman. I guess that didn't go over too well with management either, aside from the fact that I had refused to do what they had asked of me. So I knew that my time was getting pretty short at Western Gear. I quit Western Gear on my fortieth birthday.

It wasn't long before I found a job at Livermore Laboratory doing what I wanted to do—research. Lee Roberts knew that I had worked as a metallurgist, but he didn't know that I didn't have a degree until I applied for the job. He said, "Ed, I know you've been working as a metallurgist, but my hands are tied. Unless you have a degree, I can't hire you as a metallurgist. But I'll do the next best thing—I'll make you a technologist." I didn't care, because as long as I was doing the kind of work that was interesting to me, that was all that mattered. Western Gear had been basically a production line, whereas at Livermore, I worked on research projects. The physicist would come to the materials department and say, "We want a material that will withstand this number of pounds of pressure under these ambient conditions, plus at 125 degrees all the way down to 0, and we want this material to be able to hold this pressure for five years." There was no such material, so we had to basically design the alloy. That was what made the job interesting in the sense that it wasn't cut and dry. It was always something that had never been done before. A lot of the work had to do with nuclear devices and was top secret at the time. We were only responsible for making the prototype. Once the design was finalized and all the bugs worked out, then someone else took over the production of the device.

When I first started at Livermore, I made a hundred dollars less than at Western Gear. Within a year, I had made that up. Then, counting all the time I was there—a total of fourteen years—I made more money than I would have if I had stayed at Western Gear. I had told Lois, "I will be getting less money to begin with, but I think the future is brighter in the sense that there's more room for advancement." That turned out to be true. But more importantly, Lois was my safety net. She was working, and even if I couldn't find a job for a year or two, I knew that she would be willing to carry me, give me credit. Still, fortunately for me, there was no time lag from one job to the other.

MY LOST BATTALION BUDDIES

Ever since that big parade in Wichita Falls in 1945, the guys had been getting together every year in Texas around August 15th, the official V-J Day. Actually, it was the wives and mothers who really started the whole thing. From the time we were reported missing-in-action in September of 1942, they kept bugging the War Department about our whereabouts. When the War Department said they didn't know what had happened to us, they asked, "How can you lose a whole battalion of men?" The news media picked up on that, and by the time we finally returned, we were known as the "Texas Lost Battalion."[3] Soon after, the Lost Battalion Association was formed, consisting of survivors of the 2nd Battalion and the USS Houston. I had lost touch with them and didn't even know they were having these annual reunions. So I didn't start attending until 1964, when Buck Lawley, who was president that year, called me up about it. Lois was apprehensive about going because she didn't know what to expect. When we got to Odessa, where the reunion was held that year, we were met at the airport by John Owens and a bunch of other guys. John gave me a big hug and said to Lois, "Mrs. Fung, I won't hug any other man like this except Eddie because I love him." Even in '64—and we're talking about twenty years after the fact—it was as if we had just seen each other last week. The bond was so strong that even if we hadn't seen each other for twenty years, we knew we still loved each other.

We got to the reunion headquarters and right away I realized that I could recognize the faces, but with all their clothes on, I couldn't remember everybody's names. For instance, the cook who was with us all the way came up to me and said, "You remember me, don't you Eddie?" Recognizing his voice, I immediately said, "Pinky!" even though his nametag said Garth. He said, "You remember!" And I said, "To tell you the truth, I never knew that your Christian name was Garth. I always used Pinky." Then I noticed Pinky had on a beautiful pair of cowboy boots, and I was admiring them. And he said, "Eddie, you like these boots?" "Oh," I said, "they're beautiful." He started to take them off. I said, "Pinky, Pinky, the most I want to know is who made them. I don't want them. We're probably not even the same size." Afterwards, when we were alone, Lois said, "Are they all like that because you've been prisoners?" I said, "Well, the basic nature of a Texan is to be hospitable to begin with, but with Pinky, it's not a gesture—he means it. He will literally give me the boots off his feet. So I have to be careful about what I say because they'll take me literally."

The following morning I was down in the lobby and I was inquiring at the car rental agency about the rates. Paul Leatherwood, for whom I had scrounged barbering scissors when we were in camp, saw me and he asked, "Do you need a car, Eddie?" I said, "No, no, I'm just making inquiries in case I do need one." He said, "I've got cars at home. If you want a car, just let me know, and I'll have one of the kids bring it over." Lois asked me afterwards, when we got home, "Does Paul really mean that?" I said, "You're going to have to learn one thing. They always mean what they say and they say what they mean." She wasn't used to that. And I said, "That's the way we are." I tried to explain to her that we were almost like family, except for one difference: "Family, you can't avoid because you're born into it. With us, we want to stay in touch, so we're closer than family." And I said, "There's no blood involved except the blood and tears that we have suffered together."

Lois had asked me before, "What do you guys do for three days? Tell war stories?" I said, "Oh no, that's the last thing we do." And I asked her, "How many close friends do you have?" She said, "Probably three or four." I said, "Well, with this group of men, we're all close friends, and there's no need for pretense. They don't care if I'm dressed in a three-hundred-dollar suit or Levi's and a T-shirt, they know me for who I am. It doesn't matter whether I'm poor or rich. If I were wealthy, they would be happy for me. If I were poor and needed money, they would probably help me out." I explained to her that we didn't usually talk about the war, except in passing. Of course, when they met Lois, they all wanted to tell Lois stories about me. I would tell Lois, "I don't remember half of the things they're saying that I did." They would all say, "Oh, he did it all right." And I would believe them, because among friends, there's no need to color a story. Like the time this sailor by the name of Bruckner grabbed me and said, "One hundred pounds of sugar, Eddie!" For the life of me, I didn't know what he was talking about until someone said, "Don't you remember, Eddie, when you dragged that one hundred pounds of sugar from the Japanese kitchen back to the hut?" I said that I remembered the sugar, but I didn't remember it being one hundred pounds. But everyone said they remembered it was one hundred pounds because they couldn't figure out how I did it. And Lois dug an elbow in my rib and said, "But you only weighed 103 pounds!"

When Lois passed on in 1999 and I didn't show up at the reunion that year, Mrs. Pryor's daughter JoAnne was thoughtful enough to send me the rose that was presented at the memorial service in Lois' honor. Usually before the business meeting, we have a memorial service for the members or their wives who had passed on the previous year. JoAnne sent it to me with a very nice note expressing their condolences. They knew there was nothing that they could do about my loss, but they wanted me to know that they felt my loss just the same. And I knew that it was meant with all sincerity, that the heart was really in it. It's a nice feeling to know that I have friends like that—who care about me, and who will do anything for me. And it works the other way, too. Until the day I die, if any of the guys need my help, they know I'll be around to help them.

FIG. 32. *Eddie (front row, third from left) at the Lost Battalion reunion in Dallas, Texas, 2003.*

FIG. 33. *Eddie (left) with his POW buddies at the Lost Battalion reunion in Dallas, Texas, 2005: Eldridge Rayburn (back), Willie Hoover (front), and Jack Kenner (right).*

When I think about it, Lois and I did a lot of traveling together. We would drive down to Texas every year for the reunion. Then we would intersperse it with longer trips to Japan, China, Australia, Singapore, Thailand, and Hong Kong. On our first trip to Japan in 1968, I was feeling apprehensive because I didn't know how I would react to any bad memories that it might trigger. But when I saw these old soldiers in their uniforms begging with their little caps in their hands, I felt absolutely no animosity toward them. I was thinking, "We didn't have any hard feelings for them after the war, and I don't have any hard feelings now." It was very easy for me to imagine myself in that situation. And I thought, "There but for the grace of God go I."

On our next trip to the Orient, we decided to take in Bangkok. Once we got to Thailand, we hired a car and chauffeur to take us to Kanburi. The place where the camp had been was now a big bus depot. I walked up there, and the driver said, "What are you looking for?" And I said, "I'm looking for the moat that was built by POWs during the war. Ask one of the older residents if they can remember a moat around this area." He finally found someone who was there during World War II, and he said, "Oh, yeah, we remember. How come you want to find it?" The driver said, "Well, this man was there." I said, "I was not only there, I helped to build the moat."

We got to talking, and the driver wanted to show me the famous bridge on the River Kwai. I said, "We'll get to that later." I wanted to go where the Japanese headquarters used to be, where I did my best scrounging. So I said, "Let's walk down to the river." And he said, "You can't go to the river from here." I said, "This was the junction where we either split off to go to work at the river or Japanese headquarters. I know the way." But he insisted, "There's no way you can go to the river from here." I said, "Yes, there is. Ask the people at the village." Sure enough, the villagers pointed the way. When we got to the river, he said, "How did you know?" I said, "I used to work here." We went to Tamarkan, and I showed him where the anti-aircraft gun placements had been. "This is where we were bombed by the Americans," I told him. He was a professional tour guide in his mid-forties, and he didn't know any of these things. I said, "You tell the tourists all about the bridge, but there's more to the history of the railroad than just the bridge. You should find out all about it." I don't know if he ever did or not, but he was amazed to know that Americans had worked on the railroad.

We made a second trip to Thailand in 1980. We could have gone as far as the Three Pagoda Pass on the Burma side, but I didn't want to take a chance of going there unless I could apply for a visa. The Australians could easily do that because their country had been on friendly terms with the Burmese government, whereas the U.S. had not. Interestingly enough, this time the steel bridge on the River Kwai looked different to me. When I saw it in 1969, twenty-four years after the war, it looked as big as the Golden Gate Bridge. But when I went back in 1980, I saw it from a different perspective. I could reach up and almost touch the arch spans. It was kind of like these stories you hear about a person going back to his room where he grew up as a kid, and now it looks so tiny. So in '69 the bridge was still huge in my eyes, but in '80 I finally saw it in its real size.

Someday, I would like to go back to Moulmein and see if that convent is still there. I suspect that many of the people who threw packages of candy and cigarettes at us as we marched from Moulmein prison to go to Thanbyuzayat came from that building. I want to find out more about why they were willing to risk the wrath of the Japanese by being kind to us. Other than that, I would like to walk or drive along the railroad line and see what is left of the railroad, if anything. The only other prominent landmark for me would be the Thanbyuzayat cemetery. From the pictures I've seen, it looks fairly well maintained. There's only so much I can do about revisiting memories of a place from the Thailand side when it was the Burma side where we had worked and experienced our worst moments.

In 1981 Lois and I visited our ancestral villages in Enping and Toishan. From Shanghai we took a train down to Guangzhou, and from there, we took a local bus to my village, Lei Yuen. When we arrived at the village, the first person we met was a cousin who happened to be spreading rice on a cement floor to dry. He looked up, and he said, "Who are you?" I replied, "I'm Lai Kwong's brother." (Lai Kwong was the Chinese name of my older brother, Al.) He looked at me and said, "Oh," and without knowing who I was except that I was Al's brother, he said, "Are you Ah Man or Ah Wai?" (In other words, "Are you Ed or Bill?") I said, "I am Ah Man." That was when I realized that my father had sent news back to the village when I was born so that I could be added to the genealogical records. Then he said, "Oh, why are you here?" So I pulled out the map that Al had drawn from memory. After they found out who I was, they were more than happy to show me around the village, the fields, and the orchards.

The village was laid out in about four rows of houses back to back, then there was the alley way and another row of houses back to back. There were about twenty houses in each row, so that made forty houses and roughly 160 families living in the village. Each house was about twenty by twenty feet. They had a loft to store extra grain and jars of things, and the lower level was where the kitchen and bedrooms were. The village was laid out exactly the way Al had drawn it. I walked to the house where my brother had lived, and nothing had changed. It was then that I realized why people didn't stay in the village if they had a chance to go abroad, because I could see it would be hard to make a living there. The hot climate reminded me of the jungles, and the land was overworked. It was basically subsistence farming. Their cash crops were from the fishponds and the orchards. As far as rice was concerned, they were lucky if they had enough from year to year.

All of us grew up knowing we were from Lei Yuen village and that we were Enping people. Even though we didn't know what that meant, we always knew where our roots were. When I went back to the village, there was no feeling of nostalgia or recognition of any changes. It was just the fact that the Communists, instead of allowing them to keep an ancestral hall, had turned it into a school. Instead of someone bidding on the fishpond, the fish now belonged to the entire village. In the old days, from year to year, the highest bidder would be the owner of all the fish in that pond, so he could sell it all and hopefully recoup his bid and more. Lei Yuen village was unique in having two fishponds instead of just one. But other than that, there was not much to the village. Although I know I'm from Lei Yuen, I've never considered it to be home. I've never considered myself to be Chinese. My feeling has always been that I am a human being first. I just happen to be of Chinese extraction, and I just happen to be an American because I was born in the U.S. But it's very seldom that I think of myself first as a Chinese. That trip to China and my ancestral village confirmed it.

RETIREMENT

I had been thinking about retiring since I was forty-five. I enjoyed my work at Livermore, but I yearned for the freedom to do whatever I wanted whenever I wanted. By then, we knew that we weren't going to have any children, and I had made enough outside investments that we didn't have to worry about money. So I asked Lois, "Would it be okay with you if I retired?" She said, "Ed, is there any special thing you want to do right now that you have to retire at forty-five?" I said, "No." And she said, "Well, as a suggestion, you will be able to carry your health plan into your retirement if you wait until you're fifty-five. I realize that ten years sounds like a long time, but why don't you wait and see what the next project is?" I had just finished a project, and each project usually took about five or six years to complete. So I waited. Before I knew it, I was fifty-five. I didn't have any real plans. It was just a good feeling to know that I was now completely my own man. I could take off, go camping, or do nothing.

It was a couple of months later when Lois said, "Didn't I hear you say one time that you wanted to learn tai chi?" She was reading the Chinese newspaper, and she saw an announcement about a class starting right down the street from us at the Telegraph Hill Center. She said, "And you don't have to pay anything because it's under the sponsorship of the community college. Why don't you go check it out?" So I decided, "That's exactly what I have been looking for." The class was only for three hours, but I would be there practicing an hour and a half before class. Then after class, I would practice another five or six hours. I was spending about eight, nine hours a day practicing, because I've always had two left feet and lack coordination. I had a hard time seeing each move, and after I saw it, I had a hard time duplicating it. Finally, I just applied the military system of breaking the components down to the simplest basics. It took me about six months to figure out what the basics of tai chi were, and once I figured that out, there was nothing to it.

According to Master Wong, when you're first doing tai chi, you're doing it from the outside in, you're doing it as a physical exercise. Eventually, when you get good, and you get your chi (internal energy) flowing, you will be doing it from the inside out, almost as if there's an irreversible force that's carrying you through the exercise. Thinking I was pretty hot stuff after about three years, I said, "How long will it take for me to do a perfect set?" Master Wong looked at me and said, "Never." And he said, "If you can't live with that, I think you better find something else, like karate, where you can go from a white belt to a black belt. In tai chi, you are trained to achieve perfection, but you will never really get there. Because even after you get to what you think is perfection, the chances are, someone can show you how to do it better. So don't worry about perfection. Just do the best you can with every move you make." That's what I love about tai chi—there's no competition involved, not even with yourself. You're just always trying to be better. I was thinking, "That wouldn't be a bad attitude to take in life—just try to be a better person with each passing day."

In a way, tai chi has been part of my regimen since I retired. I feel a certain responsibility for keeping my body in as good condition as I can, because when I came out of the camps after the war, I realized what a marvelous machine the body is. I figured that if it could take that much abuse and still work, it should last forever if I took good care of it. So it doesn't matter how long I live, I just want to be in good health as long as I'm around. I used to run seventy miles a week. I would basically run eleven and a half miles from the house, cross the Golden Gate Bridge to the north parking lot, get a drink, and come back. I did that for about fifteen years, until I realized after I retired that it was probably not a good idea for me to keep running, because it will be rough on my knee joints. That was when I decided to switch to tai chi, but I've always kept my body active. I've never been a bodybuilder. All I look for is general conditioning, good muscle tone, and stamina. People who know me used to say, "Gee, you run so much, why don't you run competitions?" And I would say, "I don't run for competitiveness. I run just for the joy of running because I'm capable of running." I think if I were to ever run in competitions, I would probably hate it because I would not be doing it for fun anymore—it has to be fun.

The other thing I did after I retired was to go backpacking. I would walk across the Golden Gate Bridge into the Golden Gate National Recreation Area, which has some 50,000 acres, and just wander all over. I used to walk to Stinson Beach with basically a half sleeping bag. If the weather got bad, I would put a jacket on top. And I would carry supplies that would last

FIG. 34. *Eddie leading tai chi chuan class at Telegraph Hill Center in San Francisco, 1984.*

me two or three nights. Again, it was just for the pleasure of walking and recharging my batteries. I remember Lois saying, "Gee, that's what you used to do when you moved from camp to camp, and when you had practically nothing to your name but a rucksack and a G-string." I said, "Oh, no, this is quite different. I don't have to be anywhere at a specific time. I've got all the food I want, and if I run out, I can buy more. Not the same thing at all."

LOSING LOIS

Before she retired, Lois had a sudden heart attack. She was in ICU for three days, and the doctors were treating her hourly. The thought was that if she could make it through the night, she might have a chance. It was that kind of a situation. Then it was if she could pull through the next night, then the prognosis would be even better. Finally, after three days in ICU, they transferred her to a regular ward. They tried converting the irregular heart beat to regular, and the success rate at that time was only one in every three cases. It didn't convert well, so she ended up with an irregular heartbeat. That was when her heart began to deteriorate. On top of that, she had a fibro tumor, which had been detected before we were married. It grew to the size of a six- or seven-month fetus, but she refused to have an operation because it was benign. She held the Chinese belief that the body should not be cut up. So her death in 1999, ten years after her first heart attack, was due to a combination of things. I think her heart just failed, because when I saw her, it reminded me of some of the guys who had died from cardiac arrest in the camps—she had the same peaceful look on her face. My nephew Randall, who's a doctor, said to me, "Uncle Ed, if I had had Auntie in the hospital with the most modern equipment, chances are I wouldn't have been able to save her. Don't knock yourself out—nothing could have saved her."

I was away in Bakersfield visiting Jess when Lois passed away at home. That was when I started having serious feelings of guilt, because when my father died, I wasn't home—I was at the ranch. When my mother died, I was still in prison camp. And then now my wife dies, and I'm not home. It was almost as if I am never home when someone dies. I knew there was nothing I could do to change the past. And I knew I was going to miss her, but, on the other hand, I never think of her as being gone. She is an integral part of me as long as I'm alive, and I don't think even death can change that. After the funeral, I kidded my nephew Michael, who is my chief executor and has a key to my house, "Since I'm never around when someone passes on, chances are I won't be here when I pass on."

A strange thing happened when I was looking for a plot for Lois at the cemetery. Being trained as an infantryman, I picked the high ground. Without knowing it, the plot number that I picked was 342. So there's no way I can forget her plot number, because 3/8/42 was our capitulation date. And I have made it a point to visit her on both Ching Ming and Chung Yeung. The custom is that all Chinese observe Ching Ming, which is popularly known as Sweeping of the Tombs. Only some Chinese observe Chung Yeung, Festival of the Dead, when, instead of buying a steamed chicken, you buy a roast duck. The duck is to transport the dead across the river so that they can attend the fair. And you burn paper clothes and money so that they

FIG. 35. *Eddie and Lois at his 60th birthday party, 1982.*

will have new clothes to wear and money to spend at the fair. Lois's mother, on her deathbed, had instructed Lois, "I don't care about Ching Ming, but I would like you to observe Chung Yeung for me." So, since it was her mother's wish, we've always observed Chung Yeung. Now that Lois is gone, I will observe it, because even though I've never met her mother, I am still her son-in-law. And because it was Lois's wish as well, I'll continue the custom until I pass on.

REFLECTIONS

When we used to sit down to dinner at the Jowell ranch and everything had been dished out, Mr. Spencer would be asked, "Is there anything else we can get for you?" He would look up and just say, "More time." Basically, I'm not greedy, but I would love to hang around just to see what other interesting changes are in store for us. I'm still curious, but other than that, as long as I'm healthy, that's as much as I can ask. In general, I think life has treated me fairly. I've seen some interesting times and I've had some bad hands dealt to me, but that's all part of the game. You learn to play the cards the best you can. When the *Survivor* series came out, my nephews were kidding me, "Uncle Ed, you should get in that. You should be able to win." And I said, "No, no, they're just playing at it. Besides that, the premise is completely different from what we were doing in the camps. We wanted to get as many people out alive as possible, and here these guys are trying to knock each other out so that one person winds up with the money." So I told them, "We have a saying that we won't take a million dollars for the experience, and we won't take a million dollars to do it again."

In retrospect, being taken prisoner has been the focal point of my life. I was a snotty-nose kid just out for adventure, thinking that was all there was to life. But I've never regretted the war or the hardships I've suffered, because it made me a better man. It taught me to respect other people's feelings, and not to treat anyone unkindly, as I had been treated. More importantly, it gave me the self-confidence and tools to solve any problem that may come up. The thing I have to remember, though, is not to be too arrogant about it, because Mother Nature has a way of shoving things in my face to remind me that there are still things I cannot handle.

People who come to know me often ask how I was able to survive the prison camps. I tell them that it's only when you are personally put to a test that you will find out what you are made of. It basically takes guts, the will to live, and lots of luck. What we learned early on is not to project too far ahead. When we were first taken on March 8, people were talking about getting out by July 4. Then it was by Thanksgiving, Christmas, and New Year's. Then we realized it might be a matter of months and years. So, gradually, we learned to live day by day. Then we learned how to roll with the punches, to take the beatings and humiliation without striking back. The point is, you can give up your pride, but you don't have to give up your dignity.

People often also ask if I feel any bitterness toward the Japanese. I don't, because I came to understand why they treated us with such contempt. From their vantage point, no respectable soldier ever allows himself to be taken

To Edward Fung
Best Wishes,   Bill Clinton

FIG. 36. *Eddie shaking hands with President Bill Clinton at the premiere of Montgomery Hom's documentary* We Served With Pride: The Chinese American Experience in WW II, *in Washington, DC, 1999. Eddie was featured in the film.*

alive. On the other hand, I find it hard to forgive the Korean guards who took such pleasure in beating and torturing us. After the war I had no hesitation about buying a Japanese camera or television set, but even if a Korean company were to offer me their best cars, their best electronics completely free, I would never accept it. Most people can't tell if someone is Korean or not, but I can. Once when I was hiking through Mill Valley, I stopped in a small park to eat my lunch. A gentleman came by with two young girls— they couldn't have been more than four or five years old. We were sitting about ten feet apart, and the hairs on my arms started standing up. I turned to this gentleman and I said, "Your girls are partly Korean, aren't they?" And he said, "Yes, how did you know? They're half." They didn't look Korean, but I knew there was some Korean blood. I don't know how you can explain that, because these kids had nothing to do with the war. I know this is pure prejudice on my part, so whenever I come across a Korean person, I bend over backwards to be courteous. Slowly, as I get to know more Korean Americans, I am starting to come to terms with this last vestige of the prison camps.

Taking my life as a whole, I've had many more good days than I've had bad ones. But even the bad days serve a purpose. They remind me of how good I have it now, in the sense that if you have never known hunger, you will not appreciate food; if you have never been enslaved, you will not appreciate what it means to be free. When people ask if I've had a good day, and I know them fairly well, I'll say that I've never had a bad day since August 19, 1945, because nothing can be as bad as those camp days. The one little glitch was when Lois passed on, but I can accept that because I know that sooner or later, all of us pass on. The one big glitch was when I interfered with my first wife's life and inadvertently caused her mental breakdown. But I've learned that regrets do not change anything. What goes around comes around; eventually everything will work out. Besides, one regret in sixty years since the camps is not bad, so I'll settle for that. In hindsight, I've actually benefited from the camp days, because that's been my reference point. Whenever I start feeling sorry for myself, I can always say, "No, no, Ed, you've got a short memory, you've forgotten the lessons that you have undergone." One lesson I've learned well is that every moment that you're alive, you'd better take advantage of the fact and enjoy it.

CHRONOLOGY

1882	Chinese Exclusion Act prohibits immigration of Chinese laborers.
1890s	Father Fung Chong Poo crosses Canadian border and enters United States.
1914	Mother Ng Shee immigrates as the "paper wife" of a merchant.
1922	Edward "Eddie" Fung is born in San Francisco's Chinatown.
1929	Stock market crashes and the Great Depression begins.
1931	Japan occupies Manchuria.
1935	Eddie works as a live-in houseboy in Antioch; Italy invades Ethiopia.
1936	Eddie works as a meat cutter in Grass Valley; Germany occupies the Rhineland.
1937	Japan invades China and commits atrocities in Rape of Nanking.
1938–40	Eddie works as a cowboy in Texas.

1939	Britain and France declare war after Germany invades Poland.
1940	Eddie joins the Texas National Guard in Lubbock.
1941	Germany conquers most of Europe; Japan signs Tripartite Pact with Germany and Italy and begins military expansion into Southeast Asia.
Nov. 22, 1941	Eddie and the 2nd Battalion head for the Philippines.
Dec. 7, 1941	Japan attacks Pearl Harbor and U.S. enters World War II.
Mar. 8, 1942	Allied forces surrender in Java, and Eddie becomes a POW.
1942–43	Eddie works on Burma-Siam Railroad.
May 8, 1945	V-E Day—Berlin falls and Germany surrenders.
August 15, 1945	V-J Day—Japan surrenders after U.S. drops A-bombs on Hiroshima and Nagasaki.
1946	Eddie joins U.S. Army Air Corps for six months.
1947	Eddie works as a meat cutter, attends junior college, and marries first wife in Bakersfield, California.
1951	Eddie attends Stanford University on GI Bill and divorces first wife.
1953	Eddie begins work as a chemist at Western Gear in Belmont, California.
1956	Eddie marries Lois Yee and moves to San Francisco.
1962	Eddie begins work as a metallurgist at Livermore Laboratory.
1977	Eddie retires, learns tai chi chuan, and travels to Japan, Thailand, and China.
1999	Wife Lois dies of a heart attack.
2003	Eddie marries Judy Yung and moves to Santa Cruz, California.

NOTES

INTRODUCTION

1. Pardee Lowe's book, which is no longer in print, was published by Little, Brown in 1943, and Jade Snow Wong's book was published by Harper in 1950 and reprinted by University of Washington Press in 1989.

2. Quotes are taken from the dust jacket of Lowe's book and from Wong's introduction to the 1989 edition of *Fifth Chinese Daughter*, p. xi.

3. The Chinese developed an elaborate system by which laborers could still immigrate to the United States. Chinese merchants and native-born citizens were exempt from the Chinese Exclusion Act and were allowed to bring their families to this country. Upon their return from a visit to China, they would claim the birth of an offspring, usually a son, and thereby create an immigration slot that would later help bring another Chinese or fictitious "paper son" to America. Similarly, the only way Chinese women could immigrate to this country during the Exclusion period from 1882 to 1943 was as a member of the exempt classes. Immigrants whose applications were based on false documents became known as "paper sons," "paper daughters," and "paper wives." See Him Mark Lai, Genny Lim, and Judy Yung, *Island: Poetry and History of Chinese Immigrants on Angel Island, 1910–1940* (San Francisco: HOC-DOC Project, 1980; Seattle: University of Washington Press, 1999), and Erika Lee, *At America's Gates: Chinese Immigration during the Exclusion Era, 1882–1943* (Chapel Hill: University of North Carolina Press, 2003).

4. For a discussion of cultural conflict, marginalization, and hybridity as expe-

rienced by second-generation Chinese Americans in the first half of the twenti-
eth century, see Sucheng Chan, "Race, Ethnic Culture, and Gender in the Construction of Identities among Second-Generation Chinese Americans, 1880s to
1930s," in *Claiming America: Constructing Chinese American Identities during the
Exclusion Era* (Philadelphia: Temple University Press, 1998) pp. 127–64; Gloria
Heyung Chun, *Of Orphans and Warriors: Inventing Chinese American Culture and
Identity* (New Brunswick, N.J.: Rutgers University Press, 2000); and Judy Yung,
Unbound Feet: A Social History of Chinese Women in San Francisco (Berkeley: Uni-
versity of California Press, 1995).

5. As quoted in "Cowboy," in *The New Encyclopedia of the American West*, edited
by Howard R. Lamar (New Haven: Yale University Press, 1998), p. 265. For a his-
tory of the American cowboy, see Joe B. Frantz and Julian Ernest Choate, Jr., *The
American Cowboy: The Myth and the Reality* (Norman: University of Oklahoma
Press, 1955), and Lonn Taylor and Ingrid Maar, *The American Cowboy* (New York:
Harper and Row, 1983).

6. According to the U.S. Census Bureau, "Table 58, Texas—Race and Hispanic
Origin: 1850 to 1990," out of a total population of 6,414,824 in 1940, there were 4,751,112
whites, 924,391 blacks, 736,433 Hispanics, 1,785 Asians, and 1,103 American Indians
(www.census.gov/population/documentation/twps0056/tab58.pdf, September 13,
2002). For treatments of blacks and Mexicans in Texas, see Sara R. Massey, ed.,
Black Cowboys of Texas (College Station: Texas A & M University Press, 2000), and
David Montejano, *Anglos and Mexicans in the Making of Texas, 1836–1986* (Austin:
University of Texas Press, 1987).

7. For treatments of the Chinese in Texas, see Edward Rhoads, "The Chinese
in Texas," *Southwestern Historical Quarterly 81*, no. 1 (July 1977): 1–36, and Mel
Brown, *Chinese Heart of Texas: The San Antonio Community, 1875–1975* (Austin:
Lily on the Water Publishing, 2005).

8. Eddie's descriptions of a cowboy's life and character ring true when com-
pared to other accounts of West Texans in the 1930s, such as John A. Haley, *Wind-
mills, Drouths and Cottonseed Cake: A Biased Biographer of a West Texas Rancher*
(Forth Worth: Texas Christian University Press, 1995), and Barney Nelson, *The Last
Campfire: The Life Story of Ted Gray, A West Texas Rancher* (College Station: Texas
A & M University Press, 1984).

9. For a study of the experiences of different racial/ethnic groups in the armed
forces during World War II, see Ronald Takaki, *Double Victory: A Multicultural History of America in World War II* (Boston: Little, Brown and Company, 2000).

10. As quoted in the *Buckley Armorer*, February 4, 1944, p. 4.

11. For treatments of Chinese Americans in the U.S. armed services, see K. Scott Wong, *Americans First: Chinese Americans and the Second World War* (Cambridge: Harvard University Press, 2005); Christina M. Lim and Sheldon H. Lim, *In the Shadow of the Tiger: The 407th Air Service Squadron, 14th Air Service Group, 14th Air Force, World War II* (San Mateo, Calif.: JACP, Inc., 1993); Marjorie Lee, ed., *Duty and Honor: A Tribute to Chinese American World War II Veterans of Southern California* (Los Angeles: Chinese Historical Society of Southern California, 1998); and Peter Phan, "Familiar Strangers: The Fourteenth Air Service Group Case Study of Chinese American Identity during World War II," *Chinese America: History and Perspectives* (1993): 75–109.

12. Almost all of the men were captured in the first months of the Pacific war—50,000 British and Australians in the fall of Singapore alone, 42,000 Dutch and 10,000 British and Australians in Java, and 25,000 Americans in the Philippines.

13. Based on Pierre Boulle's novel of the same title, the film was produced by Sam Spiegel, directed by David Lean, and starred Alec Guinness and William Holden. In *The True Story of the Bridge on the River Kwai* (Greystone Communications, 2000), POW survivors critiqued the film for wrongfully portraying the British officer as a mad collaborator and for changing the facts that the bridge was made of wood instead of concrete and steel, and that it was destroyed by commandos rather than by B-24 Liberators.

14. Meticulously researched and highly readable, Gavan Daws' *Prisoners of the Japanese: POWs of World War II in the Pacific* (New York: William Morrow, 1994) follows four American POWs captured on Wake Island, Java, and in the Philippines through their ordeal of captivity and into their postwar lives, while Clifford Kinvig's *River Kwai Railway: The Story of the Burma-Siam Railroad* (London: Brassey's, 1992) examines the railroad's purposes, planning, and construction from the viewpoints of the Japanese soldiers, Allied prisoners, and Asian laborers. See the bibliography for other reliable sources.

15. The personal accounts most closely related to Eddie's story include: Robert Charles, *Last Man Out* (Austin: Eakin Press, 1988); Benjamin Dunn, *The Bamboo Express* (Chicago: Adams Press, 1979); Robert La Forte and Robert Marcello, *Building the Death Railroad: The Ordeal of American POWs in Burma, 1942–1945* (Wilmington, Delaware: Scholarly Resources, 1993); Rohan Rivett, *Behind Bamboo: An Inside Story of the Japanese Prison Camps* (Sydney: Argus and Robertson, 1946); and Kyle Thompson, *A Thousand Cups of Rice: Surviving the Death Railway* (Austin: Eakin Press, 1994).

16. Gavan Daws, *Prisoners of the Japanese*, p. 23.

17. For an excellent racial analysis of the Pacific war, see John W. Dower, *War Without Mercy: Race and Power in the Pacific War* (New York: Pantheon Books, 1986).

18. Frank Fujita kept a diary embellished with pictures of life in the prison camps in Nagasaki. See Frank Fujita, *Foo: A Japanese-American Prisoner of the Rising Sun: The Secret Prison Diary of Frank "Foo" Fujita* (Denton, Tex.: University of North Texas Press, 1993).

ONE · GROWING UP IN CHINATOWN

1. According to the immigration records at the National Archives, Ng Shee and Ho Li Quong were admitted as the wife and son of Ho Nin, a merchant and member of the Fun Kee Company at 832 Grant Avenue in San Francisco, in 1914. See Ng Shee, folder 13163/4–5, Chinese Arrival Case Files, San Francisco District Office, Immigration and Naturalization Service, Record Group 85, National Archives, San Bruno, California.

2. Interracial marriages between whites and Chinese were outlawed in California until 1948. However, if an interracial couple got married in another state where it was allowed, California would recognize the marriage. In 1967 the U.S. Supreme Court ruled all state antimiscegenation laws unconstitutional.

3. Foot binding was practiced in China from the tenth century until it was outlawed after the Republic of China was established in 1912. Women with bound feet were considered of the genteel class.

4. According to Ng Shee's immigration records, she had reported that her brother was a deaf-mute.

5. A Filipino delicacy said to be an aphrodisiac, *balut* is an incubated duck egg with a developed embryo of seventeen to nineteen days. It is usually boiled and eaten when the embryo is almost a full duckling.

6. Prostitution was rampant in San Francisco from the Gold Rush until the 1920s, when the enforcement of antiprostitution measures forced it to go underground. The situation for Chinese prostitutes was different than that of European or Latin American prostitutes in that most of the Chinese girls had been kidnapped, tricked, or sold by poor parents in China and brought to America to work as indentured slave girls.

7. A significant number of second-generation Chinese Americans went to China for an education or employment opportunities in the 1920s and 1930s. Most returned in the late 1930s, when war broke out between Japan and China.

TWO · A CHINESE COWBOY IN TEXAS

1. Although not a law, it is a Southern custom not to drink milk while eating fish. It may have started when people got sick drinking spoiled milk in the days before refrigeration or pasteurization.

2. The poll tax requirement of one dollar and fifty cents was passed by the Texas legislature in 1902. Poll taxes were banned in federal elections by the Twenty-fourth Amendment in 1964, and in state and local elections by the Supreme Court in 1966.

THREE · A GOOD SOLDIER

1. A noncommissioned officer is anyone at the rank of corporal to master sergeant, whereas a commissioned officer is anyone at the rank of second lieutenant and above.

2. Shortly after the big maneuver ended, the army decided to switch to smaller and more mobile divisions by eliminating one infantry regiment and one artillery battalion from each division. The 2nd Battalion was separated from the 36th Division as a result. Married officers or soldiers over twenty-eight years of age were transferred from the 2nd Battalion to the 1st Battalion, and they were replaced by incoming draftees and volunteers from the 1st Battalion.

3. The Angel Island Immigration Station was established in 1910 to examine and process all immigrants coming through the port of San Francisco, but because of the Chinese Exclusion Act, the Chinese were singled out for long detentions and subjected to intense cross-examinations to prove their right to enter. The immigration station closed in 1940 (a year before Eddie arrived on the island), after a mysterious fire destroyed the administration building. The Chinese Exclusion Act was finally repealed in 1943 as a goodwill gesture to China, a U.S. ally in World War II.

4. This is how Willie Hoover described Eddie's bravery in the cornfield to Judy Yung in a phone conversation on February 1, 2003: "I don't know where he gets hold of a jeep, but he gets him a jeep, and he gets him a set of Twin .50s, off one of them wreck airplanes. He mounted them on that jeep, and he goes out in the cornfield off the end of the runway there. He sets that jeep up out there in the cornfield, put some sandbags around it, and he sat out there and he fights back at those Zeroes coming in out there strafing the fields. So one day, I was out there in my truck by the foxhole line, and I looked up and here comes one of these Zeroes. I run off the side and dodge him, while Eddie was firing at him when he went by. He goes out, he turns around, and he comes back, and he and Eddie goes head on. And I said,

'That's the end of that,' now, I'm going to say this and I don't mean no disrespect whatsoever, but I said, 'That's the end of that little Chinaman.' I didn't know how in the world he was going to half hit that Zero. I looked at Eddie, and he swung that gun around and he's still firing and going after him. So I bet you that Zero didn't fire before he went down. But Eddie stood up there and he fought them until when we left there to go up to the front lines, there wasn't enough corn left in that field to hide a jackrabbit. I mean, he had guts; he didn't give up on anybody."

5. The Rape of Nanking, in which 50,000 Japanese soldiers tortured and murdered 300,000 civilians and soldiers in a six-week carnage of rape, pillage, and plunder, was the single worst atrocity in the Pacific war.

FOUR · A PRISONER OF THE JAPANESE

1. Made of stout bamboo, "yo-ho" poles are used in Asian countries to carry heavy loads suspended at the two ends of the pole. The Americans called it a "yo-yo" or "yo-ho" pole because of the sound natives made as they trotted under the load.

2. "Hellship" was the name given to Japanese transports used to ship POWs around during World War II. Thousands of prisoners died at sea—sick, starved, suffocated, or killed by Allied bombs and torpedoes because the ships were sailing unmarked by decision of the Japanese.

3. Five Australian lieutenant colonels were put in charge of the camps on the Burma side, under Brigadier General Varley, and their names were used to identity the work groups: Anderson Force, Black Force, Green Force, Ramsey Force, and Williams Force.

4. Because the course of the railroad ran along the rivers and through mountainous terrain with many tributaries, ravines, and dried beds, a total of 688 of these bridges had to be built. Eddie worked on three of them.

5. Slug Wright later became the manager of Oceanside, California. His story is told in Gavan Daws's book, *Prisoners of the Japanese*.

FIVE · A POW SURVIVOR

1. The exact date of Chinese New Year according to the Gregorian calendar varies each year because it is based on the lunar calendar. It generally falls between January 15 and February 23.

2. Beriberi is fluid retention caused by a deficiency of vitamin B that can lead to organ failures and suffocation from within; pellagra is a skin rash caused by a

deficiency of niacin; and dengue fever is a violent attack of high fevers and pain in the muscles and joints caused by a ubiquitous mosquito.

SIX · LEARNING TO LIVE WITH MYSELF

1. In response to war hysteria and racial prejudice following the Japanese attack on Pearl Harbor, President Franklin D. Roosevelt signed Executive Order 9066, ordering the removal of 120,000 Japanese Americans from the West Coast to internment camps in desolate areas of the United States for the duration of the war. There had been no evidence of disloyalty, and two-thirds of the population were U.S. citizens.

2. Steve "Brody" Miller died after an Allied submarine torpedoed the "hellship" that was transporting him from Java to Japan.

3. There is another Texas Lost Battalion—the 1st Battalion, 141st Infantry, 36th Division, which was surrounded by German forces in the Vosges mountains and rescued by the all-Japanese 442nd Regimental Combat Team in October of 1944.

BIBLIOGRAPHY

Brown, Mel. *Chinese Heart of Texas: The San Antonio Community, 1875–1975*. Austin: Lily on the Water Publishing, 2005.

Chan, Sucheng. "Race, Ethnic Culture, and Gender in the Construction of Identities among Second-Generation Chinese Americans, 1880s to 1930s." In *Claiming America: Constructing Chinese American Identities during the Exclusion Era*, edited by K. Scott Wong and Sucheng Chan, 127–64. Philadelphia: Temple University Press, 1998.

Charles, H. Robert. *Last Man Out*. Austin: Eakin Press, 1988.

Chun, Gloria Heyung. *Of Orphans and Warriors: Inventing Chinese American Culture and Identity*. New Brunswick, NJ: Rutgers University Press, 2000.

Clarke, Hugh V. *A Life for Every Sleeper: A Pictorial Record of the Burma-Thailand Railway*. Sydney: Allen and Unison, 1986.

Clavell, James. *King Rat*. New York: Delacorte Press, 1962.

"Cowboy." In *The New Encyclopedia of the American West*, edited by Howard R. Lamar, 265–68. New Haven: Yale University Press, 1998.

Daws, Gavan. *Prisoners of the Japanese: POWs of World War II in the Pacific*. New York: William Morrow, 1994.

De Vries, David. *The True Story of the Bridge on the River Kwai*. Documentary film. Greystone Communications, 2000. Distributed by the History Channel.

Dower, John W. *War Without Mercy: Race & Power in the Pacific War*. New York: Pantheon Books, 1986.

Dunn, Benjamin. *The Bamboo Express*. Chicago: Adams Press, 1979.

Frantz, Joe B., and Julian Ernest Choate, Jr. *The American Cowboy: The Myth and the Reality*. Norman: University of Oklahoma Press, 1955.

Fujita, Frank. *Foo: A Japanese-American Prisoner of the Rising Sun, The Secret Prison Diary of Frank "Foo" Fujita*. Denton: University of North Texas Press, 1993.

Fung, Eddie. "'There but for the Grace of God Go I': The Story of a POW Survivor in World War II." In *Chinese American Voices: From the Gold Rush to the Present*, edited by Judy Yung, Gordon H. Chang, and Him Mark Lai, 212–20. Berkeley: University of California Press, 2006.

Haley, John A. *Windmills, Drouths and Cottonseed Cake: A Biased Biography of a West Texas Rancher*. Forth Worth: Texas Christian University Press, 1995.

Hom, Montgomery. *We Served with Pride: The Chinese American Experience in WWII*. Documentary film. Waverly Place Productions, 2000. Distributed by NAATA, San Francisco.

Kerr, E. Bartlett. *Surrender and Survival: The Experience of American POWs in the Pacific*. New York: William Morrow, 1985.

Kinvig, Clifford. *River Kwai Railway: The Story of the Burma-Siam Railroad*. London: Brassey's, 1992.

Kreeft, Otto. *Birma Spoorweg: Een Visuele Herinnering* [Burma railroad: A visual recollection]. Dordrecht: Stichting Stabelan, 1998.

La Forte, Robert, and Ronald Marcello. *Building the Death Railway: The Ordeal of American POWs in Burma, 1942–1945*. Wilmington, DE: Scholarly Resources, Inc., 1993.

La Forte, Robert, Ronald Marcello, and Richard Himmel. *With Only the Will to Live: Accounts of Americans in Japanese Prison Camps, 1941–1945*. Wilmington, DE: Scholarly Resources Inc., 1994.

Lai, Him Mark, Genny Lim, and Judy Yung. *Island: Poetry and History of Chinese Immigrants on Angel Island, 1910–1940*. San Francisco: HOC-DOI Project, Chinese Culture Center of San Francisco, 1980; Seattle: University of Washington Press, 1991.

Lee, Marjorie, ed. *Duty and Honor: A Tribute to Chinese American World War II Veterans of Southern California*. Los Angeles: Chinese Historical Society of Southern California, 1998.

Lim, Christina M., and Sheldon H. Lim. *In The Shadow of the Tiger: The 407th Air*

Service Squadron, 14th Air Service Group, 14th Air Force, World War II. San Mateo, CA: JACP, Inc., 1993.

Lost Battalion Association. "History of the Lost Battalion," 2002 Roster, iv–vii.

Lowe, Pardee. *Father and Glorious Descendant.* Boston: Little, Brown and Company, 1943.

MacArthur, Brian. *Surviving the Sword: Prisoners of the Japanese in the Far East, 1942–45.* New York: Random House, 2005.

Marcello, Ronald. Interview with Edward Fung, Denton, Texas, December 21, 1977. North Texas State University Oral History Collection, Number 404, 1978.

Massey, Sara R., ed. *Black Cowboys of Texas.* College Station: Texas A & M University Press, 2000.

Montejano, David. *Anglos and Mexicans in the Making of Texas, 1836–1986.* Austin: University of Texas Press, 1987.

Nelson, Barney. *The Last Campfire: The Life Story of Ted Gray, A West Texas Rancher.* College Station: Texas A & M University Press, 1984.

Phan, Peter. "Familiar Strangers: The Fourteenth Air Service Group Case Study of Chinese American Identity during World War II," *Chinese America: History and Perspectives* (1993): 75–109.

Rhoads, Edward. "The Chinese in Texas," *Southwestern Historical Quarterly* 81, no. 1 (July 1977): 1–36.

Rivett, Rohan. *Behind Bamboo: An Inside Story of the Japanese Prison Camps.* Sydney: Angus and Robertson, 1946.

Schultz, James Willard. *Seizer of Eagles.* Boston: Houghton Mifflin Company, 1922.

Sloane, Reuben. *The Light Behind the Cloud.* Waco, TX: Texian Press, 1992.

Spiegel, Sam, and David Lean. *The Bridge on the River Kwai.* Film. Columbia Pictures, 1957.

Takaki, Ronald. *Double Victory: A Multicultural History of America in World War II.* Boston: Little, Brown and Company, 2000.

Taylor, Lonn, and Ingrid Maar. *The American Cowboy.* New York: Harper and Row, 1983.

Thompson, Kyle. *A Thousand Cups of Rice: Surviving the Death Railway.* Austin: Eakin Press, 1994.

Waterford, Van. *Prisoners of the Japanese in World War II.* Jefferson, NC: McFarland and Company, 1994.

Wigmore, Lionel. *The Japanese Thrust.* Canberra: Australian War Memorial, 1957.

Wong, Jade Snow. *Fifth Chinese Daughter*. New York: Harper, 1950; Seattle: University of Washington Press, 1989.

Wong, K. Scott. *Americans First: Chinese Americans and the Second World War*. Cambridge: Harvard University Press, 2005.

Yung, Judy. *Unbound Feet: A Social History of Chinese Women in San Francisco*. Berkeley: University of California Press, 1995.

INDEX

EDDIE FUNG AND JUDY YUNG ON THEIR WEDDING DAY, APRIL 1, 2003.

JUDY YUNG is Professor Emerita of American Studies at the University of California, Santa Cruz. Her earlier books include: *Island: Poetry and History of Chinese Immigrants on Angel Island, 1910–1940; Unbound Feet: A Social History of Chinese Women in San Francisco; Unbound Voices: A Documentary History of Chinese Women in San Francisco; Chinese American Voices: From the Gold Rush to the Present;* and *San Francisco's Chinatown.*